BLOCKCHAIN EXPLAINED

YOUR ULTIMATE GUIDE TO THE TOKENIZATION OF FINANCE

PETER GAFFNEY

KYLE SONLIN

HERWIG KONINGS

ISBN: 979-8-218-20684-0 (Hardback)
ISBN: 978-1-960346-03-2 (Paperback)
ISBN: 978-1-960346-04-9 (Ebook)

Authorsunite.com

CONTENTS

Hey Randall,

We hope you enjoy this book!
Based on our conversation last year
at the ForbesU30 Summit, we figured
this book might be useful. Maybe
Blockchain will have its own list
someday. By the way Herwig
turned 29 this year...

Sincerely,

Herwig Konings

KYLE SONLIN

FOREWORD

This book is an excellent read for anyone looking to gain a comprehensive understanding of what Blockchain technology is and how it has been applied in numerous ways since Satoshi Nakamoto in October 2008 issued his white paper titled "Bitcoin: A Peer-to-Peer Electronic Cash System." The authors provide their explanations in understandable, non-technical ways to demonstrate how this technology has played out over the past fifteen years and why it is so important to both U.S. and global capital markets, financial systems, and economies.

You don't need to be an engineer, gamer, or developer to figure out or participate in this New Age Economy, or to financially benefit from it. This book explains well all the basics one needs: cryptocurrencies, types of tokens, NFTs, smart contracts, DeFi, and CBDCs, including the authors' vision of how securities tokens can provide an important, legally compliant avenue. If you don't know what these acronyms mean or aren't familiar with these use cases, then this book is for you!

After retiring from a 35-year legal career as a securities lawyer at two top national law firms, and five years of public service at the SEC, I have been teaching Blockchain Regulation and FinTech Law to law students in Miami since January 2021. My course materials for these classes are pieced together from statutes, articles, white papers, current reports, government pronouncements, releases, and settled legal proceedings, as well as litigation pleadings, papers, and court opinions. I do not use any one book because the subject matter is so topical and ever-changing that any such text would quickly become outdated or need constant amendment. This book, however, goes a long way toward staying topical and focusing on blockchains, use cases, networks, and projects that will likely still be relevant even five or more years from now.

The three authors do an admirable job of clearly explaining the securities laws, rules, and case law applicable to various public offerings of cryptocurrencies and participants. Given the complexity of the technology and the many ways it is being applied, this guide is a surprisingly fast read. In a matter of days, readers can become fluent in the language and use cases of Blockchain. After that, it will continue to serve as a must-have reference guide. Enjoy the exploration of this new and fascinating technology!

Prof. Marc Powers
March 2023

INTRODUCTION

When *The Bitcoin Whitepaper* appeared in 2008, it ushered onto the world stage an experimental application of an existing technology to disrupt the traditional banking system as we know it.[1] Within a matter of years, at its peak the blockchain protocol held $1.28 Trillion USD in value.[2] The idea of blockchain technology wasn't new in 2008. The term *blockchain* was coined back in 2000 as a novelty stemming from roots in cryptography and distributed database technology. To whom do we owe the disruption described in *The Bitcoin Whitepaper*? A mythical, anonymous author who went by the moniker of Satoshi Nakamoto. While some have claimed to be this person, none have been able to prove it. Unlike most pioneering technologies where inventors proudly claim their fame, this one was conceived without a big business idea or any known entity behind it. The whitepaper inspired enough brilliant individuals to take up the cause it described and put it to use. The rest, as they say, is history.

Blockchain technology has inspired much in the way of nomenclature and is now often mixed in with the metaverse and referred to as crypto or Web3. With this technology underpinning the next generation of companies and internet applications, it's important to help make its adoption easy through education and standardization, which is exactly what this book aims to do. We will walk you through the journey of the blockchain's history and functionality so you can live it as if you were there all along. Copious amounts of jargon have sprung up around blockchain and crypto, so we hope you will take full advantage of the extensive glossary of terms we have painstakingly assembled in the lattermost section of the book.

Our hope is for you to achieve an understanding of how the blockchain works and why it is every bit as revolutionary as the internet has been. In the same way those who understood the internet early stood to gain massive returns and unlocked the ability to create and predict the future, we believe this book can do the same for you regarding blockchain technology.

The major concept you must grasp to comprehend this phenomenon is the problem of *trust*. Trust is the backbone of commerce, business, partnerships, and relationships. In fact, it's fundamental to humanity. How do you remove the problem of trust using technology? As explained later in the book in greater detail, it begins with a data solution that removes the need for trust. This is accomplished through the concept of radical *decentralization*. As more and more centralized points of trust failure are removed, a point is reached where it's so decentralized the information is assumed to be reliable.

Imagine a Wikipedia without the need of being powered by donations in order to store the data hosted on the website on a server. Imagine a Facebook where the algorithm can be influenced by the users. Imagine a financial system where there is enough trust for transactions without banks. This is the journey that blockchain and this book will set you on. From the inner workings of different blockchain solutions to the applications that popularized them, the history of this industry is young but has grown and evolved faster than any other technological advancement before it. We're going to walk through the stories of digital cats, massive hacks, and the failures of billion-dollar coins that were supposed to be stable. What drives this usage and how are Bitcoin and blockchain supposed to upend our financial system? If the whitepaper was too difficult to understand, then this book will break it down for you into digestible chunks.

We three authors of this book are all on the team at Security Token Advisors, a leading authority in this industry by virtue of our experience gained from tokenization projects combined with our strict understanding of the securities laws governing the very largest financial institutions and markets in the world. For us, many of these advancements and how they have been adopted by the market and treated by regulators were somewhat obvious, and have been reinforced by accurate predictions year after year by the team.

We've constructed the story in this book to follow not only the history of blockchain but also to understand the juxtaposition of anarchist anti-bankers to the willful opportunists to the technology reformers envisioning change. You will be able to see all this from our perspective and rationale, realizing how many of the events were, in hindsight, entirely predictable. This is harder to accomplish in the moment because illusions such as Fear of Missing Out (FOMO) and greed often cloud logical thinking. Thus, we have seen blockchain and crypto cycles of ups and downs occur much faster than are seen with the overall economy, making them more volatile than any other asset class.

We hope you will come to enjoy the concepts, mind-bending applications, and the rich (or not so rich) history found in this industry as much as we do. After all, it creates trillions of dollars in value out of thin air, using algorithms to develop sophisticated, complex money-making schemes in the name of anti-corporate decentralization. With a better understanding of the technology and its applications, watching it all play out in the real world with real people and firms with loads of traditional money is all the more interesting and dramatic.

Each new term comes with a new model for blockchain, a new opportunity to reinvent the world as we know it, to entirely change the way an industry operates. It's hard *not* to see the potential once you have a firmer grasp of the fundamentals. Banks are slow. Supply chains are slow. Industries are monopolized by data. The internet redefined the user experience for almost every industry, and blockchain will do the same. This is your textbook, guide, and glossary to understand this burgeoning new technology, and perhaps also participate in it so you can live and breathe future editions.

NOTES

1. The Bitcoin Whitepaper: https://www.bitcoin.com/satoshi-archive/whitepaper/
2. Global Data: https://www.globaldata.com/data-insights/financial-services/bitcoins-market-capitalization-history/

CHAPTER 1

BLOCKCHAIN FUNDAMENTALS

The core concept of the blockchain revolution revolves around the practicality of decentralization. Decentralization is the transfer of control and decision-making from one centralized party to a group, cohort, or user base. A greater number of uncorrelated groups involved typically indicates a more decentralized network. This decentralized nature creates a *permissionless* future where network users can freely contribute to the validation and upkeep of the network rather than relying on one organization's approval to do so. Decentralization focuses on not only the control and decision-making powers of an organization but also security functions, as a decentralized network will likely have multiple smaller points of failure rather than one.[1]

This decentralization is achieved through having many separate representatives (called *nodes*) validate and operate the network at hand. If one node were to go down, the network should theoretically be fine since the remaining nodes are online and capable. Even if a small handful of nodes were to go offline, the same protections should remain and the network should continue to operate. This is the advantage decentralized networks offer over centralized networks, whereby in the latter a single point of failure through the managing party could affect the entire system.

Understanding the role decentralization trends play in how society is evolving is key to recognizing what our technological future could look like. Companies and organizations have gathered large amounts of data ranging from financial to social to personal, and each company is a centralized point of potential failure. A company can be vulnerable to a cyber attack, thereby putting all users' data and network operations at stake. These risks could be mitigated through more decentralized or *distributed* networks(a network not quite decentralized but at least relies on multiple sources to reduce the overall total points of failure).

BLOCKCHAIN - DECENTRALIZATION

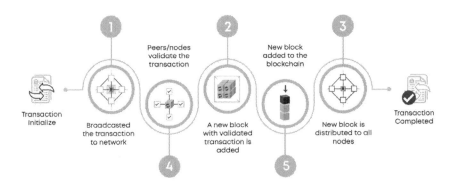

Blockchain technology is the next progression in data management and record keeping. Building on the concept of Distributed Ledger Technology (DLT), a blockchain is simply a self-updating method of keeping track of a series of transactions. DLT and blockchain allow for simultaneous access, validation, and record updating in an immutable (unchangeable) fashion where each transaction is recorded in a *hash.*[2]

This self-updating record-keeping system operates using a certain consensus mechanism to verify and confirm new transactions and records. The two most commonly known consensus mechanisms are Proof-of-Work (PoW) and Proof-of-Stake (PoS). Each one has its own mechanics to prove a transaction did in fact occur on a designated blockchain. In successful cases, the transaction will be fully recorded as a new hash, which is added to the blockchain for eternity. Any future transactions will now include that hash within its history since blockchains are immutable.

If a transaction cannot be validated by the blockchain via its associated consensus mechanism, the transaction will be rejected and will not be included in the most recent successful hash. A transaction may be rejected if it is deemed fraudulent or insufficient by the existing blockchain hashes, and this "admission process" is determined by the consensus mechanisms itself.

Proof-of-Work

Proof-of-Work (PoW) is associated with *mining*—perhaps most well-known through the practice of mining Bitcoin. Essentially, parties (individuals, firms, organizations) run computer software to make constant calculations aimed at finding a numerical key used to unlock a transaction's hash. This process either verifies or rejects transactions on-chain. The productivity of each miner is determined by the amount of processing power contributed by the computer, known as the hashing power (similar to horsepower for a vehicle).

PROOF-OF-WORK

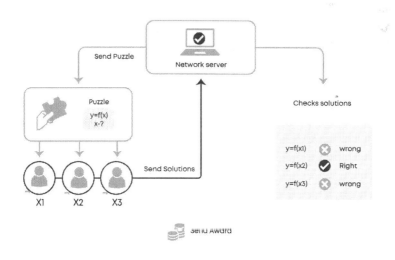

In a Proof-of-Work system, miners are competing to solve complex math algorithms, usually revolving around calculating incredibly large prime numbers, requiring immense amounts of processing power. In PoW mechanisms, there is a winner-take-all reward structure, where the 'winning' miner who finds the correct number is awarded the entire block reward. In the Bitcoin blockchain, each block of transactions averages a new prime number solution every ten minutes. This ten-minute goal is estimated by a self-correcting algorithm. If a block is solved in less than ten minutes, the next equation will increase in difficulty. Similarly, if transactions are consistently taking longer than ten minutes, the equations become less complex to align with the target time.

A miner with higher hashing power (a stronger computing system) is more likely to solve the calculation, and in return, the winning miner is rewarded with a set portion of Bitcoin. As the hardware requirements in PoW systems increase over time, the average individual likely has no chance of solving these algorithms without specialized hardware. Instead, groups of smaller computing networks can join forces, forming a *mining pool*, allowing all users to combine their individual computers into an aggregate with a higher chance of success. These pools have quickly become some of the largest individual mining operations in the world, and each contributor is awarded a proportional reward in cryptocurrency relative to the amount of hashing power they contributed to the network during a given period.

While Bitcoin was the first proof-of-work cryptocurrency, there are many others using a PoW consensus mechanism, including Monero, Litecoin, and Ravencoin, to name just a few.

Proof-of-Stake

Proof-of-Stake (PoS), on the other hand, relies on a decentralized system more akin to the Board of Directors of a corporation. Those with cryptocurrencies operating on Proof-of-Stake networks are allowed to "stake" some or all of their holdings in a designated pool. In return, these "stakers" are given a chance to participate in transactions and are rewarded for locking their holdings up in favor of verifying and validating transactions on the network. Those who stake more coins or tokens over longer periods of time typically receive a greater share of the rewards, just like a board member with two seats has greater voting power over a member with just one seat. Proof-of-Stake is typically seen as a more environmentally friendly consensus mechanism since it doesn't rely on computing power and energy, although this is actively being countered by miners who revert excess energy into renewable solutions.

PROOF-OF-STAKE

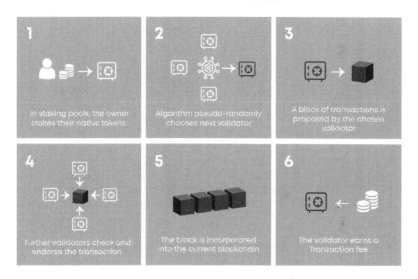

The "rewards" are usually distributed via each network's own utility token. A utility token is necessary to interact with the network at hand. It is the proprietary method for payment inside the network and is generally how the network's value is assessed. For example, to interact with the Ethereum blockchain requires one to purchase and/ or earn Ether (*ETH*). If the value of *ETH* is increasing, this indicates the Ethereum network itself is becoming more valuable or populated.

Moreover, the metric known as *Total Value Locked (TVL)* is a common measurement of a network's value. TVL is the collective value of digital assets stored in applications built on a network that has been deposited into a smart contract, typically freezing the asset for a period of time, hence the term *locked*. The greater the TVL on a network, the greater value the network has as its user base continues to contribute to the usability and breadth of the network. To date, Ethereum peaked at roughly $160 billion in TVL in November 2021, whereas competing chains had sub-$20 billion TVL.[3]

On the other hand, a waning network may be accompanied by a decreasing token value if would-be users or former users begin selling their tokens in lieu of storing or accumulating more for network usage. Nonetheless, token value is formally attributed to supply and demand which is not always in line with the fundamentals of the underlying network, so multiple factors should be considered when valuing utility tokens.

In short, imagine utility tokens as the currency to pay a blockchain protocol and its associated application's network fees in order to interact with it. Some blockchains create their own utility tokens in order to incentivize users into their networks by requiring the purchase of the unique utility token (or swap from other cryptocurrencies) in order to gain access. When looking at this from a business model perspective, the utility token may be seen as a "moat" in relation to other competing networks without an integrated transactional system. Often, this model also prevented adoption as it became more difficult to build applications due to the requirement of using a specific token, which might be fluctuating wildly at the time.

In order to store and use these utility tokens, individuals and organizations can set up digital wallets to hold blockchain-based assets. These wallets may be held solely by the owner, who would be responsible for what's known as a *public key* and a *private key*. These keys work similarly to a username and password combination.

The public key acts as a public facing address, like one's home address, which represents a touch point like a mailbox to send assets or communications to someone directly. Conversely, a private key acts as the key to the home's front door, granting access to someone's privately held property so long as you have the key. In the same way you should never share a password online, you must be very careful about sharing their private keys (or seed phrase, which is a string of sixteen words used to reset a private key).

To avoid the complexity of managing one's own private keys, many choose to use a third-party custodian like Ledger or an exchange like Coinbase to manage their assets. When using a third-party, you are provided a public key so you can still send and receive assets, but the private key is hidden, even to the account holder, and is managed on behalf of users by the company, typically an exchange. Every wallet has its own unique identifier, usually a combination of numbers and letters in both uppercase and lowercase. For Bitcoin, it's a string between twenty-eight and thirty-four alphanumeric characters. Transactions may be sent across the blockchain to another wallet identifier, which represents a transfer from one party to another. As mentioned earlier, the consensus mechanism and associated miners and/or stakers will verify and facilitate the transaction.

Users may elect to move their holdings from a personal wallet to other wallets for a variety of reasons such as staking, trading, or swapping. What makes blockchains so wide-ranging in applications and use-cases can be attributed partially to the smart contract functionality. A smart contract is just a series of *if/then* statements that can be programmatically enforced without any human intervention. In traditional industries, sensitive data has to be carefully managed by companies who are constantly threatened by data breaches, competitors, and regulation changes. With blockchain-based databases, this information can be secured digitally, but more importantly can be accessed safely by automated protocols.

Many financial processes, for example, may not need to rely on a trusted third party to operate on behalf of their customers. Instead, a smart contract application is built to complete the desired set of instructions without storing any data or charging a fee for the work. A user only has to pay the gas fees (compensation to those who participate in operating the blockchain) to record the transaction on the blockchain for a fraction of the cost they would pay a traditional middleman

Ethereum pioneered the idea of smart contract development and implementation when it launched in 2016. The first Ethereum-based application was called *CryptoKitties*, a cartoonish game centered around trading digital collectibles solely using smart contracts. Finance professionals saw their own opportunity to begin migrating existing financial services to the blockchain through borrowing and lending applications.

Rather than using existing intermediaries such as banks and alternative lenders, cryptocurrency owners are able to deposit a certain amount of their crypto assets into an automated liquidity pool managed by a smart contract. In turn, the smart contract validates and verifies the deposit, and elects to lend out the deposit amount to another user who is seeking to borrow the assets. The smart contract considers the liquidity within that specific pool and determines a feasible interest rate payable to the lender, and a feasible interest rate charged to the borrower. With enough liquidity and users, this lending mechanism is able to operate solely through lines of code (a series of smart contracts) rather than relying on human interaction as does the existing financial services industry. This concept and execution will be covered in greater depth throughout the book.

This evolution in financial services on the blockchain is what's known as *Decentralized Finance* (DeFi). So far, the market has seen protocols and services that offer borrowing and lending of cryptocurrencies, tokenized assets, and stablecoins, which are cryptocurrencies valued at $1 either through an algorithm or a Treasury backing. What DeFi has done for the financial services market, especially across decentralized trading and decentralized lending, opened the market's eyes up to something even more generalized: decentralized organizations.

Known as DAOs, Decentralized Autonomous Organizations are designed to be, as the name suggests, a decentralized and distributed organization for members to join, participate in, and ultimately shape, in an automated fashion through smart contract enforcement. The activities of each DAO vary greatly and can range from anything as novel as purchasing a collectible item to operating an organization or investment vehicle. As with Proof-of-Stake, DAOs can draw on similar "voting systems" to decide how each organization is governed and managed by its user base, token holders, and any founding members. To date, DAO tokens are largely seen as utility tokens that both reward users for participation and enable access to the perks and purpose of each DAO. The smart contracts powering DAO tokens should be seen as vehicles that offer board seats since users can collectively vote and govern the body as they see fit.

DECENTRALIZED AUTONOMOUS ORGANIZATIONS

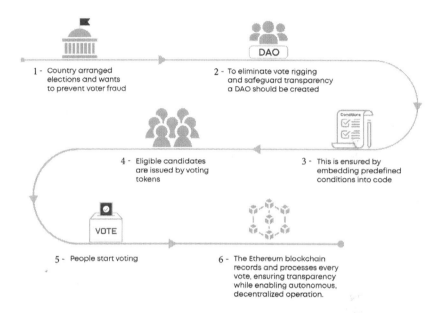

1 - Country arranged elections and wants to prevent voter fraud

2 - To eliminate vote rigging and safeguard transparency a DAO should be created

4 - Eligible candidates are issued by voting tokens

3 - This is ensured by embedding predefined conditions into code

5 - People start voting

6 - The Ethereum blockchain records and processes every vote, ensuring transparency while enabling autonomous, decentralized operation.

It is admirable to see the wave of DAOs attempting to replace companies (i.e., LLCs), although certain organizations have begun acting as unregistered investment vehicles and managers. These organizations are more likely to come under question by the Securities and Exchange Commission (SEC), much like Initial Coin Offerings (ICOs) in the 2018–2020 era. This is because both ICOs and DAOs contain elements that trigger a new series of rules that need to be followed as they are considered securities (commonly referred to as stocks).

Since its creation in 1934, the SEC was designed to protect investors, which are defined as people who hold securities. Since tokens for ICOs and DAOs seem to offer a return based on some sort of purchase (investment), the SEC is required to follow through on its job to go after token issuers who do not comply with the existing regulation. As a result, many ICOs and DAOs have been prosecuted by the SEC and forced to shut down and return money to investors.

In order to compliantly and legally offer investment securities, organizations (whether traditional or DAOs), should be issuing *security* tokens rather than *utility* tokens. Security Tokens are standard securities—instruments that represent legal financial upside or participation in a venture—that operate and settle on the blockchain like any other digital asset. The difference between a security token and a utility token comes down to the structuring and management of the token. Security tokens are typically managed by SEC-registered Transfer Agents and qualified financial professionals and personnel, and trade on National Exchanges or Alternative trading Systems managed by Broker-Dealers. On the other end of the spectrum, utility tokens are unregulated and may trade on decentralized exchanges (DEX) or centralized cryptocurrency exchanges like Coinbase, Gemini, or Binance, which are typically only licensed as Money Transmitters, not securities exchanges.

Security Tokens represent one of the more nascent verticals within mainstream digital asset conversations, although they likely present the greater value. There are already hundreds of trillions of dollars worth of assets in both the private and public sectors. The vast majority of these assets can be "tokenized" and managed on a blockchain rather than through existing manual maintenance processes. Just like DeFi solutions have begun revolutionizing the lending and borrowing markets, security tokens are poised to revolutionize the existing capital markets.

Cryptocurrencies have proven their worth by achieving an aggregate market cap of around $798 billion by the end of 2022.[4] Considering the fact there are already hundreds of trillions of dollars in existing assets such as real estate or equities, bringing these already-funded assets to the blockchain is even simpler than creating and funding new digital assets. From a scalability perspective, security tokens have the potential to quickly dwarf the market capitalizations of other digital asset verticals, as it may only take a handful of behemoths like KKR, Goldman Sachs, and Blackrock (asset managers with trillions of assets between them) to get involved and bring their asset portfolios over to the blockchain.

Lastly, but perhaps most popularly in the mainstream, the concept of unique and "one-of-one" tokens surfaced more than ever in early 2020 (remember *CryptoKitties*?). Non-Fungible Tokens (NFTs) by definition mean each token is unique and one-of-a-kind on the blockchain protocol. Fungible tokens like Bitcoin imply that one *BTC* is worth one *BTC*. Another example of fungibility is stocks. One Tesla share is worth one Tesla share. However, every diamond is one-of-a-kind and therefore considered a non-fungible item. This is due to certain programmable unique characteristics associated with each NFT known as metadata. These characteristics range from visual properties (colors, accessories, backgrounds) to scarcity tiers and limits (think *CryptoKitties*) to simply being a unique smart contract of a token (think supply chain for tracking a can of soup that was produced).

Going even further, NFTs are natively digital, as they are *minted*, the term widely used for "created," to represent pieces of art, music, tickets, passes, rewards, points, and even real-world items like collectibles, supply-chain pieces, and more. Although most widely known for digital art through collections like *CryptoPunks* and *Bored Ape Yacht Club*, NFT "sectors" are starting to branch out more into the music and entertainment industry. For instance, a song is unique and cannot be directly replaced or swapped for another song, which makes a song a viable use-case for an NFT.

Similarly, the rights to a movie or to a production cannot simply be lumped into the rights to every other movie or production since they are all inherently unique. For this reason, an NFT is a nice fit, whereas a fungible utility token wouldn't make much sense nor even be feasible for reflecting ownership compliantly and correctly. Nonetheless, while NFTs have been the "golden child" in terms of digital assets progress, certain collections are in fact walking the fine line between acting as utility to the owner and acting as a security or investment token.

NOTES

1. What is Decentralization in Blockchain? https://aws.amazon.com/blockchain/decentralization-in-blockchain/
2. Distributed Ledger Technology (DLT): https://www.investopedia.com/terms/d/distributed-ledger-technology-dlt.asp
3. Ethereum TVL: https://defillama.com/chain/Ethereum
4. Aggregate Crypto Market Cap: https://coinmarketcap.com/charts/

CHAPTER 2

CRYPTOCURRENCIES

U p until 2018, most digital assets fell under the general moniker of *cryptocurrency*, despite many coins and/or tokens solving different problems and requiring more nuanced classification. While Bitcoin was and is the original cryptocurrency, should Ether, the second digital asset, fall in the same classification if it behaves quite differently?

As the industry grew, it became apparent more detailed and precise classifications were needed. One of the most powerful features of blockchain technology is its ability to act as a building block in a series of applications and digital constructions. Building a healthy economic system around these new digital assets requires a solid foundation of understanding.

The foundational cryptocurrencies and digital assets are used in Layer 1 blockchains, or *Layer 1* for short. Layer 1, as the name implies, is the first and primary layer on a blockchain stack. Many blockchain solutions have their own associated network tokens, which are used to access and build upon the technology scaffolding of its particular distributed ledger. These tokens, which are commonly classified as cryptocurrencies, enable developers and users to make use of the development capabilities offered directly by the blockchain. Because Layer 1s are the base layers, the various applications, products, and communities built upon them rely on the Layer 1's utility token to facilitate and validate transactions.

The true value added by Layer 1s are the leverage they provide to products and services built upon them. For instance, a product built on a Layer 1 can rely on that blockchain for all transaction validations and finalizations, which is exactly the purpose for which it was designed. Without this Layer 1 solution, each new product would have to figure out and implement its own blockchain solution for transactions (i.e., Proof-of-Work, Proof-of-Stake). This would require each of these projects to reinvent the wheel, as if each app on your phone had to build its own internet. Rather than creating redundancy, Layer 1s allow developers to choose their preferred blockchains to work with and focus on the real real value creation activities of their application built on top of the Layer 1. Below are several examples of Layer 1 blockchains:

Bitcoin (BTC)

Bitcoin is the world's first digital currency allowing for secure peer-to-peer transfers across the internet. Designed in 2008 by Satoshi Nakamoto, the vision for Bitcoin was to enable any parties to transfer funds to each other in a borderless and permissionless manner. This circumvents the need for intermediaries such as banks, credit card firms, and governments by relying on a decentralized network.

Bitcoin is a Layer 1 solution originally developed as digital currency. Its main use-case has centered around acting as a permissionless store of value and transaction medium, although it's not limited to these uses. While developers could build upon the Bitcoin blockchain, the general sentiment is that Bitcoin has established itself as the most prominent version of so-called *digital gold* given its token mechanics, including a capped supply at 21 million Bitcoins and a decreasing issuance rate.

As mentioned in the proof-of-work consensus mechanism details in chapter 1, successful miners are rewarded with the assets contained in each block mined. At Bitcoin's inception, the block reward was 50 *BTC*. However, after every 210,000 successfully mined blocks, the reward decreases by 50 percent. This recurring event is widely known as the *halving*, and it occurs roughly every four years based on historical results. The third and most recent Bitcoin halving took place on May 11, 2020 in which the block rewards were reduced from 12.5 *BTC* per block to 6.25 *BTC* per block. The *digital gold analogy* primarily comes from the profile of Bitcoin: A fixed supply of 21 million with a deflationary issuance schedule to promote scarcity over new printing. The supply of gold is more or less fixed and finding new gold to mine becomes more difficult as more and more gold is mined.[1]

MINERS' REWARDS FOR SUCCESSFULLY COMPLETING 1 BLOCK

HALVE every 210,000 blocks, or an average of every 4 years

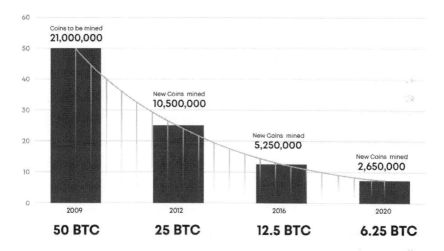

The issuance rate refers to the number of newly minted *BTC* (earned by miners) each year based on Bitcoin's age. The analogy to gold comes from the store-of-value concept that gold, which is also limited in supply, will always serve as a source of wealth no matter the situation because you will always be able to trade it for currency or livestock or other minerals somewhere. The same applies to Bitcoin where a world could exist in which the US dollar loses value while stores-of-value like *BTC* and gold hold their value.

Scalability challenges associated with Bitcoin are typically due to the blockchain's low throughput capabilities, as each block is only eight megabytes in size. While this size is only relevant in relation to the number and volume of transactions on the network, it does present a cap on the throughput capabilities of the network rather than an infinitely capable network. In situations of high enough volume, the Bitcoin network will slow down and users will experience slower traffic, which may lead to longer transaction times, higher fees, or both.

Bitcoin represents the largest and most successful implementation of the Proof-of-Work consensus mechanism, a mathematical system designed to reward users for contributing their computational resources and solving each equation. Bitcoin focuses on maintaining three core principles: being permissionless, decentralized, and transparent.

Permissionless means Bitcoin allows any user with an internet connection to utilize the network. Anyone around the world can transact using *BTC* and can feel comfortable storing their Bitcoin in a private wallet, unseizable by outside actors unless they have the private key.

Decentralized refers to the decision-making process of the network. Unlike countries that control most fiat currencies used in the traditional economy, Bitcoin is controlled by a diverse set of backers, and no one party has total control. By requiring consensus between many different groups, Bitcoin more effectively represents the objective needs of the system, with less risk of bias or intervention.

Transparency refers to Bitcoin representing a log of every transaction through its distributed ledger. Just as anyone can transact using the currency, anyone may review any and all transactions that occur on the network in a safe and secure manner.

Ethereum (*ETH*)

Largely seen as the most popular blockchain network for building new applications, Ethereum was founded in 2015 as an alternative to Bitcoin. Ethereum uses its utility token, Ether (*ETH*), to execute the innovative smart contract system now commonplace throughout the industry. Smart contracts act as automatically enforced if/then statements, allowing verified on-chain data to be sent between parties with trust in the authenticity of the records. *ETH*, the native token, is used to pay *gas fees*, small fees associated with compensating miners or delegates for the mathematical validation. The Ethereum blockchain acts as connective tissue between applications built on its native *Solidity* programming language, similar to an operating system on a computer.

The platform has leveraged both Proof-of-Work and Proof-of-Stake as consensus mechanisms, electing to transition to the latter to scale up and reduce the gas fees associated with on-chain signatures. Ethereum's supply is variable, with a current supply of over 120 million *ETH* at the end of 2022. This supply is used not only for Ethereum itself, but also for applications utilizing Ethereum as their Layer 1 blockchain solution. Ethereum acts as the market leader for decentralized applications, cryptocurrency and security token issuance, as well as NFT creation due to its intuitive programming language, ease of use, and network scalability benefits.

Since Ethereum is expansive, largely application-agnostic, and has perhaps the deepest network of developers and users on it, it also has the largest amount of Total Value Locked (TVL). As of the year end in 2022, Ethereum's Total Value Locked was $23 billion.[2] Ethereum enables multiple types of tokens and projects to be developed upon it through token structures such as the following:[3]

- ERC-20: the most general utility token model.
- ERC-721: Non-Fungible Tokens (NFTs).
- ERC-1404: Security Tokens and Digital Securities.

ERC is an acronym (Ethereum Request for Comment) serving as the standard abbreviation for protocol standards. These smart contract standards are open-source templates of code that already perform a specific function. Using these token types allows programmers and users to build more efficiently on Ethereum and also creates a standardized ontology for the industry to follow.

Avalanche (*AVAX*)

Avalanche is an open-source, programmable smart contract system for decentralized application development. It was developed by Ava Labs and launched in September 2020 with the goal of creating a more formidable and manageable blockchain network than alternatives on the market. Avalanche is made up of three separate sub-chains: Exchange

Chain (X-Chain), Contract Chain (C-Chain), and Platform Chain (P-Chain).

- The X-Chain is used for creating and trading assets.
- The C-Chain is for smart contract creation.
- The P-Chain is for coordinating validators and Subnets.

This three-pronged approach addresses the scalability problem of blockchains. Rather than having every application developed on a blockchain running on the same rails, Avalanche enables a more bucketed approach to separate transactions of different types of assets as per the X, C, and P chain designations. These three prongs are all interoperable on the Avalanche blockchain itself, so there is no barrier between them.

Avalanche runs on an Ethereum Virtual Machine (EVM). This technology stack emulates the testing environments built on the Ethereum protocol and uses the Solidity programming language. Capitalizing on the scalability and throughput of the Avalanche blockchain system while maintaining a high level of interoperability with applications on the existing Ethereum infrastructure are key to the success of this blockchain solution.

Transactions on Avalanche have a finality time of under one second. This is the period of time in which transactions are initiated and added to the blockchain ledger. A shorter finality time helps reduce network congestion as transactions can process upon finality. Even if Avalanche sees a spike in transactions, it can batch and validate transactions more efficiently as these transactions are finalized on the blockchain.[4]

Solana (SOL)

Solana moves away from the "smart contract" terminology that made Ethereum famous. Rather than referring to its tokens and projects as being smart contract driven, the Solana ecosystem just refers to them as *Programs*. Solana enables developers to program in Rust, C++, and C. Because these are well-known programming languages, it encourages everyday programmers to come over to the Solana eco-system and begin building rather than forcing developers to learn a new blockchain-specific language such as Solidity (the programming language specific to Ethereum).[5]

Solana makes use of its novel Proof-of-History consensus mechanism, which timestamps every transaction on the blockchain. These timestamps are referred to by each and every future transaction as a method of verifying their own transactions. Rather than relying on Proof-of-Stake or Proof-of-Work to confirm new blocks, Solana looks back at the ledger's historical timestamps, matching up their ledger with the historical ledger, and accepts or denies transactions and new blocks accordingly. This is designed to reduce the computing power required to maintain the network and contributes to Solana's alleged 50,000 transactions per second capabilities.[6] At the end of 2022, Solana's Total Value Locked was just over $206 million.[7]

Ripple (*XRP*)

Ripple Labs, founded in 2012, designed a payments protocol known as *XRP* with the goal of reducing global transaction fees for payments and remittances. It leverages a real-time gross settlement (RTGS) system to remove intermediaries, and was once touted as the "SWIFT Killer." SWIFT is the traditional payments and settlement service used by the existing financial services industry. The *XRP* network can handle 1,500 transactions per second, which doesn't quite overtake credit card processors, but is an improvement on the backend plumbing. With a maximum *XRP* supply of 100 billion coins, the protocol is designed for a high velocity of transactions rather than a limited store of value.[8]

Blockchain Forks

Since the blockchain is simply a length of code—one that records each transaction in a new *hash*—it can be modified as a new open-source project. The modification of a blockchain is what's known as a *Fork*. A fork can come in two forms: soft fork or hard fork.

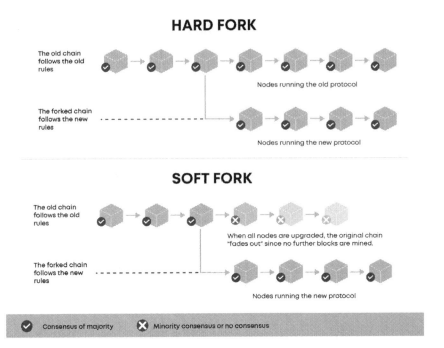

HARD FORK

The old chain follows the old rules

Nodes running the old protocol

The forked chain follows the new rules

Nodes running the new protocol

SOFT FORK

The old chain follows the old rules

When all nodes are upgraded, the original chain "fades out" since no further blocks are mined.

The forked chain follows the new rules

Nodes running the new protocol

✓ Consensus of majority   ✗ Minority consensus or no consensus

Think of a *soft fork* as routine maintenance. Soft forks are necessary for blockchain upgrades related to security issues, bugs, speed improvements, new interoperability capabilities, and so on. Soft forks are so named because the underlying utility token does not change. Users typically don't notice any of the fork's impacts because the upgrade happens seamlessly in the background, much like a smartphone auto-updating its operating system. This upgrade runs in the background and may come with new features, but on the same smartphone interface. Soft forks are known as "forward-compatible" since they do not change the user experience or interaction basics.

Soft fork proposals can be published by a blockchain's foundation, parent organization, or group of leading developers, and are voted upon by the miners and users. Approval is often by majority vote and is considered a decentralized method of reaching consensus. If approved, the proposed changes will be applied to the network and consensus mechanisms. As the soft fork is in process, the hash history is maintained through duplicate copies of all of the historical transactions.

As the miners make their choice about accepting the new proposal or rejecting it and thereby sticking with the original chain, the old nodes are either no longer recognized as the chain follows the new blockchain rules per the fork or maintain the blockchain if the fork was unsuccessful.[9]

A historical example of a soft fork is the Bitcoin SegWit upgrade. Prior to Bitcoin having a block size of 8MB, it originally had a block size of just 1MB. After pondering methods of improving this capacity and increasing the block size, Bitcoin developers and enthusiasts decided they could shift around the storage method associated with *public keys* and *private keys*. This shift in methodology would free up more space in each block, and thus improve scalability by handling a greater number of transactions in a single block. Known as *Segregated Witness* (SegWit), this initiative could be accomplished through a software upgrade rather than a new chain, and thus the SegWit soft fork was executed in August 2017 and still operates today.[10]

A *hard fork*, by contrast, is more severe, significant, and requires attention from all existing token holders. Hard forks typically end with new tokens being minted, as the fundamentals of the blockchain change drastically enough to require two separate chains. A hard fork could occur for many reasons such as a majority of token owners deciding on a different future for the blockchain or to address a severe hack of the existing main network. Think of this as an established corporation dissolving into two new companies, which may or may not now be in competition with each other.

When a hard fork occurs, holders of the original token are typically compensated for maintaining their holdings throughout the forking process. This compensation, in the form of the newly forked blockchain utility token, also acts as an incentive to begin using the new chain over the original chain. The ratio of new tokens to original holdings may be anywhere from 1:1 to 3:1 or even more. The official term for the distribution of these new tokens is an *airdrop*. The new tokens are airdropped directly to users' digital wallets in the properly determined ratio.

Think of airdropping like a neighborhood where each house has its own address. The neighborhood has passed a new ordinance and each resident is notified by mail in their mailbox. The mailbox in our blockchain example is a wallet and the neighborhood includes all the users on the network. This airdrop function can also be used for the distribution of digital assets to any range of user wallets once these wallet addresses are on record, which is a powerful tool for organizations seeking to reward their developers, users, or the community in general. Unlike your mailbox at your physical address, a wallet is more than just an inbox. In addition to being a receiver, it's also a storage solution for holding tokens representing value, access, and utility. Airdropping simply lets smart contracts send tokens with instant delivery to wallets.

AIRDROP

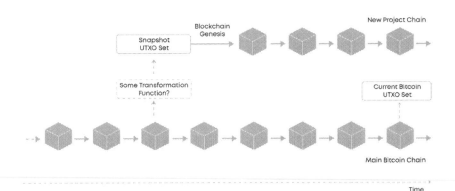

What's important to understand from a technical level is that hard-fork blockchains share all the same transaction blocks up until the exact event of the fork itself. Should a blockchain be split down the middle, 50-50 across its user base, some governance problems and questions may arise—the main question being which is the true record? Communities, however, don't typically split evenly down the middle, and the original chain usually maintains a vast majority of its user base, but the scenario cannot be ignored. Because both forks share the same previous hashes up until the forked block, the chain achieving and maintaining the strongest community will likely prevail in terms of widespread adoption and usage. This is usually defined by the following functions of a coin:

- Hash rate: The collective mining power for Proof-of-Work chains.
- Total Value Locked (TVL): The value of assets locked in a Proof-of-Stake blockchain or network.
- Market Capitalization: The total value of a network calculated by multiplying the price per token by the number of tokens in circulation.
- On-Ramps: Third parties accepting the coin for payments, deposits, withdrawals, and so on.

A historical example of a Bitcoin hard fork is *Bitcoin Cash*. In August 2017, the Bitcoin blockchain underwent its first hard fork in history, resulting in Bitcoin and the newly formed Bitcoin Cash. The preexisting Bitcoin proponents and developers were in disagreement about how to address Bitcoin's noted scalability challenges. Proponents such as Blockstream rallied to maintain the existing network while leveraging Layer 2 solutions such as sidechains through the Bitcoin Lightning network, while public *BTC* critics including Craig Wright and Roger Ver argued in favor of increasing each block size from 8MB to 32MB, which would enable greater throughput capacity but would also create a greater cost burden on storage and on load times as each block would contain up to four times more data than an 8MB block, which inherently puts the speed of a network at risk.

Since the two factions were deadlocked, the latter group decided to hard fork and branch away from the incumbent group. Thus, while sharing the same historical previous blocks, Bitcoin (*BTC*) and Bitcoin Cash (*BCH*) separated on August 1st, 2017 due to disagreement about how to best fulfill the original vision of Satoshi Nakomoto. Bitcoin holders on record at the time of the split were compensated with BCH in a 1:1 ratio to their existing *BTC* holdings. Still, since the Bitcoin Cash team failed to attract a majority of the Bitcoin network's miners, users, and proponents based on the vote, Bitcoin and *BTC* continued to reign as the original Bitcoin. This can also be measured by looking at each protocol's *hashrate*, meaning collective mining power and activity. Bitcoin's hashrate increased exponentially since the time of the hard fork while Bitcoin Cash's hashrate was overall steady and/or null in comparison. This signals that ecosystem participants favored Bitcoin over Bitcoin Cash and largely continue to do so.[11]

Another historical example of a Bitcoin hard fork is Bitcoin SV. Only a year after the hard fork described above, Bitcoin Cash went through its own split in November 2018. This hard fork was propelled by Craig Wright, who was actively seeking to fulfill his interpretation of Satoshi's vision he believed was not being fulfilled through the existing Bitcoin Cash network. Wright wished to upgrade the block size from 32MB to 128MB in order to once again address the scalability capabilities cited in the original fork from Bitcoin. However, Roger Ver was not in favor of this hard fork and instead wished to settle on a soft fork software upgrade.

This schism had ripple effects across the industry as it forced miners to not only decide which chain they would direct their computing power toward but also applied pressure on exchanges to decide if they were going to support only one of the two chains or both. This division did not reflect positively on the digital assets industry as the split was widely perceived to be a power struggle rather than a technological advancement. Some wallets and centralized exchanges chose to support the newly forked chain known as Bitcoin SV (*BSV*), which stands for Satoshi's Vision, although the major exchanges elected to support Bitcoin Cash in the immediate term.[12]

An example of an Ethereum hard fork is Ethereum Classic. Ethereum today is not the same chain as Ethereum in 2015. After a debilitating hack resulted in a $60 million loss, the original Ethereum chain was reverted to a custody provider in July 2016. As a response, the Ethereum community voted to rewind the stolen transactions to return the assets back to the previous owners. As this is a fundamental change to the historical record, an override of the blockchain would need to occur, which can only be accomplished via a hard fork that essentially erased the hack from the original ledger, secured the stolen funds, and returned the funds to the rightful owners.

In order to solidify this return of funds and prevent that same hack from occurring again, Ethereum underwent a hard fork. This hard fork changed the structure of the hashes of each block and created a new ledger, beginning at the hash immediately prior to the hacked block, known as a snapshot. The majority of computing power on Ethereum elected to move forward with the new chain and return stolen funds rather than continuing to be associated with a known hackable chain, even though this fork brought the immutability of the Ethereum ledger into question. Upon this fork, the new chain assumed its rightful position as the primary Ethereum everyone uses today. The original chain, which resolved the hack in a different way, was forced to rebrand and is known today as Ethereum Classic (*ETC*).

Ethereum (*ETH*) maintained the better part of its developer base and community to solidify itself as the "true" Ethereum, which is why it is still actionable and active. Ethereum Classic, unfortunately, suffered subsequent attacks, which can happen with greater frequency due to a lack of active developers and interest on a chain after a hard fork.[13]

Layer 2 Applications

The forking model was the original method of scaling and modifying a blockchain. Forking has since been supplanted by what are called Layer 2 solutions. Layer 2 (L2) solutions build on Layer 1s and use the Layer 1s for finality of transactions, much like products and applications built on Layer 2s do. However, Layer 2s are designed specifically with scalability in mind. They improve a Layer 1's capabilities without undergoing a full coding modification as was done with forking.

Rather than reconstructing a highway and pointing traffic to the new highway, Layer 2s can simply construct a system of floating highways enabling traffic to flow better on the same road. After all, there is no need to tear up the pavement and recreate what already exists.

The Layer 2 model has come into play for many of the Layer 1s with the overarching goal of increasing Layer 1 efficiencies. This efficiency typically comes in the following forms:[14]

1. Increasing throughput capabilities as measured in transactions per second.
2. Reducing the fees associated with each transaction.
3. Connecting multiple Layer 1 solutions or acting as a "blockchain bridge."

Layer 2s can be implemented in a variety of ways such as channels and sidechains, although they are typically separate projects and blockchains simply leveraging the Layer 1 data and processing capabilities. Take Ethereum for example, which is a prominent Layer 1 with numerous Layer 2 solutions. The official Ethereum website states, "A Layer 2 is a separate blockchain that extends Ethereum and inherits the security guarantees of Ethereum." The Layer 2 solution handles the traffic and transactions while relying on Ethereum itself to settle, validate, and store the transactions.[15]

The Layer 2 blockchain constantly communicates with the Layer 1 it is built for (Ethereum, Avalanche, Algorand, and so on) by submitting batches of transactions its network handles. This mechanism eases the constant traffic on the Layer 1 as it simply receives periodic batches of completed transactions it must store, as opposed to receiving, facilitating, and storing transactions in real-time. This is typically known as a *rollup* as transactions are all gathered and batched together. As the batch fills up, the Layer 2 solution will relay it to the Layer 1 blockchain for settlement and validation.

Rather than all these transactions paying separate transaction fees, a batch is only charged one transaction fee. This single transaction fee is divided up among all of the users in the batch, therefore reducing fees for all parties involved. Rollups can reduce transaction fees by a factor of one hundred relative to standard Ethereum transactions. A Layer 2 solution can focus on the scalability of the network while Layer 1 handles the security, data availability, and decentralization.[15]

For example, an Ethereum Layer 2 doesn't need to be the most decentralized system as long as it can batch and complete transactions. It will always answer to Ethereum, and therefore the decentralization of the network is still measured in Ethereum's decentralization sentiment. This avoids spending any resources on reinventing the wheel and enables Layer 2 to focus on value creation through scale while Layer 1 focuses on value creation through security and consistency.[15]

Nonetheless, few things are without security issues and Layer 2 solutions are no exception. While the main network security relies on the Layer 1 blockchain, it is still possible for Layer 2s to have exploitable vulnerabilities. These exploitations may result in lost funds on Layer 2 transactions and batches, and may eventually make their way down to the Layer 1 if any malicious blocks pass through.

Lightning Network

The Lightning Network is a Bitcoin Layer 2 solution enabling the processing of transactions off-chain. The Lightning network solution was proposed in 2015 and rolled out in full over the next several years. The real purpose for Lightning isn't to facilitate all transactions, but rather to bulk smaller ones. Bitcoin has the lowest throughput among most blockchains to date, and yet still has the highest price per coin at around $16,800 at the end of 2022. Gas fees on Bitcoin transactions range on average from $5 to $20. These fees are incredibly low for large-value transactions compared to traditional finance.

However, these fees make little sense regarding the classic semi-rhetorical question: *Can I buy a coffee with Bitcoin*? A $5 gas fee would at least double the price of many a coffee, and a $20 gas fee would quadruple it. Purchasing small value items with Bitcoin is not logical. Furthermore, if you are banking on the price of Bitcoin going up and not staying the same, in practice you wouldn't pay for anything until *after* you've cashed out your investment.

For smaller and more numerous transactions of this nature, the Lightning Network can take these off-chain and process on a side ledger before stamping them onto the official Bitcoin blockchain, or *mainnet*. A mainnet refers to the live ledger with real transactions. A *testnet* is a replica of a mainnet that allows developers to interact with a blockchain and build an application without affecting the current applications or status on the mainnet. It can be seen as the beta version or the sandbox mode of a blockchain application. Once developers are satisfied with their work on the testnet, they may choose to fully launch the application on the mainnet.[16] In order to use the Lightning Network, a user must have a lightning-compatible wallet. In September 2021 Twitter made crypto headlines when it enabled its *Tips* feature to let users "tip" their favorite Twitter accounts through the Bitcoin Lightning Network for payments ranging from $1–$10 or custom amounts.[17]

Plasma

Plasma is an Ethereum sidechain-driven solution that forms new "child chains" through an unlimited supply of Merkle trees. These Merkle trees are essentially smaller, fractional bits of the full Ethereum code. Rather than comparing new blocks to the entire Etheruem chain, the blocks are compared to these bits, which are small enough in size for efficiency but large enough to properly manage fraudulent transactions and replicate the minimum threshold needed for validation.

Since they are bits, they are inherently simpler and faster to traverse, meaning new transactions can be grouped into these bits and verified off-chain (on the side chains rather than on Ethereum itself). This enables the child chains to handle large traffic as it comes in, confirm the new blocks in a more efficient manner, and stamp the newly accepted transactions onto Ethereum as a batch rather than individually. Plasma, like other Layer 2 solutions, is designed to reduce gas fees through this mechanism and process.[18]

Polygon

Polygon is governed by its own ERC-20 token known as *MATIC*. As a Layer 2 solution, Polygon makes use of a series of plasma chains (side chains), zero-knowledge (ZK) rollups, and optimistic rollups to improve the scalability associated with Ethereum.

ZK-Rollups batch multiple transactions and transfers for processing off-chain. Once completed, the batch is transferred to the mainnet in a single transaction, which not only improves the speed of transactions on the Layer 1 but also typically reduces gas fees for each user involved. Optimistic rollups are designed to move even quicker, as they will simply assume transactions are legitimate and stamp them to the mainnet, surpassing the limited processing the typical ZK-Rollup can handle. Optimistic rollup transactions are typically only checked and audited in the event a transaction is called into question or the integrity of a block is challenged. This is particularly useful for high-volume activities of lower significance or monetary value as the efficiency benefits found through the optimistic rollup likely outweigh the need for individual transaction checks and buffers.[19]

ZERO-KNOWLEDGE ROLLUP

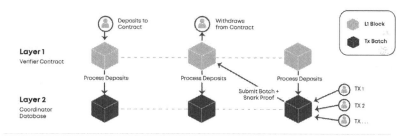

OPTIMISTIC ROLLUP

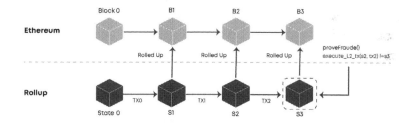

Arbitrum

Arbitrum is an Ethereum scaling solution using optimistic rollups with the operational goal of scaling the Ethereum network to a capacity of 40,000 transactions per second at a price of mere cents per transaction given its bundling and batching mechanism. Transactions are essentially added to the network's "inbox" as they are recorded on a sidechain. At any given point, the number and profile of the transactions determines Arbitrum's "chain state." Arbitrum is also DeFi-compatible with other applications on Ethereum through the Ethereum Virtual Machine (EVM), which is the software bedrock and operating system of nearly all Ethereum-based applications.[20]

Accumulate

Accumulate is an identity-based Layer 2 solution designed for interoperability across multiple Layer 1 chains. Rather than utilizing 28-digit wallet identifiers, Accumulate makes use of "username" style codes to identify individual, group, or enterprise wallets across a number of different Layer 1 solutions. Its multichain architecture enables greater throughput up to 70,000 transactions per second (TPS).[21]

Immutable X

Immutable X is one of the pioneering solutions addressing the scalability of Ethereum-based NFT transactions. When NFT trading volume spiked over the course of 2021 and 2022, Ethereum gas fees were quoted at an average between $25–$50 per transaction, with numerous cases quoted in the hundreds of dollars for gas fees alone. The purpose of Ethereum became stronger than ever through the NFT craze, but the accompanying gas fee spike also put a spotlight on the scalability problem of the network under this immense transaction volume.

Immutable X designed a solution for minting and transacting NFTs with zero gas fees in a peer-to-peer manner. The solution takes thousands of transactions in a single batch and utilizes the ZK-Rollup feature to transfer and validate them before stamping them to the Ethereum mainnet. At a 9,000 transactions per second throughput, Immutable X seeks to reduce the NFT-driven volume on the mainnet and provide a suitable solution across various NFT Marketplaces.[22]

With an understanding of Layer 1 and Layer 2 relationships, the next question is how these various blockchains interact with each other. It's evident all Layer 2s on the same Layer 1 blockchain make use of the same common base layer, but how do different Layer 1s interact with each other, if at all?

Working backwards, this is where blockchain bridges come into play. The industry recognized that while Layer 1s have the capacity to grow and respond to market demands, the ecosystem would inherently be inhibited if none of the Layer 1 projects could move across blockchains since they would not be maximizing the user bases or the full range of applications. This would continue to perpetuate the competition among blockchains. While beneficial for new development and features, competition would demarcate all of the users and separate them into their preferred blockchains and only their associated projects.[23]

The response was to develop *bridging* solutions, sometimes even referred to as Layer 0 solutions, meaning a base layer to Layer 1s. If Layer 1s are the foundations of buildings, imagine bridges to be the tunnels underneath and between these buildings. As projects flow downward from the Layer 2 solution to the Layer 1 solution such as Ethereum or Avalanche, they can also be sent across to another Layer 1. This transaction is facilitated by the bridging solution. The blockchain bridge typically supports several consensus mechanisms such as Proof-of-Stake, Proof-of-Work, Proof-of-Activity, and so on, to facilitate this desired interoperability.

Another analogy to understand this is a global map. Imagine each country was a Layer 1 solution. All of the individual states, regions, and territories would be examples of Layer 2 solutions for better governance and batching of people (i.e., states/provinces, counties, cities). These solutions are great within each country, but a totally different set of rules or structures may apply in other countries. There must be a solution to enable cross-border interactions or else people would be limited to just one country.

Transportation solutions like planes, ships, and railroads may be used to transport humans and goods across borders and into countries all over the globe. This is what the bridge does in the blockchain world. Much like transportation services were developed after society recognized the need for cross-border interactions, bridging solutions were developed after the industry recognized the need for interoperability and limited barriers across blockchains. Examples of bridging solutions include Polkadot and Cosmos.[24]

Much of the existing digital assets landscape is built on Ethereum. This means the cost of switching blockchains is not only defined in literal expenses, but also in the cost of converting your user base to a new workflow. The boom of DeFi applications, NFTs, DAOs, and so on all largely rode on the back of Ethereum. Most early entrants-turned-whales (whale is a term designating a cryptocurrency holder who falls in the top percentiles of holders relative to the general public) store their assets in Ether, and build and manage their projects on Ethereum.

For whales and early adopters, there is not a strong incentive to migrate away from Ethereum as there may be for new entrants and users to look at competing solutions. Although the nature of digital assets is still quite new relative to other periods of technological revolution, it seems Ethereum is the incumbent blockchain being disrupted by other Layer 1s, with each one competing to present itself as the "David" to Ethereum's "Goliath."

Aside from the speed and transactions capability, security and interoperability are two other factors investors and users typically take into account when analyzing Layer 1s, and blockchains in general. Interoperability is simply the ability of one blockchain to seamlessly interact with another blockchain, such that the end user doesn't detect even a blip or bump in the process. Interoperability has long been a goal of developers and contributors to the ecosystem because it's become evident that having an industry of competing chains will only divide the audience into silos rather than building a collectively strong, fortified, single "digital assets user base."

To counter the problem of "siloed solutions" unable to interact with each other, developers have been building the *bridge solutions* mentioned earlier. For example, you might hear the phrase *Avalanche Ethereum bridge*, which refers to a solution enabling Avalanche-based tokens to interact with Ethereum-based wallets and services. This creates efficiencies between wallets that support *AVAX* and wallets that support *ETH* and Ethereum-based tokens, as there may indeed be certain limitations when it comes to retail-level wallets.

Having an effective and secure bridge between two or more blockchains is comparable to having strong enough glue to keep an entire puzzle together. The more solidly connected those puzzle pieces, the stronger, more intact, and smoother the entire puzzle. Should the glue fail to hold over time, those puzzle pieces will slowly separate and eventually fall out of place, thereby effectively undoing the master image.

In this scenario, blockchain communities can be seen as the puzzle pieces, with the entire digital assets ecosystem being represented by the final assembled puzzle. Proper bridges and interoperable solutions enable all blockchain users to contribute to the common goal of the final image. In a demarcated and singular blockchain-based industry, the grand puzzle will likely fail to hold, if it were to ever complete itself in the first place.

Lastly, the word "secure" deserves further consideration. A common saying in the industry is: "You can choose two of the following: speed, security, and scalability." The phrase, while originally an old programming phrase, was applied to blockchains as competitors delivered more speed and scalability to the industry. Scalability is typically defined as the ability to increase the throughput of a network, measured in transactions per second. However, the raw capabilities of a network are only one facet of success. Arguably, the network's community and resources are more indicative of scaling successes than sheer capacity.[25]

Security is a critical part of digital assets since they do in fact represent monetary value. When faster chains like Solana come to the forefront, it is often accompanied by overlooking how security and up-time are real problems for the network. This may cause users to adopt the faster chain for the sake of convenience while downplaying network security and uptime.

When discussing blockchains, uptime is typically a pillar of a successful network as it describes the amount of time the network was functional and operational for its user base. A decentralized network should have maximal uptime relative to a centralized network since the points of failure are diluted. That being said, should a network go offline for any amount of time, users will likely be unable to transact value across the respective blockchain until it comes back online.

For example, Solana (*SOL*) experienced 9 days in the month of January 2022 where it had either partial or major system outages and degraded performance. One of the appealing attractions of Solana was indeed its speed in transaction execution, and yet users may have suffered during these periods of weaker network health.[26]

There is likely no winner-take-all scenario for any one blockchain. Each chain serves to improve on the one before it in some manner, which is not always simply speed or throughput capacity. This technology is moving faster than any other technical revolution before it, and competition breeds new blockchains on a regular basis.

Similarly, certain blockchains may deem their chains *secure enough* from a risk-reward standpoint when factoring in the sheer speed and traffic capabilities relative to the rest of the competitive landscape. As previously mentioned, the emphasis going forward will likely be put on interoperable solutions that open up a multi-chain world, and may even shine some light on verticals blockchains may begin to specialize in such as asset tokenization, value transfer, or privacy solutions.

While interoperability is an important feature for some, it would be irresponsible not to understand the current mechanisms for maintaining, upgrading, and modifying blockchains.

NOTES

1. See https://www.coinbase.com/learn/crypto-basics/what-is-bitcoin and https://www.investopedia.com/tech/what-happens-bitcoin-after-2 1-million-mined/

2. See https://www.defipulse.com/

3. See https://blog.tokensoft.io/erc-1404-one-year-later-1bf2d8c93432 and https://medium.com/knowledge-centre/erc-token-standard-and-their-types-445f875a0d0b

4. See https://academy.binance.com/en/articles/what-is-avalanche-avax

5. See https://thenewstack.io/solana-rust-developers/

6. See https://solana.com/news/proof-of-history

7. See https://defillama.com/chain/Solana

8. See https://www.gemini.com/cryptopedia/ ripple-xrp-cryptocurrency-fiat-bridge, https://smartasset.com/financial-advisor/ripple-xrp, and https://www.litefinance.com/blog/for-beginners/ripple-killer-of-payment-systems/

9. See https://www.investopedia.com/terms/s/soft-fork.asp and https://freemanlaw.com/hard-and-soft-forks-a-detailed-and-simplified-explanation-of-how-blockchains-evolve/

10. See https://www.investopedia.com/terms/s/segwit-segregated-witness.asp and https://www.sofi.com/learn/content/segwit-segregated-witness/

11. See https://www.investopedia.com/news/all-about-bitcoin-cash-hard-fork/ and https://startuptalky.com/bitcoin-cash-vs-bitcoin/

12. See https://www.gemini.com/cryptopedia/bsv-what-is-bitcoin-sv

13. See https://www.gemini.com/cryptopedia/ethereum-classic-etc-vs-eth#section-the-origin-of-ethereum-classic and https://www.investopedia.com/terms/e/ethereum-classic.asp

14. See https://academy.binance.com/en/articles/what-is-layer-1-in-blockchain

15. See https://ethereum.org/en/layer-2/

16. See https://academy.bit2me.com/en/que-es-testnet/

17. See https://cointelegraph.com/bitcoin-for-beginners/what-is-the-lightning-network-in-bitcoin-and-how-does-it-work, https://privacypros.io/tools/bitcoin-fee-estimator/, and https://blog.twitter.com/en_us/topics/product/2021/bringing-tips-to-everyone

18. See https://academy.binance.com/en/glossary/plasma

19. See https://www.benzinga.com/money/what-is-polygon/

20. See https://decrypt.co/resources/what-is-arbitrum-speeding-up-ethereum-using-optimistic-rollups, https://decrypt.co/resources/ethereum-virtual-machine, and https://coinmarketcap.com/alexandria/glossary/ethereum-virtual-machine-evm

21. See https://accumulatenetwork.io/

22. See https://www.theblockcrypto.com/data/nft-non-fungible-tokens/marketplaces, https://www.immutable.com/, https://docs.x.immutable.com/docs, and https://cointelegraph.com/news/ethereum-gas-fees-drop-to-lowest-levels-since-august-2021

23. See https://coinmarketcap.com/alexandria/glossary/layer-0

24. See https://docsend.com/view/tdgbf4sfmyd7sr3m

25. See https://www.binance.com/en/blog/fiat/layer-1-blockchain-tokens-everything-you-need-to-know-421499824684903155

26. See https://status.solana.com/uptime?page=4

CHAPTER 3

UTILITY TOKENS

U tility tokens are digital assets that may represent access to an underlying blockchain ecosystem, act as the transactional currency inside these ecosystems, or support governance of chains and projects. These tokens do not legally or compliantly promise token holders any equity ownership, debt distributions, revenue sharing, or profit-sharing from the blockchain protocol. Instead, utility tokens may simply act as a key to facilitate transactions on the blockchain and associated decentralized applications.

As explained in the previous chapter, applications can be built upon Layer 1 blockchains. These applications, projects, and add-ons usually require the Layer 1 utility token for access and interactions. Since the mainnet is responsible for finality of transactions, that chain's utility token will be transacted at some point in time when interacting with these applications in order to power the blockchain.

For example, a user wishing to interact with a lending service built on Ethereum will likely need to purchase *ETH* in order to gain access to the service. Ethereum is the network, and *ETH* is its network utility token. When interacting with the lending service, a user may be paid in a service-native token, meaning the token originated within the service's ecosystem and used solely within that ecosystem. The token, in this case, is largely a transactional token as it is used to pay users or collect user fees.

It became popular to speculate on a blockchain's future success by purchasing its utility token. This thesis is largely driven by the "network token" model: As the network becomes more popular, usable, and crowded, the utility token will appreciate in value by virtue of more users demanding the token for access to the ecosystem.

Initial Coin Offering (ICO)

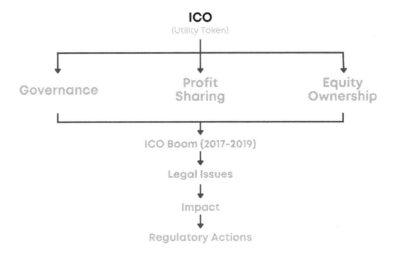

The network token arguably has a stronger value proposition than a purely transactional currency since it may see demand from two types of users:

1. Those who wish to speculate and/or invest in future growth of the network.
2. Those who wish to access other applications built on the blockchain itself and need the asset in bulk to lock in the price.

Recognizing Ethereum as a network and foundation for accessing a vast range of other applications across industries like financial services, supply chain, art, and music gives it a stronger value proposition than Ripple (*XRP*), which is solely a transactional currency.

Does the value of XRP really need to appreciate over time if it exists to facilitate many transfers? Does the value of ETH really need to appreciate over time if it exists to facilitate and secure the operations of numerous applications, goods, and services?

The latter question is more of a leading question that highlights Ethereum's utility token (*ETH*) as a multifaceted digital asset. Access to the Ethereum ecosystem is safeguarded by the *ETH* utility token. *ETH* acts as a ticket to the Ethereum ecosystem and everything in it, much like a ticket provides someone with access to a music festival, sporting event, professional conference, and so on.

Nonetheless, transactional coins are an important piece of the ecosystem because of the need for a reliable and designated method of transacting value. Bitcoin was created as the original transactional currency, but there is no one-size-fits-all solution in society—Bitcoin is no exception. Bitcoin's stigma as a transaction token has largely shifted to its utility as a network token in the sense that it solely has store-of-value and transactional properties, but it relies on the strength of its network to hold value.[1]

Network Valuation

Regarding a network's value, Metcalfe's Law describes how *a network's impact is measured as the square of the number of nodes on the network (n^2)*. As the number of nodes increases, the impact of the network, otherwise interpreted as the value or the traction of the network, grows at an even greater pace. Taking this into a Bitcoin perspective, the narrative surrounding Bitcoin as a store-of-value and transactional solution grows with every new user added.[2]

METCALFE'S LAW

Number of nodes increases with n^2

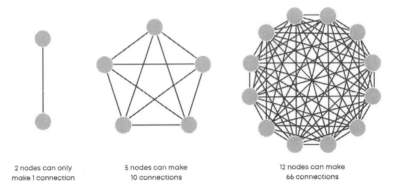

| 2 nodes can only make 1 connection | 5 nodes can make 10 connections | 12 nodes can make 66 connections |

Due to Bitcoin's high price per coin in fiat terms, the idea of spending it on small purchases or sending small amounts of money can be a daunting idea. Bitcoin can be broken down into much smaller parts, with the smallest measurement being the satoshi. There are 100 million satoshis (known commonly as sats) in just one bitcoin. Rather than listing something as 0.0005 *BTC*, it can be listed as 50,000 sats, which at a price of $20,000/*BTC*, for example, would represent $10 in spending money. This is an improvement over using a full Bitcoin for your daily spend, but it still comes with additional challenges, such as the scalability of the Bitcoin blockchain.

While the Bitcoin architecture works well, it only allows for 3–7 transactions per second (tps), which doesn't satisfy the needs of Visa, for example, which averages 2,000 tps on an average day, and has the capacity for nearly 65,000 tps if everyone was using a credit card at once. Given this, Bitcoin has been facing an inherent battle of establishing itself as a global transaction currency versus a reserve asset that the digital gold narrative reinforces.

To account for this future outlook, other transactional coins like Ripple (*XRP*), Litecoin (*LTC*), and Monero (*XMR*) entered the industry at a higher supply of circulating tokens relative to Bitcoin, with a potential goal of suppressing the USD value and being more viable as a payments or transactional solution.

Financial Uses for Utility Tokens

As the ecosystem developed during 2017–2018, the term "platform coins" became more commonly used. The platform coin is a hybrid between a network token and a transactional token. As mentioned earlier, projects can be developed on top of a Layer 1 blockchain such as Ethereum. These projects may, but aren't required, to have their own tokens associated specifically with the project's ecosystem. A project's token may act as both an access token to the project and a payments or rewards facilitator for the project.

Aave is a good example of an entirely different use case for cryptocurrency technology. Aave is an open-source liquidity protocol built on Ethereum. Users are able to purchase *AAVE*, which acts as a utility token to operate the Aave network, which is built on the Ethereum blockchain. Users are able to deposit *AAVE* tokens into what's known as a liquidity pool—a smart contract pool to store digital assets for the facilitation of lending, trading, or other decentralized activities—and earn a yield on those deposits. The rewards are paid out to liquidity providers in the form of *AAVE* and other cryptocurrencies.[3]

Not only do users need to purchase the *AAVE* token to gain access to the platform (network token), but they also accept transactions in the form of the *AAVE* token (transactional token). This two-pronged approach provides cheaper exchange rates for traders around the world while giving the *AAVE* token and similar token-enabled projects a stronger value proposition relative to just a network token or just a transactional token.

Many of the early network and transactional tokens were thrust into the spotlight during the ICO boom between 2017 and 2019. An Initial Coin Offering (ICO) is a method of fundraising by issuing a utility token to the general public and positioning buyers of this token as investors. Utility tokens throughout this era had all sorts of features, promises, and stipulations ranging from governance capabilities to profit sharing to equity ownership in the projects issuing these tokens.

Unfortunately, these ICOs were very rarely registered as securities and therefore were operating as illegal fundraising vehicles. Security tokens and tokens representing real world assets are discussed in further detail in Chapter 7.

Just under $20 billion was raised globally through Initial Coin Offerings between 2017 and 2019. Quarter 1 of 2018 saw the peak of capital raising through ICOs, amounting to $6.8 billion. This coincided with the peak of Bitcoin's price at $19,834 in December 2017, which may have signaled a shift in investors chasing outsized returns through *altcoin* promises. *Altcoin* is a slang term derived from *alternative coin* and simply represents any token that is not Bitcoin. Although the industry has since matured significantly, it is still common to refer to smaller, newer projects as altcoins, and this was especially pertinent throughout the ICO boom when many of these fly-by-night altcoins originated. Someone could take an ERC standard token, come up with an idea for a use case and inherent value for it, and then mint it instantaneously. In a matter of minutes you'd have yourself a currency anyone around the world could buy using their own cryptocurrency.[4]

Most ICOs never had any warnings about the risks of participating in the ICO and were largely insider schemes commonly referred to as *pump-and-dumps*. Per TokenData, "The data shows that ICOs raise a majority of their capital (58 percent) through private rounds and pre-sales. They do so by giving presale participants an average 'Bonus' of 34 percent on the ETH:Token exchange rate compared to participants in the main/public stage of the ICO. Unsurprisingly, the size and timing (lock-up) of the 'bonus' are often the subject of debate and can lead to controversy among token sale participants and in secondary trading."[5] This pre-sale feature enabled insiders of the projects to buy coins at a hefty discount before the coin hit the public market on a cryptocurrency exchange. It then followed with the dumping of those coins by insiders while the demand for them was hot.

Unfortunately, this put the public at an asymmetrical disadvantage since public investors were left competing with each other to "time the top." Since insiders had already purchased these digital assets at a discount, they had a much higher chance of price appreciation than the public, and therefore a more sizable opportunity for capital gains. As prices rose parabolically throughout the ICO boom, insiders were able to achieve returns of 5x, 10x, 50x, and even over 100x.

These insider sales had to be met with public buyers, however, and as the steam wore off, many public retail investors were left holding coins of these projects with limited or no investor protections. The resulting aftermath of the vast majority of ICOs was upwards of 90 percent losses over the course of 2018 and 2019, as evidenced by the industry's market cap which climbed from $80 Billion in July 2017 to $800 Billion in January 2018 but then fell back to $100 Billion in December 2018.[6]

Not all ICOs were set up as fly-by-night projects. While the ICO craze was indeed a dark stain on the reputation of digital assets due to its "scammy" sentiment, it did show the power of these assets as fundraising vehicles outside the standard angel investing, venture capital, and private equity models in which high-net-worth individuals and organizations control nearly all the market share. The ICO era showed the democratization of access digital assets ushered in. There were some cases of successful decentralized projects and missions that still exist and are even thriving, as described below.

Filecoin (*FIL*)

Filecoin is a decentralized data storage network that relies on its *FIL* utility token to facilitate transactions among users. Rather than relying on one data provider and storage system (such as Amazon Web Services, Google, Apple, or Dropbox), Filecoin distributes the storage responsibilities across all users and nodes on the network. This reduces the concern over a single point of failure and ensures that user data cannot be controlled or monetized by one corporation or group.

The *FIL* utility token is used for data interactions. Users pay to store their files on the network, and can also get paid to store files from other users on a network. In general, users likely play on both sides of this equation. Since *FIL* is the utility token here, users may allocate their resources accordingly based on if they require storage or if they wish to generate gains for providing storage. *FIL* is a true utility token as it is required for all aspects of the Filecoin network rather than acting as a spoof token for some service that could easily be facilitated with *ETH*, for example.

FILECOIN

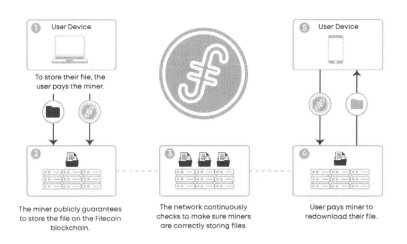

Filecoin raised $257 million in 2017 through its ICO. While users may have purchased tokens under the guise of capital appreciation and as a bet on the decentralized file storage network itself, the function of *FIL* is strictly utility for storage purposes. Roughly three years later, Filecoin launched its mainnet in October 2020 and now maintains over 2.5 billion gigabytes of storage, which is enough to hold more than 10,000 copies of Wikipedia. This can be interpreted as a symbol of functionality of both the network and the *FIL* token as utility, rather than as the pseudo-investment that was so rampant during the ICO boom.[7]

Chainlink (*LINK*)

Chainlink is a blockchain platform and service that enables the connectivity among blockchain-native activities (on-chain) and external information and factors (off-chain). Essentially, Chainlink is a decentralized data oracle that draws a wide variety of data for specific uses within smart contracts and blockchain apps to leverage its technology. For example, Chainlink can draw stock pricing data, financial data, novelty data (like sporting game scores and statistics, betting lines, weather reports, and so on), and other desired insights necessary to operate a unique program on-chain. In short, Chainlink is a middleware between the external world's infrastructure and the blockchain world's infrastructure, enabling useful communication and interactivity between the two.[8]

Chainlink is governed by its *LINK* token, which was issued in September 2017 as the platform came to market and raised $32 million across 1 billion *LINK* tokens. The supply of *LINK* was dispersed among investors, among the parent company (SmartContract.com), and among nodes who support the sustainability and growth of the network. The platform works with and serves other digital assets platforms such as Aave, Compound, and Synthetix among its almost 1,000 oracle networks. This has culminated in over 6.6 billion on-chain data points and $7+ Trillion transaction value enabled by 2023.[9]

NOTES

1. See https://medium.com/capriole/has-metcalfes-law-stopped-working-for-bitcoin-45209e02c4bb

2. See https://www.techopedia.com/definition/29066/metcalfes-law

3. See https://www.gemini.com/cryptopedia/what-is-a-liquidity-pool-crypto-market-liquidity and https://aave.com/

4. See https://www.statista.com/statistics/804748/worldwide-amount-crytocurrency-ico-projects/ and https://www.wsj.com/articles/bitcoin-hits-all-time-high-of-19-786-topping-record-from-december-2017-11606750573

5. See https://mailchi.mp/tokendata/tokendata-weekly-newsletter-289971

6. See https://coinmarketcap.com/charts/

7. See https://docs.filecoin.io/about-filecoin/what-is-filecoin/ and https://decrypt.co/resources/filecoin

8. See https://www.investopedia.com/chainlink-link-definition-5217559

9. See https://messari.io/asset/chainlink/profile/launch-and-initial-token-distribution and https://data.chain.link/?_ga=2.244675205.1876347526.1676129272-718383571.1676129272

CHAPTER 4

DECENTRALIZED FINANCE (DEFI)

The traditional financial services landscape began its migration to the blockchain through what's known as DeFi or *decentralized finance*. Much like the financial services industry is broken into various verticals such as sales and trading, banking, lending, and asset management, the DeFi space consists of multiple decentralized programs, platforms, and protocols offering a similar range of services. Some of the most prominent DeFi applications include the following:

- Trading
- Lending and Borrowing
- Derivatives
- Stablecoins
- Digital Asset Management
- Yield Farming (staking on steroids)

Before delving into these five categories, it is important to understand one of the most fundamental mechanisms in DeFi: *Staking*.

Staking is the act of depositing digital asset funds into a smart contract and locking them up for a period of time in order to provide liquidity to the smart contract and its associated function. Stakers are rewarded with yield for locking up their assets, much like a person is rewarded with interest for depositing their funds in a bank. An analogy to this is a bank asking you to deposit money into a new account. Let's say a new local bank emerged and are incentivizing new accounts with a high interest rate. Though 10 percent sounds unheard of for a bank to offer just for you depositing and holding your dollars there, this was the case in DeFi. In fact, some staking strategies, referred to as Yield Farming, earned aggregate yields above 1,000 percent during nascent and volatile times.

Liquidity

Liquidity is a key facet of the digital assets ecosystem. Liquidity is essentially defined as the ability for an asset to be swapped for cash or cash equivalents. The more liquid an asset is, the easier and more ready it is to be converted into its equivalent value of cash. The less liquid an asset is, the more difficult it is to convert that asset into cash at the *fair market value*. Examples of very liquid assets include large-cap stocks, US treasury bonds, and cash in bank accounts. These are all typically simple and available to swap since there are prevalent buyers at multiple pricing levels. Less liquid assets include real estate properties, private investment fund interests, and pre-IPO shares, since there is usually a lack of marketplaces for these, or simply little demand for active buyers.

The measure of market liquidity may come from the depth of an order book, which shows the buyers and sellers of an asset at various price points, and this activity is signified by trading volume, which shows how much value of and how many times an asset was traded in a given period of time. The greater the order book depth, the more liquid an asset will be since it indicates a greater bench of active buyers and sellers. Essentially, a deeper order book can absorb more buying or selling pressure at given price points than a thin order book. This is important because a key component of asset liquidity is the ability to convert from asset to cash or cash equivalents without affecting the market price greatly. The more liquid an asset will be, the more readily convertible it is to cash at each price point; the more readily an asset is convertible to cash, the less likely it is for that asset's price to fluctuate with trades.[1]

To date, trading venues and order matching systems for assets have been done through brokerages, exchanges, and marketplaces, robustly built out with organic buyers and sellers, market makers who incentivize and maintain order book depth, and a range of brokers and agents who help connect buyers and sellers. There is a great deal of help from third parties on most centralized exchanges and marketplaces to ensure liquidity and active trading. This is where much of the investors' confidence in buying and selling on a trading venue comes from.

The story in decentralized finance is a bit different, however. Since there is no centralized party managing liquidity, the ability for users to successfully buy, sell, swap, or use digital assets in decentralized applications relies solely on the users in the ecosystem. These users must be incentivized to establish and maintain a reliable two-sided marketplace in order to make DeFi transactions as efficient as possible.

The mechanics of staking follow the original Proof-of-Stake consensus mechanism explained earlier. Users may lock their coins or tokens into a smart contract to help validate the network's operations. Those with a greater portion of assets staked have a greater chance at attaining rewards, much like those with the strongest computing power have a greater chance of mining blocks in a Proof-of-Work system. Proof-of-Stake relies on a relatively decentralized network of contributors to validate transactions.

The more *fragmented the value* is across the network, the more decentralized the network. In other words, a network that has twenty operators (nodes) each with 5 percent of the computing power is likely to be determined as more decentralized than a network of one hundred nodes where one node contributes 90 percent of the computing power and ninety-nine nodes make up the remaining 10 percent of computing power. Even though the latter option has a greater raw number of nodes, the proportional computing power is still heavily concentrated in one large operator. If this operator were to go offline or turn malicious, the whole network is compromised. In the former example, power is distributed evenly across the twenty operators, so even if one or a few operators go offline or turn malicious, the majority of the network will remain operational.

This concept of power distribution is an important principle to keep in mind throughout this chapter and in general. The DeFi mission relies on decentralization and not just in the sheer number of users but in decentralization of the power and value itself. This is where staking comes into play. On the surface level, applications reward stakers for locking up their assets and enabling the application to serve its designated function, such as trading or lending. Deeper than that, however, staking incentivizes a more decentralized network, which is a stronger network as a result of having a larger Total Value Locked, which in turn means more DeFi applications can build on top of the existing infrastructure and available liquidity.

True decentralized networks have no one central point of failure, weaving a net of connections to support the protocol. Through staking rewards, users are incentivized to directly contribute to the Proof-of-Stake consensus mechanism, and every user added is another step towards a more decentralized network. As the number of users and the amount staked increases, these networks will find themselves well-positioned on the centralization-decentralization spectrum.[2]

At the end of 2022, roughly $50 billion worth of assets, after peaking at $180 billion in December 2021, were staked in the DeFi ecosystem across all applicable chains.[3] Specifically, *Staking Rewards* tracked roughly 180 yield-bearing assets and calculated an average interest rate of 7.63 percent.[4] The yield on Ethereum, noting 3.89 percent at the end of 2022, is typically lower than that of the industry average. This makes sense because Ethereum is the most expansive and widely used Layer 1 at the time of writing. Users do not need to be highly incentivized to stake their *ETH* for rewards since the user base is already solidified and aligned with the long-term mission of Ethereum.

Smaller and lesser-known yield-bearing assets may offer above-average yields because users may require higher rewards to commit capital into these chains via staking. For example, NEAR Protocol averaged 8.93 percent, Tron averaged 3.95 percent, Avalanche averaged 9.11 percent, and Algorand averaged 6.82 percent interest rates, noted as *staking rewards*, at the time of writing. Higher yields like this are not simply limited to smaller chains, however. The yields are a reflection of supply and demand in decentralized liquidity pools. A high yield may also indicate investors are looking to borrow high amounts of the asset, and therefore the pools, in efforts of maintaining enough supply, will incentivize stakers by offering higher yields.[5]

Nonetheless, it's important to note how higher yields may also indicate a lack of liquidity in the associated staking application or pool. In traditional financial practices, a higher risk is generally accompanied by a higher return to compensate investors for taking that risk. While stakers may find themselves in an opportunity to generate 15–20 percent yields, they should also be aware a particular staking application offering those yields likely has a greater risk than a staking application offering 5 percent yield on the same asset. It is possible for a staker to become too large a contributor to the liquidity provided in an application, and rather than acting as a miniscule liquidity provider, they now have a position large enough to manipulate the results in the pool, drastically altering the reward structure for other users.

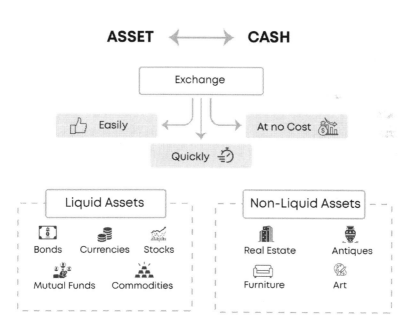

In short, liquidity is not a guarantee in the DeFi ecosystem and is managed as best as possible through the algorithms backing the platforms. The complex algorithms calculate liquidity thresholds and adjust for higher yields, but stakers should understand how a lack of liquidity can trap or hurt them in their ability to liquidate their own positions.

Staking is the basis of much in the DeFi landscape and is one of the building blocks for understanding this side of digital assets. The concept's most applicable sub-verticals are Decentralized Trading and Decentralized Lending and Borrowing. These, along with additional DeFi applications, are explained below.

Decentralized Trading

A decentralized exchange, known as a DEX, relies on no middle centralized party to facilitate trades. Centralized exchanges like Coinbase, Gemini, and Binance all match orders on behalf of their user bases without relying on the blockchain and therefore not always resulting in a traditional, on-chain transaction that powers DeFi in its entirety, hence its name. They store their users' assets, and therefore have access to the users' private keys. The DeFi community generally prefers non-custodial, peer-to-peer solutions enabling them to maintain full control over their own assets. The idiom "Not your keys, not your crypto" became popular to reiterate to new entrants how your keys represent the access to your crypto and nothing else does. Therefore, key security is of utmost importance and many consider sharing your key with anyone other than yourself a security risk.

Since there is no centralized middle party matching orders or effecting trades, DEXes rely on smart contracts to execute instantaneous peer-to-peer trades. Assets remain in the users' wallets all the way up until the moment they are traded in a smart contract, as opposed to transferring funds to a centralized exchange's control before being able to place any trades. There are three types of DEXes:[6]

- *Order Book:* Compiles a record of buy and sell orders to match against other orders on the DEX, much like users would place Limit Orders on a centralized exchange or bids on eBay.

- *Swaps:* This most commonly used DEX relies on liquidity pools and algorithmic balancing to facilitate instantaneous trades at market price.
- *Aggregator:* Aggregates all liquidity pools and/or order books across designated DEXes to better facilitate large trade orders (i.e., minimizing slippage by drawing portions across multiple sources versus using one singular liquidity pool).

Since the Swap DEX is the most commonly used type, it is important to see how things work under the hood. This type of DEX is known as an Automated Market Maker (AMM) since it relies on the underlying smart contracts to automatically find a price between buyers and sellers making use of the DEX. The AMM will measure the liquidity provided and stored within its smart contract, known as a *Liquidity Pool* in this context, against the trade order being sent to the liquidity pool. Traders must pay gas fees to compensate the DEX for each transaction, which vary based on the speed of execution desired and effected.

In general, large orders tend to "move the market" more significantly than smaller orders, which means large orders may be filled at varying prices above or below the intended market price. The difference between one's intended trade price and the executed trade price is called slippage. Slippage can occur upward on buy orders or downward on sell orders and is the result of a market order exceeding the amount of liquidity at the intended trade price. See the examples below for reference within a centralized order book context.

SLIPPAGE

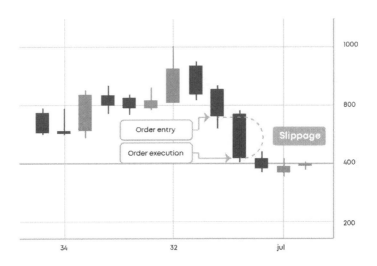

Assume Asset A is priced at $100, and there are fifty shares offered for sale at $101. There is another block of fifty shares offered for sale at $102, and another block of fifty shares offered for sale at $103. A trader may see the market price at $100 and place a market buy order for 150 shares at an intended price of $100. However, since the first sell order begins at $101, the trader ends up filling those fifty shares and then continues buying, purchasing the available shares in the order book across each of the prices: $101, $102, and $103, for a total of 150 shares at an average price of $102. This results in slippage of $2 per share (or 2 percent).

On the other hand, that trader could place smaller orders and fill fifty shares at a time for more calculated pricing. The larger the size of the trade, the greater the chance of slippage as it will fill and absorb more depth within the order book, thus leading to a wider range of fill prices.

On the flip side, slippage can occur with sell orders that drive the price of the asset downwards greater than expected. Take a similar scenario as above where Asset A is priced at $100. Assume there are outstanding buy orders at $99, $98, and $97, with fifty shares available at each price. A sell order of 150 shares would fill the first fifty at $99, the second fifty at $98, and the remaining fifty at $97. This results in an average sell price of $98, which may be less than the trader's intended sell price. This too may be exacerbated with the size of the trade, which is why understanding liquidity and order book depth is an important facet of trading.[7]

SLIPPAGE USE CASE

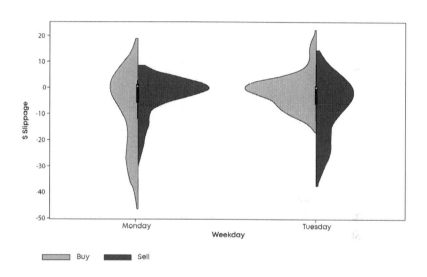

Unfortunately, DEXes do not solve the slippage challenges existing in centralized order books. In fact, DEXes have their own slippage that is a function of the underlying swap algorithm covered below.

Liquidity Pools

AMM's rely on the *constant product formula* to calculate the liquidity in a liquidity pool at any given time and trade. The formula $x * y = k$ represents *Asset 1 * Asset 2 = Constant*. That constant is indicative of the total amount of liquidity in a pool. The amount of liquidity in a pool is calculated by the product of the amount of Asset 1 and Asset 2, which can be represented by any digital assets. These pairs of digital assets are known as a *trading pair*, and nearly any range of trading pairs can be created through a DEX.

Since trades are executed against that liquidity pool, buy orders will drain liquidity while sell orders will add liquidity. For example, if an AMM user were to buy Asset 1, there would be less of Asset 1 in that liquidity pool upon order execution. Since k is a constant amount of liquidity, the price of either Asset 1 or Asset 2 must increase to ensure the product of Asset 1 and Asset 2 still equals that k constant. In this scenario, some amount of Asset 1 was purchased by a user and therefore removed from the liquidity pool. By nature, the price of Asset 1 will now have to rise in order to maintain the constant product formula. Conversely, if one were to sell Asset 1, this would increase the supply of Asset 1 in the liquidity pool and therefore decrease the price of Asset 1. This is the mechanism that drives pricing and execution in an AMM.[8]

HOW AUTOMATED MARKET MAKERS WORKS

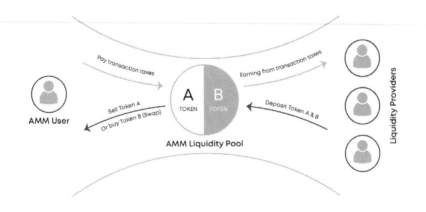

The constant k can be increased as new liquidity providers (LPs) contribute to the liquidity pool, although LPs must contribute an equal amount of Asset 1 and Asset 2 to maintain the proper proportion at the time of contribution. This is why trades will affect the pricing of Asset 1 and Asset 2, but additional liquidity provision can increase the constant k, and therefore increase the depth of the pool itself. LPs are rewarded for their contributions via pro rata shares in transaction fees that occur within the pool, with larger LPs enjoying a larger share of the transaction fees.[9]

DEXes are still susceptible to both price slippage (a change in price caused by external movements), but the above examples are more specifically defined as measures of price impact (a change in price caused by someone's own trade). However, in a swap DEX like an Automated Market Maker, slippage is not calculated against the order book but against what the expected trades were to be on the DEX.

Some DEXes offer a slippage tolerance feature for users to select prior to placing a trade. The slippage amount selected essentially acts as a tolerance level for the trader, only allowing trades to be executed at or below that tolerance level, and rejecting the order or filling only a portion of the trade order up until the slippage tolerance level is reached in a trade scenario. Again, liquidity pools with *deeper* liquidity from providers will safeguard against slippage better than *thinner* liquidity pools or liquidity pools offering less reserves and having a lower constant k.[10]

Another negative externality to the DEX landscape is *impermanent loss*. Impermanent loss occurs when the price of a liquidity provider's asset size changes relative to the base price at deposit. The price of an asset in a liquidity pool is subject to supply and demand based on other traders and liquidity providers in the pool. Prices of the tokens involved will vary and move based on those mechanics, which are largely out of a single LP's control. While an LP may be collecting a portion of trading fees, they are still susceptible to exiting the liquidity pool at a lower dollar value than when they entered based on how the DEX prices the exit. There is also an opportunity cost factor whereby it may be better to deploy capital into another application (or even simply hold an asset) rather than facilitating the trade of underlying assets.[11]

LIQUIDITY POOL

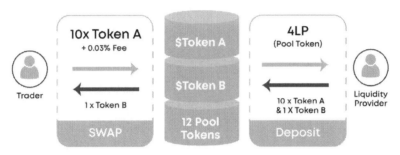

Liquidity Pool

Uniswap

Uniswap is the most popular and widely used Ethereum-based AMM with a TVL of $3.31 billion at the time of this writing. Since Uniswap was built on Ethereum in 2018, it supports nearly all ERC-20 tokens and therefore has a deep bench of ERC-20 trading pairs. Additionally, Uniswap has its own utility token known as *UNI* that offers governance rights and voting to token holders, allowing LPs to submit proposals to change interest rates and adjust the protocol's incentive systems.

The protocol currently charges transaction fees of 0.3 percent per trade (although this can vary with asset pairs and types like stablecoins, exotic pairs, and so on), which are distributed in pro rata fashion among its many stakers. When Liquidity Providers contribute an equal amount of *ETH* and the ERC-20 token designated in a pool's trading pair, they receive what's known as a *pool token* symbolizing this contribution. This pool token is what accrues value as an LP's right to their proportion of the 0.3 percent transaction fees. From the Uniswap documents themselves, "Anyone can become a liquidity provider (LP) for a pool by depositing an equivalent value of each underlying token in return for pool tokens. These tokens track pro-rata LP shares of the total reserves, and can be redeemed for the underlying assets at any time."[12]

The pool token can be moved freely around the ecosystem and is eventually burned (destroyed) when it is redeemed for the originally deposited funds. With this, Liquidity Providers can deploy funds into a liquidity pool, generate gains through transaction fees, and redeem their pool token for the principal deposit.

Uniswap had a record quarterly volume to date in Q4 2021, totaling $238 billion worth of transactions. This equates to $714 million in transaction fees to be dispersed among the network's liquidity providers. In the same timeframe, Coinbase generated $2.5 billion in net revenues and $840 million in net income on $547 billion in trading volume. Throughout 2022, Uniswap was responsible for $620 billion worth of aggregate trading volume, and reached $1 trillion in lifetime trading volume by May 2022.[13]

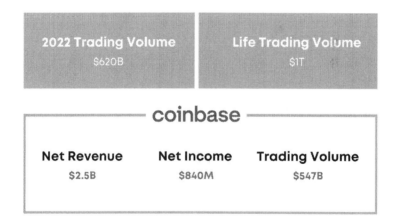

Uniswap

Q4 2021: Record Quarterly Volume: $238B

2022 Trading Volume	Life Trading Volume
$620B	$1T

coinbase

Net Revenue	Net Income	Trading Volume
$2.5B	$840M	$547B

SushiSwap

SushiSwap is a fascinating story of a rollercoaster ride of a journey. The platform took the open-source code of Uniswap and launched an alternative with better incentives and lower fees for the same assets, causing an avalanche of users to move to the platform overnight and resulting in what's called a *vampire attack* on Uniswap. Essentially, SushiSwap was a hard fork of Uniswap that began supporting a greater range of digital assets than did Uniswap. While Uniswap is solely a platform for swapping assets in a peer-to-peer manner, SushiSwap was established in August 2020 to include a more full-suite package of trading tools and capabilities. Examples of SushiSwap features through the "Bento Box" include liquidity mining, margin trading, and additional value generation through the *SUSHI* utility token.

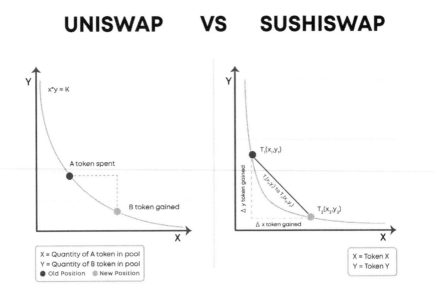

Here's a retelling of this story using blockchain terminology: Since SushiSwap is a hard fork of the Uniswap smart contract protocol, founding developers were determined to figure out how to encourage users to pool liquidity using their solution rather than Uniswap.

To do so, SushiSwap attracted users to stake their *UNI* tokens on the SushiSwap framework to begin generating higher-than-average yield and rewards. Returns for staking on SushiSwap were higher than on Uniswap, so this incentive worked quite well in siphoning off the Uniswap user base. The term *vampire attack* comes from the draining of liquidity from Uniswap and then coming over to SushiSwap in a bloodsucking fashion. SushiSwap secured $810 million directly from Uniswap liquidity pools in a matter of days.

SushiSwap's trading mechanism is quite similar to that of Uniswap's. The AMM operates according to the constant product formula and facilitates trades, so business as usual. The unique features come through the concept of *liquidity mining* through its *SUSHI* utility token. While *SUSHI* acts as a governance token like *UNI* on Uniswap, SushiSwap enables investors and users to generate excess yield on top of the trading fees collected and shared.

Liquidity Mining, in this context, is the act of generating yield through one action, and parlaying it into another yield-generating activity. With SushiSwap, users can provide liquidity to trading pools and earn a share of the trading fees. Those trading fees may then be redeployed into the same of other trading pools on the SushiSwap ecosystem, thus generating even more yield. It is called liquidity mining because a user can continue to "mine" and exploit these yield-generating opportunities in a cascading pattern.

It is possible to generate yield across three or four (or more) liquidity pools all beginning by staking a digital asset in just one pool. As a user begins generating yield and re-deploying those yield rewards into other pools, the term *yield farming* becomes applicable, which is a more expansive version of liquidity mining, and is explained in its own brief section later in this chapter. For now, think of liquidity mining and yield farming as a "yield-on-yield return" strategy, and one that is available directly on the SushiSwap platform.

Additionally, users can stake their *SUSHI* tokens in return for *xSUSHI*, which represents a token receiving 0.05 percent of all trading fee allocations. Upon redemption, users may retire their *xSUSHI* for their original *SUSHI* tokens plus an accrued interest or yield. Staking enables SushiSwap to improve operationally and maintain the network, making this incentive to users mutually beneficial to the network itself.[14]

Balancer

Another DEX known as Balancer was established in 2018 by a company now called Balancer Labs. Balancer is a unique AMM compared to Uniswap and SushiSwap because its liquidity pools are not limited to just two assets. Instead of a rigid trading pair, Balancer pools may encompass up to eight different assets in one pool. Rather than relying on the constant product formula, Balancer pools rely on the allocation of the pool across each of the 2–8 assets, and this allocation makeup will determine the prices of each asset as the allocations fluctuate while trades are executed.

The rationale for this allocations model was largely inspired by real portfolios. Uniswap, SushiSwap, and other AMM's, while successful and feasible, had a limitation whereby liquidity providers always had to provide the same dollar amount of each asset in the pool. If an LP wanted to contribute *ETH* and *USDC* to a Uniswap pool, they would have to contribute roughly 1,200 *USDC* for each *ETH* at the end of 2022.

Balancer acknowledged real portfolios are rarely constructed in this manner. Instead, they rely on diversification of assets for risk and volatility mitigation. Drawing on that, Balancer pools may consist of up to eight digital assets with the understanding that executed prices will remain more stable if the liquidity is concentrated in one pool, but against multiple assets. If an asset in a six-asset pool sees a large sell order, for instance, the change in allocation makeup within the liquidity pool will be spread amongst the remaining five assets rather than applied only to the other asset in the trading pair. This should serve to reduce volatility, all other things being equal. Balancer labels itself as an "Automated Portfolio Manager" through this logic, and through the possibility of trading these mini-indexes, although it is still certainly a trading mechanism more than anything else.[15]

MULTI ASSET POOLS BALANCER

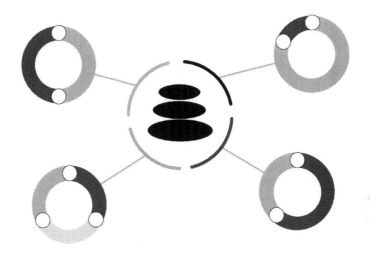

For example, a Balancer pool could contain *ETH* and *BAL* in an 80 percent to 20 percent ratio. The pool will adjust prices to maintain this ratio as trades are executed through it. On the macro level, the Balancer DEX will scan all of its pools and seek to provide traders with the best execution price for whatever asset is in question. If there are multiple *ETH* pools, the Balancer DEX will select the lowest-priced *ETH* to fill a buy order with, for instance. As trades execute and pools get rebalanced (repriced), the prices among assets should converge and become more consistent with greater volume. This principle gets more complex with 3–8 assets in a pool, but maintains the same allocation-focused pricing mechanism.

Now, liquidity pools consisting of multiple assets are bound to see some mispricing among assets in other liquidity pools, both in the Balancer ecosystem and elsewhere. As prices of assets fluctuate, trades may find and trade on these mispricings to take advantage of the price differentials, otherwise known as the spread. These traders are known as *arbitrageurs* in what is called an *arbitrage strategy*. Arbitrage opportunities exist when the same asset is priced differently on two or more exchanges, marketplaces, or venues, and generally serve as a risk-free investment opportunity for traders since they could purchase the asset on the lower-priced exchange and sell it on the higher-priced exchange, earning an instantaneous and predictable profit.

Balancer's other differentiating factor is how transaction fees are set by the liquidity pool manager rather than a fixed or predetermined floating rate. This results in a competitive atmosphere as pool creators must determine what transaction fee they are comfortable with in relation to other pools supporting the same blend or range of assets. Liquidity providers then have their choice of pool to enter based on these yields, and receive *BAL* tokens in exchange for their deposits. These *BAL* tokens accrue interest based on trading fees on a weekly basis.

Keep in mind that arbitrage strategies are usually high-frequency trading strategies relying on heavy volume and low price spreads. This is a positive for liquidity providers since it generates a substantial amount of trading fees. Understanding this dynamic, arbitrageurs are encouraged by liquidity providers and are crucial to the pricing mechanisms across pools, which makes for a symbiotic relationship.[16]

Lending and Borrowing

The next logical piece of the financial services system to bring to the blockchain is lending and borrowing. Typical lenders, such as banks, credit card providers, private credit firms, or even FinTech lenders ("robo-lenders") will set their own rates, terms, and conditions, as well as criteria for prospective borrowers. These criteria usually revolve around credit scores, existing assets, income, living expenses, and a potential multitude of other lurking variables. While FinTech-driven applications have brought some efficiencies to the borrowing arena, there is certainly more to be desired.

Moreover, it's quite rare for individuals to act as lenders to other borrowers. Peer-to-peer lending services like Happy Money, Peerform, and Upstart are not nearly as popular as the FinTech lending giants like SoFi, Avant, loanDepot, Rocket Loans, and Lending Tree. On the lending side, the firms themselves dominate the loan origination scene and provide little room for individual investors to act as lenders. This creates a barrier to a major piece of the economy. After all, public credit markets in the United States are double the size of equities markets.[17]

Digital assets were created to democratize access to capital at the base layer. This principle can be applied to debt and credit on both sides of the equation, meaning both borrowers and lenders. Certain borrowers do not get approved by banks or alternative lenders, and have little to no access to capital except under draconian terms. Conversely, individuals have little access to act as a lender and generate yield on their capital, thereby forcing them to look for opportunities elsewhere.

DeFi has carved out its own lending vertical similar to the trading mechanics previously explained. The idea of using AMMs and staking to produce yields and facilitate loans is extremely prevalent. As of the end of 2022, DeFi lending platforms had around $38 billion in TVL across all chains, with the most prominent ones developed on Ethereum, Cardano, Binance Smart Chain, and Avalanche. Total Value Locked is a commonly used metric for lending platforms, as with trading venues, to show the depth of a platform. Services with higher TVLs have deeper liquidity pools and therefore can handle larger and more frequent transactions with improved execution. It is not the be-all and end-all metric to measure the success or adoption of a blockchain protocol.

Much like a DEX removes the intermediary responsible for matching trade orders in favor of a peer-to-peer swap, a decentralized lending platform removes the lender and underwriters and enables for peer-to-peer loans on digital assets. Similar smart contract governance and guidelines facilitate these loans within liquidity pools, which essentially creates a peer-to-peer lending ecosystem. Since there are no credit scores or similar vetting processes associated with digital asset lending as of now, most of these services rely on collateralized loans in order to sift through transactions.

LENDING PLATFORM

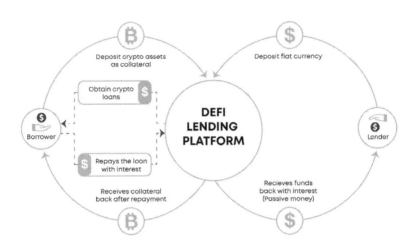

A borrower may initiate a loan request by depositing a certain amount of digital assets as collateral into a smart contract. The smart contract will verify this collateral and determine the loan amount based on the *Loan-to-Value* and collateral ratios that a liquidity pool or service requires. Upon verification, the smart contract will distribute the loan to the borrower, which is provided by the liquidity providers to the liquidity pool facilitating the loan. The liquidity providers will receive pro rata distributions in any interest generated by these lending activities. The interest rates are largely based on the supply and demand of each digital asset itself and therefore will vary heavily based on the market and the individual token positions. Through this mechanism, liquidity providers become peer-to-peer lenders to a wide range of borrowers, which is a rare opportunity for non-institutional entities.[18]

MakerDAO

MakerDAO is one of the earliest and longest-standing DAOs in the industry. While being structured as a DAO, the organization serves as a decentralized lending service. The mechanism of Maker is relatively straightforward: A user can lock up *ETH* in exchange for a loan in the form of the *DAI* stablecoin.

Users would be able to lock their *ETH* into Maker smart contracts, which then create Collateralized Debt Positions (CDPs). Maker contracts are typically overcollateralized with a 150 percent collateralization ratio, meaning the initial collateral must be equivalent to $1.50 for each *DAI* created and borrowed to account for price changes and slippage in the event of liquidation. Interest rates are determined by the DAO's users and by supply and demand factors. Loans can be closed by returning the *DAI* in exchange for the initial *ETH* collateral.

A pressing question revolves around the overcollateralization factor. On the surface level, it seems that overcollateralization of a debt position creates little value to the borrower. Since the initial collateral is greater than the loan needed, why would the borrower not just liquidate a portion of the collateral and use those funds for the desired financial activities?

Selling a digital asset such as ETH will usually cause a taxable event at a corresponding capital gains tax rate. It will also lower the investor's exposure to that asset as the investor will now have less ETH than before. Asset owners who are comfortable borrowing against their assets likely feel either 1) they do not want to lose any upside potential associated with the asset, or 2) do not want to create a taxable event, and therefore prefer to borrow new funds for financial activity, even if the nominal amount is less than that of the collateral.

In the case of Maker, CDPs require 150 percent of collateral locked up in ETH to borrow DAI. Borrowers can then make use of DAI throughout the broader DeFi ecosystem in other staking, lending, swapping, and yield farming activities, among others. They can take the borrowed DAI and deploy the funds into these other services with the goal of participating in new projects, generating excess yield, or taking advantage of arbitrage swapping and trading opportunities. Of course, investors could simply put the original ETH to work in DeFi applications, but that would generate an unleveraged return.

With the CDP mechanism through Maker, investors can generate leveraged returns that are potentially amplified through the borrowed

DAI, all the while maintaining ownership of the original ETH, which could also be appreciating in value and therefore providing the borrower with additional DAI funds. However, a depreciating ETH price may eventually cause the CDP to close out should it fall below the required collateralization ratio, thus force selling the ETH collateral and leaving the investor with only the borrowed DAI, which is usually inherently *less* than the original value of the collateral at the time the loan was initiated.

If a user believes the value of *ETH* will appreciate in the near future, it may be wise to open a CDP on Maker in exchange for *DAI*. As the value of *ETH* increases, the strength of the CDP increases as the associated CDP now has a greater collateralization ratio. The borrower could create additional *DAI* and continue borrowing funds under the same *ETH* position that was originally collateralized, thus taking advantage of the increase in value of *ETH* without having to open new loans each time.

For example, suppose a borrower deposits one *ETH* at $1,500 into a Maker contract. The borrower may receive 1,000 DAI in exchange as specified by the platform's Collateralized Debt Position (CDP) guidelines requiring a 150 percent collateralization rate. In this example, as the price of *ETH* moves upwards toward $2,000, the borrower's CDP can now acceptably act as collateral for up to 1,333 *DAI* per the 150 percent collateralization ratio. Given this, the borrower can make use of an additional 333 *DAI* off the same initial *1 ETH* deposit without needing to open a new CDP. This can be a very powerful tool for borrowers who are anticipating an appreciating *ETH*.

Leverage

Q4 2021: Record Quarterly Volume: $238B

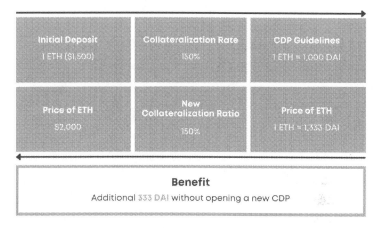

Initial Deposit	Collateralization Rate	CDP Guidelines
1 ETH ($1,500)	150%	1 ETH = 1,000 DAI
Price of ETH	**New Collateralization Ratio**	**Price of ETH**
$2,000	150%	1 ETH = 1,333 DAI

Benefit

Additional 333 DAI without opening a new CDP

On the other hand, if the value of *ETH* were to decline from an initial price of $3,000 toward $2,000, a portion or all of the *ETH* would be liquidated in a Maker CDP to cover the borrowed 2,000 *DAI*, plus interest owed. In a market downturn, borrowing on Maker against *ETH* puts the borrower at a higher liquidation risk as each position is at a greater risk of closure in more volatile economic conditions. Higher collateralization rates provide a greater cushion and mitigate liquidation risk, ultimately making the lenders more apt to offer loans, which is important for scale in this context as MakerDAO is open for anyone to participate in its ecosystem.[19]

Aave

Aave became one of the most widely used two-sided lending platforms for users in the DeFi space during 2020 and 2021 after being built on the Ethereum blockchain in 2017. The service makes use of a similar liquidity pool functionality made popular by Uniswap. The smart contracts that automatically form peer-to-peer lending opportunities on Aave require deposits from users who act as lenders and can receive interest on those deposits and borrowers who are willing to pay higher interest rates for those loans. Since the pool executes these loans, the "*P2P*" terminology in this case means *pool-to-peer* lending.

Users deposit (stake) their digital assets in a liquidity pool, receive specially designated tokens in return, and 0.09 percent share in flash loan volume. Liquidity pools with a surplus of collateral will typically offer lower yield, although a surge in demand for the liquidity pool's lending asset may drive yield upwards even in saturated pools.

If a user deposits *ETH* into an Aave liquidity pool offering 7 percent yield to lenders, the user will receive an equivalent amount of wrapped *aETH* while the *ETH* is staked. The "*aETH*" represents one share of *ETH* wrapped in the Aave protocol, and is used as a measure of account to distribute accrued yield and fees to the depositor. Upon close, the lender may redeem the *aETH* for their original *ETH* and keep accrued yield in the form of *AAVE* tokens.[20]

On the other end of the pool, a user is able to borrow at 80 percent Loan-to-Value (LTV), meaning they must deposit 1.25x the amount of collateral as they are looking to borrow. Borrowers must also pay interest that fluctuates based on supply (liquidity in the pool) and demand (number of borrowers and amounts borrowed), and usually end up paying slightly higher rates than the yield offered to lenders.[21]

As of December 2022, Aave supports Avalanche, Fantom, Polygon, Arbitum, and more Layer 1s aside from Ethereum, with a Total Value Locked (TVL) of $3.66 billion across more than thirty liquidity pools.[22] Given its wider range of asset support relative to Maker, Aave provides an opportunity for users to capitalize on arbitrage or yield-generating activities specific to these supported assets. For instance, if a user sees the price of ChainLink (token ticker *LINK*) varies on two exchanges, they may wish to borrow *LINK* on Aave, transfer it to sell on the exchange with a higher priced *LINK*, buy the same amount of *LINK* on the lower priced exchange, and enjoy this price spread as gross trading profit. To retire the loan, the user would transfer the purchased *LINK* to Aave and close out the original loan. After any interest is paid by the user, they are left with their original collateral and the trading profits minus interest as net profit.

While this concept is powerful, it is limited to well-capitalized cryptocurrencies since the pricing of these assets is quite efficient on most exchanges. Instead, traders could make serious profits through larger-sized arbitrage opportunities with thinner spreads (price differentials). Enter *flash loans.*

Flash loans became popular on Aave when savvy borrowers began writing their own programs to execute massive loan-driven arbitrages in a swift manner. The general approach is as follows:

1. A user borrows cryptocurrency without collateral,
2. buys a large quantity of Asset A on one exchange,
3. transfers Asset A to another exchange where it's priced higher,
4. sells Asset A for a profit,
5. transfers the remainder to Aave and closes the loan position

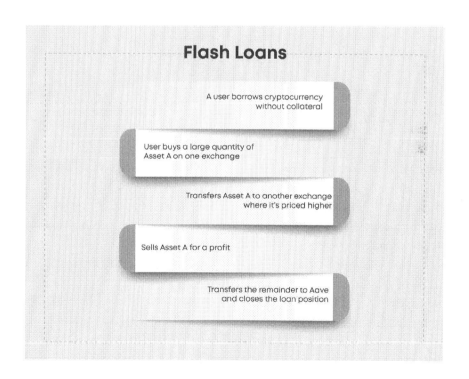

Flash Loans

A user borrows cryptocurrency without collateral

User buys a large quantity of Asset A on one exchange

Transfers Asset A to another exchange where it's priced higher

Sells Asset A for a profit

Transfers the remainder to Aave and closes the loan position

The key to flash loans is how all five steps occur at once in a single transaction. Rather than all five steps executing separately, the flash loan is designed to only execute if all five are confirmed to be executed. This makes the flash loan an all-or-nothing approach. Either all five steps will be executed, or the transaction simply will not happen. This makes flash loans relatively low risk to the borrower as they will only end up borrowing assets if the arbitrage execution is guaranteed. These trades, similar to high-frequency trading strategies on Wall Street, account for significant liquidity in a system.

These five steps can be executed together through a savvy coder and algorithm. Flash loans are not a strategy that can be taken advantage of by a typical trader or DeFi enthusiast. Instead, they require smart contracts or comparable computer science programming to check the five-step process to ensure all steps will hit prior to executing. Flash loans can also be executed on a smaller scale, although the approach may require patience and the right mispricing opportunities. This makes it more appealing for larger prizes such as when Aave issued $138 million of flash loans in a twenty-four-hour period in July 2020.[23]

Compound

Launched in September 2018, Compound consists of openly accessible smart contracts that enable the lending and borrowing of Ethereum-based digital assets. The interest rates paid and received are based solely on supply and demand in each smart contract, and loans can be closed at any time. Yield is accrued in real-time and distributed solely through the smart contract-enforced ecosystem.

Much like Aave has its *aToken* wrapping structure to represent interest-generating tokens to lenders, Compound offers a *cToken* to a lender. This cToken represents the lender's initial deposit plus any accrued interest, and these cTokens are minted whenever a new deposit is made or staked in the smart contract. Upon redemption, the lender will receive the initial deposit and interest payable in the same denomination, and then the cToken is burned. This ensures the number of outstanding cTokens is equal to the deposits staked by the lenders.

For example, a user can deposit 1,000 *USDC* into a Compound liquidity pool and receive 1,000 *cUSDC*. Upon redemption, the user will be returned the 1,000 *USDC* plus any accrued/owed interest in the form of *USDC*. The 1,000 *cUSDC* is burned to designate the withdrawal of the 1,000 *USDC* deposit and balances the books.

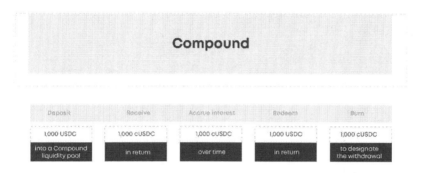

On the borrower's side, initial deposits must be made as collateral before being able to borrow any amount of assets. The collateralization ratio is not fixed on Compound. It is a function of the depth of liquidity in each asset's pool. Compound uses liquidity as a determination of the quality of assets in each pool and sets the collateralization ratio and Loan-to-Value guidelines accordingly. This is where interest rates become purely reliant on supply and demand within each liquidity pool.

Since interest rates on Compound float according to supply and demand fluctuations, lenders are incentivized to contribute assets to smaller, less liquid pools paying higher yields while borrowers are incentivized to close loans in less liquid pools and borrow from more liquid pools charging lower interest rates. While there will likely never be a perfect equilibrium, this two-sided incentive mechanism keeps liquidity pools competitive and offers yield strategies for users of all ranges and needs (i.e., low yield, medium yield, high yield).

As an added piece of compensation to users on Compound, both borrowers and lenders receive pro rata distributions of each Compound block mined via *COMP* in a 50:50 ratio, meaning 50 percent to borrowers and 50 percent to lenders for maintaining the integrity of Compound's liquidity pools. *COMP* is the protocol's governance token. Each *COMP* token comes with one vote to changes and decisions made regarding the Compound protocol, and the token has its own value. Therefore, users can hold *COMP* with the goal of voting on protocol decisions or sell *COMP* tokens as an additional piece to their total returns.[24]

Yield Farming

Yield Farming became popular throughout 2020 and 2021. It was even quoted as "the rocket fuel of DeFi" by CoinDesk.[25] This title is due to the sheer volume and expansion of the ecosystem yield farming triggered.

Yield Farming is the process of generating yield in one liquidity pool and transferring and staking the yield elsewhere for additional yield in a separate liquidity pool. The phrase "yield-on-yield return" was on the lips of many DeFi participants as the ecosystem was truly unlocked and allowed to run wild for one of the first times in history. The generalized process of yield farming is as follows:

1. User stakes tokens into a liquidity pool and generates yield,
2. then takes that generated yield and stakes it into a different liquidity pool, now generating additional yield on the original yield,
3. and then takes that yield-on-yield and stakes it in yet another liquidity pool.

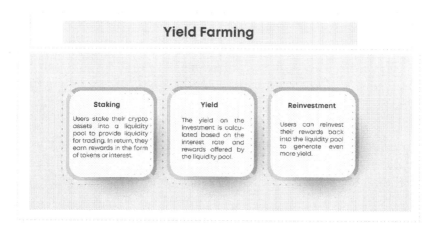

Yield Farming

Staking

Users stake their crypto assets into a liquidity pool to provide liquidity for trading. In return, they earn rewards in the form of tokens or interest.

Yield

The yield on the investment is calculated based on the interest rate and rewards offered by the liquidity pool.

Reinvestment

Users can reinvest their rewards back into the liquidity pool to generate even more yield.

This process can encompass as few or as many liquidity pools as the user wishes. A more skilled yield farmer may be able to navigate a handful of liquidity pools at once, while a novice or a mere enthusiast may feel more comfortable practicing with just one or two liquidity pools. Of course, the more a user re-stakes their yields, the higher the total return potential since they are making their principal stretch even further with each additional liquidity pool and associated yield.

This is what was meant by "expanding the money supply" across the DeFi ecosystem earlier. The more pools being used by a yield farmer, the greater the amount of capital available for lending to borrowers, which inherently increases the supply of digital asset currency in the ecosystem.

This is not without its risks, of course, and skilled yield farmers must be aware of the cascading effect one failed liquidity pool can have on the rest of the positions. Without careful monitoring, high-yield liquidity pools could dry up or be drained of liquidity, leaving a user with either reduced yield or with the inability to exit a position if the remaining liquidity cannot facilitate the transaction.

What is unique about yield farming is how it is simply an overarching term to describe compounded yield strategies in the DeFi ecosystem. Not only can yield farming be done by staking assets and generating yield first, but it can also be started by borrowing funds.

For instance, if a user is able to borrow *ETH* at a 2 percent interest rate, they may take the *ETH* and deposit it into a liquidity pool generating 5 percent interest. The real yield for the *ETH* exposure is now 3 percent. This process can be applied to multiple pools, or even expanded to multiple borrowing pools and multiple yield-generating pools. It simply comes down to the numbers (yield) and the user's ability to manage risk and execute. Without risk management in the borrowing approach, it's quite possible for a user to lose value and not meet a collateralization ratio, thereby causing them to be liquidated, closed out of a position, and lose the principal investment.[26]

Collateralized Lending Rates

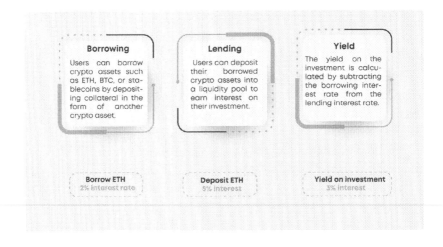

Borrowing
Users can borrow crypto assets such as ETH, BTC, or stablecoins by depositing collateral in the form of another crypto asset.

Lending
Users can deposit their borrowed crypto assets into a liquidity pool to earn interest on their investment.

Yield
The yield on the investment is calculated by subtracting the borrowing interest rate from the lending interest rate.

Borrow ETH
2% interest rate

Deposit ETH
5% interest

Yield on investment
3% interest

For example, Curve (*CRV*) is an ERC-20 token currently providing 5.96 percent yield to stakers on Aave. Balancer (*BAL*) is also an ERC-20 token providing just 0.24 percent yield to stakers, but charging 2.21 percent interest to borrowers. There exists an opportunity for a savvy yield farmer to execute the following:

1. Borrow BAL at 2.21 percent interest.
2. Swap BAl for *CRV* on Uniswap.
3. Stake CRV for 5.96 percent yield.

This is a 3.75 percent nominal spread on the Balancer and Curve yields, or a bit lower when accounting for the Uniswap transaction fee. Nonetheless, this is a 3+ percent yield to the yield farmer based on borrowed funds. Assuming these two interest rates remain relatively constant, the position will be profitable. Should the borrow rate on *BAL* begin rising and the yield on *CRV* begin falling, the yield farmer will want to reassess to ensure profitability. If profitability is no longer there, the position should be closed out. The Uniswap step can even be skipped if the user has access to another liquidity pool on the same asset at a higher yield or has access to a multi-asset pool (i.e., a general ERC-20 pool like in Balancer).

These sample yields are just examples from Aave. During the summer of 2020 and throughout 2021, protocols like SushiSwap and PancakeSwap (built on the Binance blockchain) were offering yields in the double and even triple digits. These were mainly on smaller market cap, less liquid coins in general, but nonetheless presented incredible opportunities for those who could take advantage of them and deploy the proper balance of capital, attention, and iterating.

As a final note to yield farming, in a way it is bringing the leverage back to individual users. Taking yield from one asset and generating yield on an additional asset indefinitely is not very different from the banking model that enables banks to repledge an individual's deposits and assets. Sometimes multiple institutions are even pledging the same asset. The most famous banking collapses and crashes are due to either under-collateralization or over-pledging, and these are lessons to which yield farmers should pay attention.

The more liquidity pools added to a yield-generating strategy, the further away the user is from their principal investment in the initial liquidity pool, thereby increasing the risk and net exposure for an investor. Proper risk management, quantitative limitations, and additional liquidity to avoid margin calls are all useful in staying afloat during volatile times, especially as liquidity pools could dry up or as demand for these assets ebbs and flows.

Derivatives

Derivative contracts and products are key in any robust financial market. These include futures, forwards, swaps, options, and some other smaller specialty products developed to support investors' strategies across a range of products. Stock markets, commodity markets, and bond markets all rely on derivatives to provide investors with a two-sided market alternative to the basic buy-and-sell functionality.

Derivatives may be used to bet on future events, hedge one's exposure, structure favorable conversion scenarios, and more as strategies are developed and made use of. The digital assets market is no different. Originally, there were only the Buy and Sell choices, which meant asset prices were clear functions of buy and sell pressure on order books (whether centralized or decentralized).

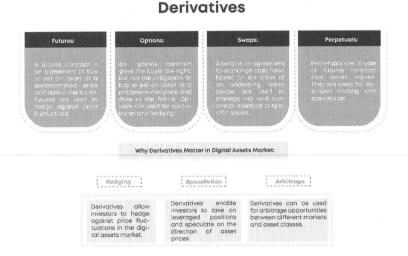

Typically, derivatives are offered by centralized parties like the Chicago Board of Options Exchange (CBOE) and the Boston Options Exchange (BOX). These parties are responsible for creating and offering derivative products to a wide audience of traders, investors, and institutions on a variety of exchanges and access points.

In order to bring this same fluidity to the decentralized digital assets markets, a variety of DeFi solutions have emerged. These services enable the creation of new synthetic products representing a variety of digital assets and act as either futures, options, perpetuals, swaps, and so on at the discretion of the product creator. Other DeFi users can trade these and make use of them in their own strategies to hedge or speculate.[27]

Synthetix

Synthetix is one of the most popular derivatives protocols in the industry. Synthetix (a very clever and well-suited name) enables the creation of synthetic assets that track another asset without having to officially own the asset. Much like a trader can purchase Call Options on a stock to bet on the stock's appreciation without officially owning the stock itself, traders in the DeFi space can bet on the upside or downside of digital assets through Synthetix.

Each synthetic asset created on Synthetix is known as a *synth*. A synth can be backed by or represent anything with a reliable price feed. Examples include not just cryptocurrencies like *BTC*, *ETH*, and *SOL* but also existing of stock, commodities, bonds, indexes, or other verticals in digital assets such as liquidity pools and yield farming strategies (more on this later). The goal is that any type of flowing asset can have a decentralized derivative created for it without waiting on guidance, execution, or oversight from a traditional institution. Moreover, the inclusion of real world assets or assets not on-chain (i.e., not blockchain native) serves to create a bridge between decentralized investors and traditional investors.

Decentralized investors do not need to register with brokerage firms or wealth management intermediaries to gain access to these traditional assets if they choose not to. Instead, they can get access to a decentralized representation using the same digital asset wealth and transaction tools they are familiar and comfortable with.

It is important to note how synths are not formally backed by the assets they represent. It would be wrong to say that an Apple ($AAPL) synth is backed by $AAPL stock, or that it can be redeemed for a share of $AAPL stock. Keep in mind synths are derivatives and are solely representations of assets as a method for investors to gain their desired exposure without physically owning the asset.

Per the standard value-add of the decentralized ecosystem, synths are swappable or tradable for other digital asset products without going through an intermediary. Synthetic is built on Ethereum, making it compatible with other ERC-20 tokens in protocols like Uniswap or Aave. The combination of synths in these Ethereum-based applications brings a whole new realm of power to the investor as they can swap and trade various asset types and classes via synths, all under one umbrella.

To create synths, users must stake Synthetix Network Token (*SNX*) of *ETH* and maintain a certain collateralization ratio throughout the life of the position. The protocol works similarly to the previously covered DeFi services in that a user may open up a position through staked assets, maintain a proper collateralization ratio, and manage the position among any volatility or pricing changes. The creation of a synth essentially works as a debt product, and users are free to close out their positions, repay a small amount of "interest" as a fee, and open other synths with the same process. The performance of the synth, which is verified by each one's associated price oracle, determines the status of the position. Collateralization ratios on Synthetix can be as high as 600 percent to ensure above-average system protection.

If a synth was created on $AAPL stock and the price of $AAPL has been depreciating, this price will be fed to the synth and the synth will show a decrease in value. At a certain point, the value of the synth will need to meet the required collateralization ratio and the position will be liquidated and closed. In this scenario, the user loses all or some of their originally staked *SNX* or *ETH*.

In other scenarios, synths will perform with upside and generate gains for users. In the case of an $AAPL synth appreciating in price, the user is free to close the position whenever they deem fit, use a portion of the gains to pay the synth fee, and open a new synth on the same or different product. Imagining a series of multiple successful synths, conclusions can be drawn to traditional options strategies that roll-over gains and disperse among multiple positions or even take more concentrated positions with greater magnitude.[28]

dYdX

Drawing on naming inspiration from the calculus notation for derivatives, dYdX focuses on decentralized margin trading for digital assets. If centralized exchanges like Coinbase and Gemini are being disrupted by DEXes like Uniswap and SushiSwap, then margin and derivative-enabled exchanges like Kraken and Bitfinex are being disrupted by the likes of dYdX.

Reaching over $3 trillion in trading volume during the month of July 2022 alone[29], centralized cryptocurrency exchanges have shown the proof-of-concept for heavy interest in derivatives within this market. The dYdX protocol works similarly to other DeFi applications in relying on a two-sided marketplace made up of stakers and borrowers.

In order to trade on margin, a trader is essentially taking out a loan, usually short-term but not always, to deploy into a trade or a series of trades. The platform currently requires a minimum collateralization ratio of 125 percent to protect lenders on dYdX, especially amid market volatility. Once users are able to stake their desired amount, they are free to borrow funds up to the 125 percent collateralization ratio, which can be increased with either additional funding or gains from trading activities.

New dYdX products can be issued at many points of leverage, which is essentially the amount of credit extended beyond the asset and its price. For instance, trading one *ETH* with no leverage means the spot price and price fluctuations will be equal to the position's value at any given time (minus trading fees potentially incurred upon exit). With leveraged products, users can get up to 20x leveraged on select digital assets through dYdX, essentially opening them up to returns otherwise requiring twenty times the amount of capital as the existing position to achieve.

Leverage is an especially popular tool during times of prosperity and bull markets. Investors may be feeling a bit more comfortable or confident in the market's upward trend and seek to amplify their earnings potential beyond the spot price activity. This causes an influx to the sheer number of leveraged positions and the total amount of leverage in the market relative to the actual spot price and spot valuations.

As more users look to open up leveraged positions, services like dYdX become more popular and find themselves in higher demand. The influx of demand then typically has an appreciating effect on the price of *DYDX* in order to access the derivatives ecosystem.

On the other hand, downturns or bear markets can be extremely detrimental to leverage traders, as their collateralization ratios are breached and positions are liquidated at a more rapid rate. This risk is amplified with greater amounts of leverage (i.e., 20x leveraged positions will be liquidated before 5x leveraged positions, all other things being equal). For this reason, the protocol lowered its maximum leverage from 25x to 20x in January 2022 to stabilize its users and pools during the market downturn.

The protocol has been adding traditional trading features such as stop-loss, limit orders, and other necessities to build greater depth and a greater range of services in a decentralized manner, which is a necessity for a maturing market.[30]

Stablecoins

A key facet of the DeFi ecosystem (and digital assets ecosystem in general) is the *stablecoin* vertical. Stablecoins will be covered in greater depth throughout this book, but it is important to have a basic understanding of how they fit into the industry and common practices. For more information on stablecoins, see Chapter 5.

Stablecoins are digital assets designed to have a stable, reliable value rather than being price-fluctuating cryptocurrencies. Since the birth of cryptocurrencies and the digital assets industry, an increasing number of people and organizations have come to enjoy, respect, and make use of the blockchain benefits previously not enabled. Features such as borderless payments and transactions, near instantaneous settlement, and self-custody are all powerful additions to the existing financial services framework.

Nonetheless, people still respect and rely on the strength of the US Dollar and other fiat currencies and measures. This is where stablecoins come into play. Stablecoins leverage all the blockchain benefits while also maintaining the strength and reliability of existing currencies and stores of value.

Stablecoins are pegged to some currency or asset in order to maintain reliability and consistent value. These pegs can come in multiple forms including fiat currency, commodities, other cryptocurrencies, or even algorithms. For the sake of simplicity, assume fiat pegs and commodity pegs fall under the same umbrella (fiat stablecoins) and algorithmic pegs and cryptocurrency pegs fall under the same umbrella (algorithmic stablecoins).

Fiat stablecoins are backed by a range of fiat currencies such as the US Dollar, the British Pound, the Euro, or an ounce of gold. The value of one stablecoin will always equal the value of its fiat peg. Stablecoins are usually minted and burned as users deposit fiat and withdraw fiat, respectively. This ensures the *fiat-to-stablecoin* ratio is always *1-to-1*, or at whatever predetermined ratio a stablecoin protocol may operate under.

Users can trust their stablecoins to always be equal to the amount they are dealing in without concern of volatility risk or exchange rate changes among cryptocurrency pairs (i.e., the *ETH/BTC* price is constantly fluctuating). This is useful for those looking to make use of cross-border or immediate transactions that require a stable value because all it takes is a crypto wallet address and the representation of fiat currency can be transferred.

Algorithmic stablecoins are not backed by fiat or physical assets. Instead, they are pegged to a series of calculations and designed to maintain a certain price point. These protocols usually rely on some reserve of digital assets or some form of digital asset collateral, and have arbitrage strategies in place to enable users to actually maintain the stable price point. Pricing of algorithmic stablecoins is measured in the stablecoin itself rather than in fiat currency, and users will often price other digital assets in reference to the stablecoin rather than in fiat terms. Algorithmic stablecoins are less tangible than fiat stablecoins, and therefore are geared more toward the DeFi crowd than large institutions and/or traditional players.

Nonetheless, the important takeaway is how stablecoins can be used in the aforementioned DeFi applications such as staking, lending, yield farming, and decentralized trading much like cryptocurrencies and other digital assets. Stablecoin strategies may offer even greater precision to users or traders since the asset prices will be constant while yield and gains may change. In fact, demand for stablecoins began growing in tandem with "DeFi Summer" in 2020 and beyond as they became more desirable across various DeFi applications and strategies.[31]

Decentralized Asset Management

As one of the last main components to financial services, DeFi has its own Asset Management protocols and services much like financial advisors, robo advisors, and wealth management services exist in the traditional world. Rather than using a third party to manage digital assets, which goes against the decentralized thesis in which DeFi thrives, developers created their own solutions to asset management. Some of these solutions include automatic portfolio balancers, DeFi indexes and baskets, yield strategies, and other "bundle" packages to investors who want exposure to DeFi applications and performances but would prefer to be more hands-off. Several of these are described below:

Set Protocol

Set is an interesting asset management tool that allows users to create, manage, and share portfolios of ERC-20 tokens. Similarly to how indexes and ETFs streamlined the purchase of certain categories and baskets of stocks, Set enables the management of baskets of Ethereum-based applications and tokens.

Known as Sets, each portfolio or basket becomes represented as an ERC-20 token itself, which can of course then be traded, staked, or utilized across the Ethereum ecosystem. Given this, users can gain exposure to other people's exposures by buying Sets, and can even create their own portfolios based on a variety of Sets. This offers great precision to investors, but also comes with unique risks. One of the easy questions is: *Why should an investor trust or use another person's set?*

This is where Set's brilliance reveals one piece of digital assets to be covered in depth later in this book regarding securities law and registration. There are limited protections to investors beyond their own diligence on Sets. On the flip side, the argument can be made that investors can easily construct the same Set as an existing set, and rather than reinventing the wheel, they are simply buying exposure into that basket. In any scenario, Set shows the power of DeFi asset management and derivatives all at once, since users can create Sets that then become tradable and become potential additions to other portfolios.

Arguably Set's flagship product, the DeFi Pulse Index tracks Etehreum-based DeFi applications and tokens meeting certain criteria. The DeFi Pulse Index (DPI) is available to investors as an ERC-20 token and is reconstituted on the first of every month.[32]

Yearn.Finance

Yearn.Finance is aptly named as its focus is automating yield-generating strategies on behalf of investors and users. The protocol is essentially an algorithm that scouts the highest yields available in the Ethereum ecosystem. Users are able to stake capital into various Vaults that have their own risk-reward ratios and profiles, and therefore provide access to ranges of yield pools.

Yearn's ability to pool capital from many investors and deploy it into one pool (at scale) is more efficient and cost-effective than each individual user staking on their own. Not only do users get access to Yearn's proprietary algorithm, but they also see reduced aggregate transaction fees since one Yearn transaction may very well be the same price as each individual transaction. Rather than individual users paying this fee, only the controller of each Vault pays the gas fee. Yearn has rolled this service out to *ETH*, stablecoins, and other Ethereum-based assets.

The governance token *YFI* enables users to vote on the direction of the protocol, including new developments associated with farming strategies and distribution. The maximum supply of *YFI* is only 30,000 tokens, making it one of the scarcer assets in the market.

While owning the *YFI* token doesn't provide any revenue share or performance upside, the token became in extreme demand and peaked in May 2021 at an average price of $82,000, even reaching $96,000 on Coinbase.[33]

Wrapped Tokens

Aside from specific applications, one interesting feature of DeFi is the ability to *wrap tokens*. Wrapping is the process of creating a synthetic asset to represent a digital asset on another blockchain. The process of wrapping enables users to interact with assets across multiple blockchains rather than the asset's native blockchain.

For example, one could wrap Bitcoin on the Ethereum blockchain and call the asset Wrapped Bitcoin (*wBTC*). The value of *wBTC* is pegged to the value of *BTC* so the wrapped version maintains the same valuation as the actual, targeted asset. A user can then take the *wBTC* and make use of it on the Ethereum blockchain. The user can trade their *wBTC* on a DEX like Uniswap, stake it in a lending pool on Aave, or deploy it into another Ethereum-based smart contract or application.

To wrap tokens, users must send their base currency or asset to a custodian, such as Coinbase, Gemini, or Anchorage, who then holds the asset in safekeeping and issues the proper amount of a wrapped token.

Wrapped Tokens

Bringing Assets to New Blockchains

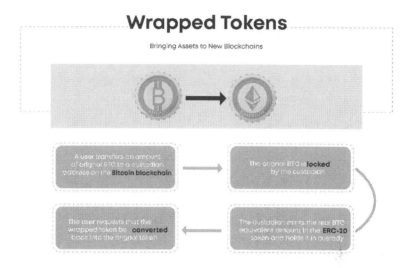

A user transfers an amount of original BTC to a custodian address on the **Bitcoin blockchain**	The original BTC is **locked** by the custodian
The user requests that the wrapped token be **converted** back into the original token	The custodian mints the real BTC equivalent amount in the **ERC-20** token and holds it in custody

Wrapped tokens are arguably one of the first examples of cross-chain interoperability, even if indirectly. Once a token is wrapped, it can be used frictionlessly within the host blockchain's ecosystem. Since original assets are held in custody, the wrapped token's peg is always accurate and in a proper ratio. Nonetheless, arbitrage opportunities may exist in short-term price fluctuations between the original token and the wapped token, which may present a lucrative opportunity for traders, stakers, or yield farmers alike.[34]

NOTES

1. See https://www.capitalone.com/learn-grow/money-management/liquidity/
2. See https://academy.binance.com/en/articles/what-is-staking
3. See https://defillama.com/
4. See https://www.stakingrewards.com/
5. See https://www.stakingrewards.com/
6. See https://www.stakingrewards.com/
7. See https://www.gemini.com/cryptopedia/decentralized-exchange-dex-crypto#section-decentralized-exchange-evolution
8. See https://www.investopedia.com/terms/s/slippage.asp
9. See https://coincodecap.com/what-is-an-automated-market-maker-amm-2021
10. See https://www.gemini.com/cryptopedia/amm-what-are-automated-market-makers#section-automated-market-maker-variations
11. See https://help.1inch.io/en/articles/4585109-what-is-price-impact-vs-price-slippage-in-defi and https://academy.shrimpy.io/post/what-is-slippage-how-to-avoid-slippage-on-defi-exchanges
12. See https://academy.binance.com/en/articles/impermanent-loss-explained
13. See https://docs.uniswap.org/contracts/v2/concepts/protocol-overview/how-uniswap-works and https://decrypt.co/resources/what-is-uniswap
14. See https://messari.io/article/state-of-uniswap-q4-2021, https://www.theblockcrypto.com/post/135383/coinbase-q4-2021-earnings-revenue, https://www.nasdaq.com/articles/half-of-uniswap-liquidity-providers-are-losing-money, https://u.today/ethereum-decentralized-exchange-uniswap-records-620-billion-in-trading-volume-this-year, and https://www.coindesk.com/business/2022/05/24/defi-trading-hub-uniswap-surpasses-1t-in-lifetime-volume/
15. See https://3commas.io/blog/what-is-liquidity-mining-and-how-does-it-work
16. See https://decrypt.co/resources/what-is-balancer-automated-market-maker-amm-defi, https://academy.shrimpy.io/post/what-is-balancer-bal, and https://www.gemini.com/cryptopedia/balancer-crypto-automated-pools#section-how-balancer-works

17. See https://www.investopedia.com/articles/investing/092315/
    7-best-peertopeer-lending-websites.asp and https://www.fool.com/
    knowledge-center/5-bond-market-facts-you-need-to-know.aspx

18. See https://www.finextra.com/blogposting/21620/explore-the-world-
    of-digital-profits-with-defi-lending-and-borrowing-
    platform-development

19. See https://learn.bybit.com/defi/what-are-dai-and-makerdao/ and
    https://www.coindesk.com/learn/how-does-makerdao-work-under
    standing-the-central-bank-of-crypto/

20. See https://decrypt.co/resources/what-is-aave-inside-the-
    defi-lending-protocol

21. See https://coinmarketcap.com/alexandria/article/how-does-aave-work

22. See https://defillama.com/protocol/aave

23. See https://news.bitcoin.com/zero-collateral-138-million-in-
    defi-flash-loans-issued-in-24-hours/

24. See https://www.gemini.com/cryptopedia/what-is-compound-and-
    how-does-it-work, https://decrypt.co/resources/compound-defi-
    ethereum-explained-guide-how-to, and https://www.ulam.io/blog/
    how-compound-protocol-works/

25. See https://www.coindesk.com/learn/what-is-yield-farming-the-rocket-
    fuel-of-defi-explained/

26. See https://www.coindesk.com/learn/what-is-yield-farming-the-rocket-
    fuel-of-defi-explained/ and https://blockworks.co/what-is-yield-farmin
    g-what-you-need-to-know/

27. See https://finematics.com/derivatives-in-defi-explained/

28. See https://academy.binance.com/en/articles/what-is-synthetix-snx and
    https://www.gemini.com/cryptopedia/synthetix#section-governance

29. See https://www.reuters.com/technology/crypto-derivatives-volumes-
    surge-312-trillion-july-cryptocompare-2022-08-11/

30. See https://academy.shrimpy.io/post/what-is-dydx-explaining-the-
    popular-crypto-derivatives-dex, https://coinmarketcap.com/rankings/
    exchanges/derivatives/, https://dydx.exchange/blog/max-leverage-
    reduction, and https://decrypt.co/resources/dydx-ethereum-margin-
    trading-platform-explained-learn

31. See https://www.theblockcrypto.com/data/decentralized-finance/
    stablecoins

32. See https://www.gemini.com/cryptopedia/set-protocol-erc20-set-token-tokensets-asset-tokenization#section-what-is-set-protocol and https://indexcoop.com/defi-pulse-index-dpi

33. See https://coinmarketcap.com/currencies/yearn-finance/ and https://www.coinbase.com/price/yearn-finance

34. See https://cointelegraph.com/altcoins-for-beginners/a-beginners-guide-to-understanding-wrapped-tokens-and-wrapped-bitcoin and https://www.makeuseof.com/what-are-wrapped-cryptocurrency-tokens/

CHAPTER 5

STABLECOINS

The inception of the *stablecoin* came in 2014 through a group known as Tether Limited. While Bitcoin was still largely under the radar to the general public, those who had been following the developing digital asset landscape for a few years likely caught on to the unpredictable price volatility accompanying the asset. We saw price reductions regularly of up to 60–90 percent, which is a death sentence for most assets. This volatility made Bitcoin more difficult to use and next to worthless within Decentralized Finance.

Tether Limited decided to leverage the same technology maintaining Bitcoin, but in a less volatile fashion. The digital asset Tether (*USDT*) was born under the guise of being pegged to the US Dollar, thus making each *USDT* worth $1. The term Stablecoin was officially coined to depict digital assets pegged to either an existing fiat currency, a commodity, or even a monetary algorithm. The goal of this type of digital asset is to maintain a steady price and value, thus making transactions more predictable and feasible, and increasing the usability of digital assets in the real economy and eventually for use in DeFi applications.

Bringing in something stable and strong like the US Dollar would open up the digital assets realm to many more use cases. The promise of near instantaneous, cost-efficient, and borderless transactions is a net benefit to users everywhere, especially in countries and regions where stable banking is inaccessible and credit extensions and services are a farce. The stablecoin concept aims to solve these problems by offering a trusted currency with the flexibility of digital assets.

There are two main types of stablecoins: fiat stablecoins and algorithmic stablecoins. Fiat stablecoins are more actionable for the majority of the financial services ecosystem since each stablecoin is backed by its corresponding fiat currency, such as the US Dollar. The mechanisms governing fiat stablecoins typically create (mint) new stablecoins as new US Dollars are deposited from customers or users, update the records of US Dollars on hand, and issue the stablecoin to the depositor. If the depositor wishes to return a stablecoin for USD, the exchange may happen and the stablecoin will be destroyed (burned) to ensure the proper 1:1 ratio of circulating stablecoin to USD collateral.

Algorithmic stablecoins are not directly backed by a fiat currency, and therefore rely on their own calculations and mechanics to maintain a stable price representation. For explanation purposes, crypto-backed stablecoins are also considered as algorithmic stablecoins since the widespread separation in the stablecoin world is fiat-backed versus not fiat-backed. Another way of visualizing this is centralized versus decentralized stablecoins.

ALGORITHMIC STABLECOINS

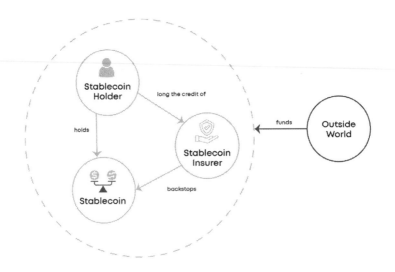

Since algorithmic stablecoins don't have typical reserves, they rely on a proprietary algorithm to balance supply and demand of the stablecoin to maintain each designated stable value. Known as a *peg*, this designated stable value, which is unique to each algorithmic stablecoin, must remain constant in order to ensure the stablecoin's value. Some algorithmic stablecoins rely on an overcollateralization of other crypto assets (such as *MKR* and *DAI*) while others may rely on a basket of crypto assets to ensure value to the stablecoin (such was the attempt with *UST* and *LUNA*).[1] Examples of fiat-backed and algorithmic stablecoins are described below.

Tether

As previously mentioned, Tether was the first stablecoin entrant into the digital assets market in 2014. Tether Limited had the goal of pegging each Tether (*USDT*) to the USD dollar in a 1:1 ratio. The rationale behind this was to provide a greater on-ramp to crypto investments from new users and existing digital asset holders and investors. Rather than needing to wire dollars from a bank, rely on ACH deposits, or purchase cryptocurrency with credit cards, an investor could simply hold a digital representation of the US Dollar in the same wallet holding other digital assets. This would bring efficiencies to the buy and sell process associated with digital assets and would reduce friction across the legacy and digital worlds. Given the demand for improved processes among existing digital asset users, Tether (USDT) rose in market capitalization so rapidly it emerged as the number-three largest cryptocurrency by market cap spot behind Bitcoin (*BTC*) and Ethereum (*ETH*), to the tune of $65+ billion in value at the end of 2022.[2]

While Tether proclaimed a 1:1 ratio of *USDT* in circulation to US Dollars held in reserve, there were accusations of miscalculations and misrepresentations of the true underlying dollar figure. Consequently, in October 2021, the Commodity Futures Trading Commission (CFTC) levied a $41 million fine on Tether Limited for these misrepresentations, misleading statements, and marketing regarding the true collateralization of the digital asset.

Tether Limited revealed *USDT* was backed by cash, commercial paper, and related liquid money market products. While mostly liquid, Tether's reserves consisting of this trifecta of asset types were not consistent with its initial promise of being "fully-backed by US Dollars," and the CFTC made it clear this misrepresentation would not be tolerated or excused.[3]

The actions of Tether paved the road for future stablecoin roll-outs. While not officially fined until around seven years after inception, Tether still had its own public perception troubles throughout the ICO days of 2017 and 2018 with much murmuring of mis-collateralization and misuse of funds. This shined a light on priorities for stablecoin providers and issuers to focus on, one of which was transparent and audited reserves.

USD Coin (USDC)

The *USDC* stablecoin was launched as a joint venture between two companies. One was Circle, a leading payments and infrastructure company in the digital assets space since 2013. The other was Coinbase, one of the more marquis wallet and exchange providers and the first digital assets company to go public via IPO. The development and issuance of "USD Coin" took place in May 2018. It was designed to improve on the path Tether set forth four years prior. All *USDC* reserves are held as either cash or cash equivalents like US Treasuries and dollar-denominated money market products. To prove this and maintain confidence for its positioning in the industry, the accounts at regulated US financial institutions holding the reserves backing *USDC* are audited by Grant Thronton, LLP, who issues monthly attestations of the reserve holdings.[4]

This approach has been particularly well-received by the industry and industry participants, as readers can see the exponential growth pattern in *USDC* market cap that seemingly began around the same time Tether was facing its prominent fine. From 2021 through mid-2022, *USDC* enjoyed an increase in market capitalization from just a few billion dollars to nearly $54 billion, a symbol that industry participants were now exploring and emphasizing the usability of stablecoins.

The joint venture between Circle and Coinbase known as *Centre* had the vision of maintaining an efficient and exact record of the number of US dollars in circulation through the representation that *USDC* provided. Rather than setting a fixed supply of *USDC*, Centre is able to mint new *USDC* as it receives new USD or equivalent deposits. Likewise, Centre is able to burn *USDC* as it records and facilitates withdrawals of US dollars. With this record keeping mechanism, the ratio of *USDC* to cash and cash equivalents should always be one-to-one. This takes incentive out of trading *USDC* since the price will not necessarily move with supply and demand between parties, but will rather be transferred by the third-party supplier itself. Today, the stablecoin sits right behind *USDT* in market capitalization ending 2022 with over $44 Billion in supply.[5]

Gemini USD (GUSD)

As a direct competitor to *USDC*, Gemini rolled out its own stablecoin to rival Coinbase's foray around the same time. Gemini promised to improve on *USDC* by not simply including cash equivalents in its reserves, and instead limiting its reserves solely to the US dollar. Every *GUSD* is backed 1:1 by a US dollar held in an FDIC-insured bank, and reserves are audited on a monthly basis by the private accounting firm BPM.[6]

While *GUSD* is more of a "pure-play" fiat-pegged stablecoin than *USDC* and competing stablecoins, its market capitalization pales in comparison to the aforementioned options. As of mid-2022, *GUSD* has an aggregate market cap of just under $200 million, peaking at around $400 million at the end of Q1 2022.[7] This shows the lagging adoption that *GUSD* faces relative to *USDC*. Whether this is a factor of Coinbase's strength relative to Gemini's or simply a difference in the integration process with other industry players and infrastructure providers is unclear. As regulatory bodies step into the digital assets industry with more clarity and guidelines, it's possible *GUSD* is better positioned than competing stablecoins and finds itself with a positive catalyst to close the gap.

TerraUSD (UST)

The "Terra Ecosystem" was designed as its own mini-ecosystem within the digital assets and DeFi spaces. Terra took the concept and execution of DeFi and recreated its own sub-ecosystem within it. The Terra utility token known as *LUNA* was the Proof-of-Stake governance token to maintain and grow the ecosystem and its services such as staking, lending, and trading. Particularly unique was how Terra's vision was to recreate and redesign global eCommerce. In order to fulfill this, the organization rolled out a series of stablecoins pegged to a wide range of fiat currencies like the US dollar, the British pound, and the Japanese Yen. For comparison's sake, the focus will be on the USD stablecoin called TerraUSD (*UST*).

By utilizing *UST* to make cross-border payments for goods and services, Terra reduced fees typically charged by credit card companies and banks, which are especially hefty when changing jurisdictions and regions. Instead, users can send stablecoins all throughout the Terra ecosystem with predictability and execution.[8]

What made *UST* different from the previously covered stablecoins is its peg, meaning the collateral backing its currency to maintain a consistent price. The stablecoin *UST* wasn't backed by US dollars, but rather by an algorithmic representation of the US dollar. The algorithm was incentive driven and designed to maintain a net value of $1 per *UST*, and this maintenance was handled largely by the utility token *LUNA* and its investors and traders. Holders of *LUNA* were able to elect to burn $1 of *LUNA* in order to mint a *UST*, which was consistently worth $1. The same is true vice versa, holders of *UST* can redeem their tokens for equivalent amounts of *LUNA*.

Should the value of *UST* ever not be $1, arbitrageurs would come into play and burn and redeem tokens accordingly to narrow and close any spread. This is a similar principle to Exchange-Traded Funds (ETFs) in the traditional capital markets where ETFs rely on what's known as Authorized Participants to burn and redeem baskets of stocks that make up the ETF itself, and do this until the ETF's Net Asset Value (NAV) is in line with the underlying holdings. In the case of Terra and its associated ecosystem, users were able to freely act like Authorized Participants, not just institutional entities.[9]

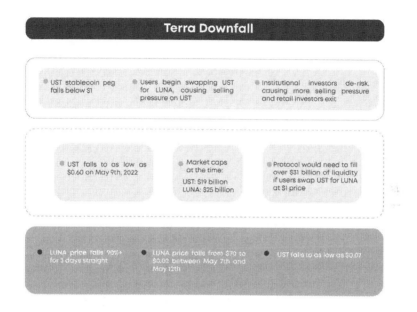

Since its inception in late 2020, TerraUSD grew to a troublingly large size for not actually being backed by real assets, achieving a market capitalization of $17 billion by the beginning of May 2022. What followed was a spectacular collapse of the stablecoin as a result of liquidity problems from one of *UST's* largest holders, (which was later determined to be linked to the Alameda-FTX scandal).

On May 7th roughly $2 Billion dollars was unstaked (removed from the ecosystem) and was subsequently liquidated for cash. This caused a drop in the price of *UST* (known as slippage) and led to the price of the supposedly "stable" *UST* falling below $1. The resulting depegging led to more people selling *UST* and removing liquidity from the protocol. The algorithmic function then kicked in, minting large amounts of *LUNA* to cover the demand. This in turn caused the overall price of LUNA to fall, further depegging the stablecoin tied to it.

Death Spiral: The Terra Crash and UST De-Peg of 2022

Since algorithmic stablecoins are based on artificial pegs or crypto reserves, the stability of these types of stablecoins are a direct function of the mathematical equations operating as intended. On a smaller scale, the algorithm should hold true, and the stablecoin's value should remain intact as retail traders and firms help maintain its peg. A larger, institutional-level scale is where these algorithms become stressed and the real examination begins.

In May 2022, the Terra ecosystem suffered arguably the most severe collapse of a major digital asset through a concept now known as the *Death Spiral*. The Death Spiral describes a situation where the peg of a stablecoin breaks and the value falls below one US dollar, causing a negative feedback loop where users redeem their stablecoins and further push the price down, ultimately resulting in both coins racing to the bottom and becoming completely worthless.

In Terra's case, the stablecoin *UST* is minted by burning *LUNA*, which is the reserve currency backed by other digital assets like *BTC*, *ETH*, *AVAX*, and so on. This minting always happens in a $1 to $1 ratio of UST to *LUNA*. If the price of *UST* is ever greater than $1, users can swap $1 of *LUNA* for $1 of *UST*, which is now trading above the dollar mark. That enables them to capitalize on the risk-free arbitrage opportunity and book profit. Additionally, as more UST are minted, the supply will become diluted and the price will fall back to the $1 level as intended.

The Death Spiral, however, focuses on the other side of the peg. If the *UST* peg falls below $1, users will begin swapping $1 of UST for $1 of *LUNA*, which is more valuable in relation to the UST at that point. On May 7th, 2022, the *UST* value fell to $0.99, which was not the first time this happened as the system is designed to briefly fluctuate based on the mechanism. However, certain institutions with *UST* funds locked into DeFi applications and strategies decided to de-risk their positions upon this de-peg, and began selling off their *UST* to avoid further losses.

Over the next couple days, this selling pressure leaked to retail investors and caused additional exits, sending the price of the *UST* stablecoin as low as $0.60 on May 9th, 2022. At this point in time, the market caps were $19 billion for *UST* and $25 billion for *LUNA*.

Keep in mind *UST*'s market cap was based on a price of $0.60. Should users begin swapping their *UST* for LUNA at the $1 price, the protocol would need to fill over $31 billion of liquidity, which at that point was nearly $6 billion greater than *LUNA*'s total market cap. Effectively, not all *LUNA* holders would be able to exit their positions at the current price, and many would struggle to get any repayment at all.

This incited a classic bank run in which *UST* users swapped their *UST* for *LUNA* and then sold their *LUNA* at a rapid rate, essentially resulting in a race to the bottom. The aftermath was detrimental as the price of *LUNA* fell 90+ percent for three days straight in a collective price change from around $70 to just $0.02 in the period between May 7 and May 12. Users who purchased *LUNA* at this two-cent mark experienced additional downfalls as the price fell as low as $0.00008. In this same time, *UST* fell to as low as $0.07, which was a far cry from its $1 peg.

Over $40 billion of market capitalization was washed away in this historical week across TerraUSD (*UST*) and Terra (*LUNA*), and the functionality of algorithmic stablecoins was called into question. With tens of billions of dollars evaporating, an official crypto winter kicked in, and we saw the unraveling of other faulty systems. The disaster put further spotlight on the need for transparency and properly pegged collateral for stablecoins. Even the interest of legislators and regulators was piqued, putting stablecoins in the full purview of the law.[10]

MakerDAO (DAI)

MakerDAO deserves credit for ushering in the first algorithmic stablecoin in 2017. The original vision of MakerDAO was to enable a DeFi ecosystem where users can borrow, lend, and transact digital assets in a stable manner without relying on an intermediary. Even if a digital asset is backed by the USD in an escrow account, users are still relying on the escrow account holder and must still have faith in the deposit and withdrawal process. To circumvent the need for a reliable reserves holder, Maker created the algorithmic stablecoin model.

DAI can be backed by a variety of assets like *BTC*, *ETH*, and *USDC*, rather than simply pegged to one fiat currency. The stablecoin can be purchased on most major centralized exchanges and decentralized exchanges, or can be borrowed from Maker itself in what's known as a Collateralized Debt Position, which was previously dubbed the *Maker Vault*.[11] *DAI* uses a Target Rate Feedback Mechanism (TRFM) to adjust interest rates and yields on borrowers for lenders to help maintain that $1 per token valuation. Additionally, new *DAI* can be minted as *ETH* is deposited as collateral, and burned upon the withdrawal of said collateral. As a last resort, governance tokens known as Maker (*MKR*) can be bought and sold to further collateralize positions and contribute to *DAI*'s peg to the US Dollar. These three features in tandem serve to ensure consistent valuation of the *DAI*.[12]

Since *DAI* is an algorithmic stablecoin, it also has no borders. Its crypto-first nature makes it a popular option in developing nations and regions, and internationally in general. As covered in chapter 4, MakerDAO was one of the earliest DeFi applications in the digital assets industry, and users can receive loans in *DAI*. The stablecoin sits as the eleventh-highest cryptocurrency at the end of 2022 with almost $6B in value.

Pax Dollar (USDP)

Paxos developed a Stablecoin-as-a-Service operation geared towards institutions and larger players rather than retail investors. Paxos is a company that's been in business since 2012 through its cryptocurrency exchange itBit and was awarded the very first New York State Department of Financial Services Trust Charter for Digital Assets in 2015. It continued its regulatory progress through the stablecoin issuance of PAX in 2018 (rebranded *USDP* as of August 31, 2021), receiving SEC permission to pilot stock trade settlement on the blockchain in 2019. Most recently it received preliminary approval for a national Trust bank charter in 2021.[13]

With an institutional focus, *USDP* is backed in a 1:1 ratio by US dollars. The token itself is issued by Paxos Trust Company, which also holds the reserves in state-regulated accounts and receives regular audits.[14] The combination of Paxos' closely regulated and safeguarded assets and its experience in the digital assets industry creates a strong value proposition for institutions looking to leverage the digital capabilities when it comes to the US dollar. Ranking thirty-ninth as of the end of 2022, the stablecoin reached nearly $1 Billion in market capitalization.

Binance USD (BUSD)

Binance, as the largest global exchange as of mid-2022, naturally threw its hat in the ring full of stablecoins. The Binance USD stablecoin (*BUSD*) is fully backed by the US dollar in a 1:1 ratio and regulated by the New York Department of Financial Services (NYDFS). Interestingly, Binance does not issue and manage *BUSD* itself. Instead, Binance is a client of Paxos, making *BUSD* an example of Paxos' previously covered Stablecoin-as-a-Service.[15] As of the end of 2022, BUSD has amassed a $17+ billion market cap, making it one of the larger stablecoins.[16]

NOTES

1. See https://decrypt.co/resources/what-are-algorithmic-stablecoins
2. See https://coinmarketcap.com/currencies/tether/
3. See https://www.sofi.com/what-is-usdt-tether/
4. See https://www.gemini.com/cryptopedia/what-is-usdc-stablecoin-circle-crypto#section-why-use-stablecoins-like-usdc
5. See https://coinmarketcap.com/currencies/usd-coin/
6. See https://www.gemini.com/cryptopedia/gusd-stablecoin-gemini-dollar#section-gusd-and-transparency
7. See https://coinmarketcap.com/currencies/gemini-dollar/
8. See https://www.gemini.com/cryptopedia/terra-luna-coin-fiat-stablecoin#section-the-terra-crypto-platform-accessible-and-interoperable
9. See https://cryptobriefing.com/can-terras-ust-hold-its-peg-cryptos-top-algorithmic-stablecoin-unpacked/
10. See https://wilfordlam.medium.com/the-biggest-collapse-in-crypto-history-the-fall-of-ust-luna-d025e47dcea2, https://www.coindesk.com/learn/what-is-luna-and-ust-a-guide-to-the-terra-ecosystem/, https://coinmarketcap.com/currencies/terrausd/historical-data/, and https://coinmarketcap.com/currencies/terra-luna/historical-data/
11. See https://www.gemini.com/cryptopedia/dai-stablecoin-what-is-dai-token#section-how-dai-tokens-work
12. See https://learn.bybit.com/altcoins/a-beginners-guide-what-is-dai-and-how-does-it-work/ and https://decrypt.co/resources/makerdao-guide-learn-explained-decrypt-3-minutes
13. See https://paxos.com/company/
14. See https://help.paxos.com/hc/en-us/articles/360042318531-Pax-Dollar-USDP-
15. See https://www.binance.us/en/busd
16. See https://coinmarketcap.com/currencies/binance-usd/

CHAPTER 6

CENTRAL BANK DIGITAL CURRENCIES (CBDC)

Perhaps the closest bridge between governments and traditional currencies and digital assets is what's known as a Central Bank Digital Currency (CBDC). One of the main points of attraction to cryptocurrency is its nature as programmable money. Being able to program and operate a money system through computer code is a powerful concept. It largely removes the need and desire for paper money, can help make transactions smoother from both initiation and settlement perspectives, and can even reduce steps and intermediaries that payment processors traditionally employ.

However, many cryptocurrencies are decentralized or distributed with little or even zero centralized parties managing them. The management of a currency, in the more traditional sense, includes anti-fraud and counterfeit monitoring to currency supply expansion or contraction activities to reserve backing decisions. Governments typically do not favor the idea of a decentralized currency as it takes away their power and positioning to maintain a hold on all those points. Thus, most governments (but not all) do not publicly acknowledge Bitcoin, Ethereum, or other digital assets as legal tender or as true currencies.

Still, the capabilities and precision afforded to communities through digital assets and their code-based mechanisms are too powerful to ignore. Digital assets are rightfully considered an upgrade from paper money and even existing digital value transfer methods such as ACH and Real-Time Payments. It would be irresponsible and irrational for government entities and central banks to overlook this money revolution. This is where the idea of the *digital dollar* comes into play.

CBDC would differ from a cryptocurrency or a stablecoin as it would be legal tender in the issuing party's jurisdiction. The United States Federal Reserve website directly states, "While Americans have long held money predominantly in digital form—for example in bank accounts, payment apps or through online transactions—a CBDC would differ from existing digital money available to the general public because a CBDC would be a liability of the Federal Reserve, not of a commercial bank."[1]

Additionally, 5 percent of adults in the United States (roughly seven million households) do not have a bank account, with an additional 13 percent of US adults having bank accounts but using expensive alternative services like money orders, payday loans, and check-cashing services for their day-to-day money management activities. On a global scale, there are 2.5 billion unbanked people, according to the World Bank Group. One of the goals of CBDCs is more expansive and inclusive access to money since these digital dollars, which are legal tender, can be held in digital wallets and used in day-to-day functions rather than relying on banking service providers. As such, individuals would have limited counterparty risk as they are dealing with the central bank issuer directly rather than interacting with intermediary banks and parties.[2]

Suppose the United States were to pass a CBDC plan. This plan would include developing and minting *dollar-valued* tokens, which are different from dollar-backed tokens like the majority of stablecoins. A CBDC token itself would be the exact equivalent of a US Dollar. The digital dollar, in this scenario, would become a part of the money supply and not simply a digital representation of it.

For further emphasis, envision the amount of USD Coin (USDC) in circulation, which was roughly $45 billion at the end of 2022. Since *USDC* is a dollar-backed stablecoin, for each *USDC* minted and issued there should be an equivalent amount of cash and cash substitutes held in a treasury with the issuing parties. The addition of $55 billion worth of *USDC* does not increase the US Dollar money supply by $55 billion, or even by any nominal amount. USDC is simply a digital representation of the underlying dollars held in the treasury.

CBDCs, however, would count as part of the money supply. An addition of $55 billion in a US Dollar CBDC would indeed increase the money supply by $55 billion. The CBDC would be minted and issued in a similar fashion to how existing US dollars are printed and issued from the Federal Reserve to banks and third parties. Understanding this, CBDC minting and management would fall under the supervision and responsibility of the Federal Reserve. As such, any activity involving a CBDC, including payments, transfers, and storage will be under the supervision of the Federal Reserve. This is the point where opinions typically become split.

One of the key tenets of cryptocurrency is the idea of self-sovereignty, meaning an individual should have the utmost control over their assets. This includes the ability to store, transfer, and accept value without government or regulatory interference. This is largely the basis of Bitcoin and subsequent cryptocurrencies, which are intended to be a global, permissionless currency enabling any individual to transfer value for any good or service available to them.

Under a government or central bank's supervision, CBDCs or digital dollars could have an additional layer of programming that would provide the issuing entity with extra control over individuals' money and activities in the form of monitoring, surveilling, and even locking or restricting. Think about the US Dollar in its existing form. Individuals are free to transact and manage their money as they see fit. Government controls largely come in the form of taxation, audits, and financial reporting for transactions greater than a designated amount of value, among others. These features can likely be heightened through digital dollars because of the same efficiencies inherent to cryptocurrencies and digital assets.[3]

Some people have an adverse reaction to this reality when they realize programmable money can result in unfavorable circumstances for the money holder. In a decentralized network, it is very unlikely that currency can be switched *off* or that accounts and holdings get frozen. However, a centralized, legal digital dollar will almost certainly give these controls to the issuing party such as a central bank. This means the central bank or government entity would be able to not only issue digital dollars to its civilians, but would also be able to easily pause, freeze, seize, and otherwise control those same assets. Activities like taxation and government payments would become more or less seamless in a fully digital environment, although those same efficiencies also shift power toward the government entity.

This is particularly concerning when looking at the corporate backdrop surrounding digital assets. There have been reports and accounts detailing individuals whose bank accounts have been flagged, locked, or frozen citing cryptocurrency transactions and transfers among banks, credit cards, and digital asset marketplaces and processors. Banks obviously must comply with Anti-Money Laundering (AML) and Bank Secrecy Act (BSA) guidelines in addition to other financial regulations, so it is possible they are simply playing their role in being diligent regarding crypto transactions interacting with their clients' bank accounts. However, ordinary customers who have been flagged or have had accounts frozen understandably have an opposing opinion to that sort of capability being given to the everyday dollar, which would be the case with a CBDC.[4]

An interesting distinction in the world of CBDCs is "wholesale" versus "retail" CBDCs. Wholesale CBDCs can be viewed as similar to holdings in a central bank. These reserve holdings would be used in monetary policy activities as tools like setting reserve requirements and ratios, interest rates, and government printing. This would primarily be an interbank tool to improve efficiencies between the central bank and corporate institutes.

Retail CBDCs are more public-facing. This includes many of the ideas covered in this chapter thus far such as day-to-day legal tender for transactions, value storage, and money management. This group of CBDCs would be active in the economy from small businesses to purchases and payments alike. Again, this would enable the CBDC holder (individual) to source money from the central bank directly rather than working with a traditional banking entity. Still, it is unlikely banks and commercial entities would be entirely cut out of the picture even with retail CBDCs as they are the prime money distribution channels and still serve other roles within the financial services world.[5] To better understand the general concept of a CBDC, there are a number of examples and similar developments in action described below.

El Salvador Declares Bitcoin "Legal Tender"

Perhaps the most progressive government move regarding cryptocurrency and digital assets can be seen in El Salvador. In June 2021, El Salvador announced its intention to make Bitcoin (BTC) legal tender in the country. This legislation went into effect in September 2021, making El Salvador the first country to deem BTC and any cryptocurrency legal tender. The primary motivations for this act included the following:

- More efficient and real-time remittance payments.
- Provide a financial outlet to unbanked individuals within El Salvador (which amounts to roughly 70 percent of the country's population).
- Become a more globalized country and reduce reliance on the US Dollar (and other countries and their central banks).

Citizens will be able to decide if they wish to manage any Bitcoin or other digital assets in a self-custodial wallet over which they have full control and responsibility, or in a third-party or bank custodian. Given the oversized portion of unbanked citizens in the country, it's likely self-custody will prevail.

To onboard citizens into this initiative with their desired Chivo Wallet app, the government provided an incentive to citizens in the form of a $30 bonus (in BTC) and fee-free transactions versus existing fiat-to-Bitcoin ATMs, whose fees can be as much as 20 percent per transaction.

With the price of Bitcoin at the end of 2022 having declined by roughly half since the June 2021 announcement and more than 65 percent since the September 2021 start date, Bitcoin adoption momentum has largely slowed in El Salvador. Much of the Chive Wallet downloads were driven by the $30 sign-up bonus rather than the longer-term goal and intention of utilizing Bitcoin as an everyday means of exchange.[6]

Bahamian Sand Dollar

The Bahamas set a precedent for CBDC in its decision to issue the Sand Dollar in September 2020. The Central Bank of the Bahamas issued the Sand Dollar, which is backed by the Bahamian Dollar, which in turn is pegged to the US Dollar, in order to penetrate the E-Money market through a mobile app.

The country's central bank has been navigating challenges along the lines of proper receipt and ticketing of Sand Dollar transactions (specifically for goods and services throughout the Bahamas), setting anti-money laundering (AML) guidelines and thresholds to be inclusive yet functional, and bank and credit union adoption. At the end of 2022, one of the nation's six retail banks began piloting the Sand Dollar, and one of the largest five credit unions completed the assessment to become a provider of Sand Dollar wallets.[7]

New York Federal Reserve and 12-Bank Consortium

One facet a CBDC addresses is the interoperability and standardization of a digital currency. The existing stablecoin market deals with a number of differing coins, mostly all working to represent the same or similar underlying fiat currency (such as the USD). On the fiat side, all banks in the United States support the US Dollar as standardized and uniform. Multiple digital asset custodians supporting the same tokenized US dollar can be viewed similarly to the existing banking landscape. There would likely be little need for custodians to decide which stablecoins to support and to omit, as the true digital dollar would be standardized.

To explore and confirm this realization, researchers with the Federal Bank of New York made another discovery regarding stablecoins. They found the process of locking up US dollars to maintain a 1:1 peg as new fiat-backed stablecoins are minted unfairly and inefficiently affects banking activities.

Banks are required to abide by certain reserve requirements by maintaining free cash and cash equivalents on hand at all times. Suppose there was a new issuance of $100 million worth of fiat-backed stablecoins. The issuing party would be required to maintain $100 million worth of US dollars, and this responsibility usually passes through to the banking partner. The banking partner now cannot truthfully count that $100 million toward their free cash reserves since those dollars technically are being used in circulation for whatever stablecoin activity the users see fit, whether for exchange trading, decentralized staking, centralized lending, and so on.

Should enough stablecoins be issued this way, the bank will have to continuously cut into their revenue-generating activities in order to maintain enough free cash to meet the reserve requirements. This, obviously, does not help the bank's financial status and will not be well-received as part of the future business model. Additionally, it would be considered "murky waters" for the bank to lend or deploy capital that technically backs the stablecoins in circulation, which then locks the capital up in a stagnant position.

Instead, researchers with the New York Fed propose tokenized bank deposits take the place of stablecoins on a wide scale. The tokenized deposits would represent liabilities to the bank much like a standard commercial deposit would, rather than raw cash. Instead of locking cash up in the stablecoin issuance process, security tokens can represent the deposits made by customers and have the same effect as a stablecoin, meaning a stable-priced digital asset that can be used in the digital assets ecosystem and economy. It was stated, "Bank depositors would be able to convert their deposits into and out of digital assets – the tokenized deposits – that can circulate on a DLT platform. These tokenized deposits would represent a claim on the depositor's commercial bank, just as a regular deposit does."[8]

A wise way of implementing this would be to establish stronger regulatory guidelines for banks or the issuing parties to ensure deposits are properly covered with an equivalent or near-equivalent amount of assets. Rather than raising the alarm that a tokenized deposit approach would lead to undercollateralized activities, this could be an avenue to bring other tokenized asset concepts and roll-outs into the mix. The rotation of tokenized deposits with tokenized treasury funds and cash equivalents may create a strong and liquid enough combination to bring this digital solution to market on a wide scale.

Bank of America proclaimed CBDCs indeed have the ability to not change money itself, but rather to change the way money is exchanged in the coming fifteen years. As a word of caution, CoinDesk noted in its coverage that, "CBDCs aren't without their risks. They may drive competition with bank deposits, and could lead to a loss of monetary sovereignty and inequality among countries globally." Many of these points likely come down to the ability to drive adoption of a digital currency versus existing forms on a global scale, and not just within United States borders.[9]

Regulated Liability Network

Back in May 2022, Thomson Reuters offered a straightforward question: Can banks and other financial institutions better manage their risk and offer faster settlements by "tokenizing" their liabilities on blockchain networks?[10] Again, as we've learned in this publication through pioneers like Arca (ArCoin), JP Morgan (repos and TCN), and HQLAx (digital collateral registry), the answer is indeed yes.

A large consortium consisting of Citi, Goldman Sachs, Barclays, OCBC Bank, Bank of America, Bank of New York, Wells Fargo, BondEvalue, Payoneer, Paypal, SETL, and Linklaters gathered and birthed an upgraded solution from stablecoins and CBDCs known as the Regulated Liability Network (RLN).

The RLN's general process would look similar to what's been seen in the previous cases in which assets can be digitized and transferred among banks on the network as tokens are minted, transferred, and burned in a single coordinated transaction where all parties involved are relying on the same ledger, thus enabling the achievement of real-time settlement.

In the initiative's whitepaper, RLN representatives explain how the primary objective is to first tokenize dollars (create digital dollars) before moving into other assets like stocks, bonds, alternatives, and so on. It's all part of a greater effort to develop sovereign digital currencies not limited just to the liabilities of a central bank. One of the RLN plans is to also develop blended digital currencies (currency baskets) in which a basket of currencies is tokenized so as to not rely on just one such as the US Dollar or the Euro. This is a bit more complex on the functional side, although if successful it could provide an avenue to dampen the worries around CBDCs.

It looks like the end goal of the RLN is to tokenize and swap such a wide range of assets that CBDCs and stablecoins are rendered less desirable since users can effectively swap value stored in real estate assets, private fund interests, and debt products for other products without the need for digital cash settlement.

To bring things full circle, Citi, HSBC, Wells Fargo, Mastercard, and the New York Federal Reserve announced their collective twelve-week pilot testing of a central bank digital dollar in November 2022. The success and the outcomes of this pilot testing may have significant implications for a future decision either in favor of the RLN, the CBDC, or a calculated blend of both based on desired activities (i.e., bank financing, payments, cross-border transactions).[11]

SWIFT Network

While not necessarily developing CBDCs, SWIFT (Society for Worldwide Interbank Financial Telecommunication), which underpins a vast majority of the current global capital markets infrastructure, demonstrated and proved its infrastructure could successfully serve as an interconnector of multiple blockchains, tokenization platforms, and cash representatives. This is important to internalize because the rails would also likely include CBDC support as CBDCs come to market.

SWIFT's Chief Innovation Officer Tom Zschach stated, "Digital currencies and tokens have huge potential to shape the way we will all pay and invest in the future. But that potential can only be unleashed if the different approaches that are being explored have the ability to connect and work together."[12] This is obviously a huge initiative for the tokenization industry as SWIFT is responsible for connecting almost twelve-thousand financial institutions consisting of four billion accounts across two-hundred countries. That sheer amount of distribution and coverage cannot be ignored, especially when SWIFT's original mission was to bridge geographies, currencies, and technologies. As we've learned with asset tokenization and seen through prior examples, "cross-ledger" is becoming the new "cross-border," meaning SWIFT is working toward adapting its interoperable mission to also include a multi-chain and multi-asset future of capital markets, including CBDC transaction support.[13]

NOTES

1. See https://www.federalreserve.gov/cbdc-faqs.htm

2. See https://www.investopedia.com/terms/c/central-bank-digital-currency-cbdc.asp, https://www.gao.gov/blog/more-7-million-u.-s.-households-have-no-bank-account.-why, and https://borgenproject.org/unbanked-population/

3. See https://www.federalreserve.gov/faqs/what-is-a-central-bank-digital-currency.htm, https://www.investopedia.com/terms/c/central-bank-digital-currency-cbdc.asp, and https://coinmarketcap.com/currencies/usd-coin/

4. See https://decrypt.co/39226/banks-still-blocking-crypto-transactions

5. See https://www.investopedia.com/terms/c/central-bank-digital-currency-cbdc.asp

6. See https://www.pwc.com/gx/en/financial-services/pdf/el-salvadors-law-a-meaningful-test-for-bitcoin.pdf, https://www.nber.org/digest/202207/el-salvadors-experiment-bitcoin-legal-tender, and https://coinmarketcap.com/currencies/bitcoin/

7. See https://www.globalgovernmentfintech.com/bahamas-central-bank-cbdc-sand-dollar-first-two-years/

8. See https://www.pymnts.com/cryptocurrency/2022/fdic-chair-calls-stablecoins-a-top-concern-as-ny-fed-calls-them-unnecessary

9. See https://www.coindesk.com/business/2023/01/17/bank-of-america-says-cbdcs-are-the-future-of-money-and-payments/

10. See https://www.thomsonreuters.com/en-us/posts/investigation-fraud-and-risk/banks-tokenizing-liabilities/

11. See https://regulatedliabilitynetwork.org/

12. See https://thetokenizer-io.cdn.ampproject.org/c/s/thetokenizer.io/amp/2022/10/07/ground-breaking-swift-innovation-paves-way-for-global-use-of-tokenized-assets/

13. See https://www.coindesk.com/business/2021/12/23/banks-swift-messaging-system-to-experiment-with-tokenized-assets-in-early-2022/

CHAPTER 7

COMMERCIAL SOLUTIONS

A side from maintaining a portfolio of whitelisted digital wallet addresses to send cryptocurrencies, stablecoins, and utility tokens to, solutions have been developed for commercial-grade crypto integration too. This is a necessity to move away from the Wire, ACH, and Credit Card standards across small businesses and financial services alike. This chapter will cover not only payments services for business and large organizations, but also banking services for businesses and organizations that are now relying on cryptocurrency or incorporating digital assets into their daily operations.

Crypto Payments Services

Payment processors like PayPal, Square (Block), and Coinbase Commerce offer streamlined transfers of funds for the buying and selling of goods and services. The typical transaction will:

1. Establish the amount a buyer is looking to spend.
2. Check the buyer's connected digital asset wallet for sufficient funds.
3. If sufficient, transfer the funds from the buyer's wallet to the seller's business wallet address.
4. Completion time will vary with the digital asset selected, but will usually be finalized within mere minutes.
5. The cryptocurrency may be held or converted into USD or stablecoin.

Payment Processors

One of the obvious questions is: How does the seller protect against volatility from the time of transaction to fiat conversion?

Some of these payment processors offer what's known as a *volatility shield*. This shield locks the USD value of the purchase in at the time of transaction and ensures the amount is delivered to the seller. This comes with risk to the payment processor, as a thinly-traded cryptocurrency may be more susceptible to short-term price movements than the typical asset, leaving the downside exposed and the processing company liable to cover the difference on behalf of the seller.

The shortlist of companies that offer commercial-grade payments solutions include the following:[1]

- Coingate
- Coinbase Commerce
- BitPay
- NOWPayments
- AlfaCoins
- CoinPayments

These processors typically compete on the fee structures, which range from fixed fees to percentages of transaction sizes. The fixed fees are seen as favorable to higher-sized transactions than the percentage fee, since a parity point will be reached where the fixed transaction fee is miniscule relative to the transaction size. The percentage fee structure is similar to a credit card processing fee, and still needs to undercut the incumbent processors like Visa and Mastercard in order to drive traffic towards the digital asset crowd, and ultimately gain traction.

The average percentage transaction fee on a crypto payment processor sits between 0.5–3 percent depending on the size of transactions, which presents favorable opportunities when looking at the average credit card processing fee of 1.5–3.5 percent. It becomes even more favorable for cross-border or international payments as credit card processors may levy their own processing and conversion fees, tacking on another 1–3 percent per transaction, thereby bringing the true international transaction cost up to 2.5–5 percent or more.[2]

Lastly, when comparing the commercial capabilities of cryptocurrency transactions to the typical bank wire fees of $20–$30 per domestic transaction and $20–$50 per international transaction, the case for cryptocurrency solutions becomes even more apparent and only grows as the volume of transactions grows.[3]

One important topic is the integration of stablecoins into existing payment processors. Since stablecoin transactions need no volatility shield yet benefit from the same blockchain value drivers like near-instant settlement, they present one of the more feasible options in the payments space.

Stripe began piloting the integration of *USDC* into its payment processor with a select group of creators on Twitter in April 2022. For the technicals, "Payments will occur via the Polygon (*MATIC*) network, a Layer 2 blockchain known for its low fees, fast transaction speed, innovative zero-knowledge technology and integration with Ethereum (*ETH*)."[4]

Stripe had planned on leveraging these capabilities to 120 countries by the end of 2022, and inherently expanding its pool of creators and earners on Twitter to solidify the proof-of-concept.

In addition to charging transaction fees to customers and vendors for access into crypto networks, many centralized exchanges built upon traditional banking business models for these new digital assets and currencies. Just like banks, the main revenue stream for many cryptocurrency custodians by 2022 revolved around making loans to other institutions using the available assets on its platform. As users store their assets on an exchange like Coinbase or Gemini, they were offered opportunities to earn an interest rate by consenting these platforms to lend out their capital for other investors to use as liquidity for more institutional trading. In a process known as *rehypothecation*, the crypto exchanges would invest earmarked user funds, known as the *float*, into high-risk opportunities, aiming to generate great returns, allowing them to pay back to users while still making a profit. Under the guise of *staking* and other terminology, these platforms discovered a rude awakening when in 2022, many investment funds and beneficiaries of these loans went bankrupt, leaving the exchanges without any recourse to recover any of the borrowed customer funds.

This began a cascading effect where customers of exchanges rumored to be affected by the lending collapse began withdrawing any available funds still left, contributing to bank runs across the industry, with firms like Celcius, BlockFi, Gemini, FTX, and many others facing billions of dollars in liabilities. Some firms, like Celcius or Gemini, had terms and conditions in place to protect against claims of fraud, while others like FTX are rumored to have been acting without its customers' consent.

In the time since these firms fell from grace, the SEC has acted quickly to condemn these firms, enforcing the position that yield-based products backed by customer funds constitute the sale of unregistered securities allowed only by licensed firms that provide eligible investors with proper documentation. In a series of settlements ranging from tens to hundreds of millions of dollars per violation, most firms have ceased from offering services like these to US customers, severely impacting future business models, and opening the question of many: are crypto exchanges actually banks?

Digital Asset Banks

Not all banks and institutions are free to work with cryptocurrencies and digital assets on a federal level. The federal bank charter is one of the highest and most encompassing distinctions in the financial services industry. With a federal bank charter, organizations are able to take deposits, manage customer assets, make money transfers, lend, and much more under the guidance of the Office of the Comptroller of the Currency (OCC).

Without a federal bank charter, institutions may receive state charters (which provide some but not all services) or must piece the process together through the application and reception of things like custodial licenses, investment adviser designations, and money transmitter licenses (MTL), of which the New York BitLicense is infamous for being one of the most difficult and costly money transmitter licenses to obtain as it enables the transfer of digital assets through the State of New York. Previous cases have shown the cost of BitLicense to be in the low-to-mid six figures and the application takes hundreds of hours in filings and discussion, with one such case cited as taking 1,200 hours to complete.[5]

While state chartered crypto banks in Wyoming like Kraken and Custodia still have certain national capabilities, they cannot yet take funds from business or customers based in New York without a BitLicense, which is superseded by a federal bank charter. Additionally, the levels of insurance and reserve requirements vary between federal and state banks. The Wyoming-based banks are not FDIC (Federal Deposit Insurance Corp.) insured and are therefore required to maintain 100 percent of digital asset value in reserve to protect their customers.[6]

This, and a variety of other nuances and differences between federal banks and other designations, simply add to the competitive advantage that comes with having a federal bank charter. Federal banks with cryptocurrency capabilities become one-stop-shops for clients, which can range from retail to accredited to institutional. Below are the existing federal crypto banks as of May 2022.

Anchorage Digital

Anchorage Digital is perhaps the most prominent name in the discussion of federal crypto banks. Originally a pure digital assets custodian founded in 2017, Anchorage received national banking approval from the OCC in January 2021 to enable it to operate on a federal level. This approval brought new capabilities, including insured stablecoin deposits, institutional-caliber custody, and all general operations associated with traditional banks. This approval put Anchorage on par with existing national banks like Chase, Bank of America, and Citibank.[7]

Beyond general digital asset custody, Anchorage is also one of the leading custodians in the security token and digital securities world. The firm is integrated with a number of SEC and FINRA-registered Broker-Dealers (BD) and Alternative Trading Systems (ATS), transfer agents, security token issuance platforms, and third-parties that support the tokenized asset space and infrastructure. Since custody is seen as the base layer and foundation within the digital assets ecosystem, as it is where investors expect their funds to be securely held and managed, Anchorage has shown its ability to execute even on some of the more regulated and strict sides of compliance.

Protego Trust

Shortly after the approval of Anchorage Digital, the OCC approved Protego Trust Company for the same federal bank charter in February 2021. Indicated by its name change to Protego Trust Bank, the organization began allowing clients nationwide to store, trade, lend, and even issue digital assets. Mutual clients of Protego could begin borrowing and lending to each other via digital assets, much like they could with US dollars in traditional banking. The key difference here is how US dollar transactions could happen in an interbank fashion, meaning between multiple different banks, whereas digital asset lending transactions are limited to intrabank only through Protego.

Again, the competitive advantage of a federal bank charter is shown as Protego began attracting both retail and institutional clients who wished to take advantage of the digital asset services and were limited to Protego's internal clients. At this point in time, users are not yet able to partake in certain interbank activities via digital assets, creating an increased demand for Protego's services and therefore improving the bank's client profiles and onboarded accounts.[8]

Paxos

As the third federally regulated crypto bank, Paxos (originally a stablecoin issuer as noted earlier) achieved the OCC's approval in April 2021 to operate with banking activity on a federal level. While Anchorage and Protego both converted their existing trust practices into a formalized bank, Paxos took a different approach. They set up a de *novo charter*, which is an entirely new entity.

This applies a bit more pressure on Paxos to ensure their operations are up to speed and can meet certain requirements, but may also provide benefits as new procedures could be formed completely under the pretense of the banking guidelines. Its current operations, which include stablecoin-as-a-service, custody and exchange services, and a cryptocurrency over-the-counter brokerage, will remain as the main driving force behind the organization. Ideally these services will strengthen with the backing of the bank and associated benefits like digital asset insurance, future lending (not yet approved), and asset management.[9]

It is worth noting that all three entities (Anchorage, Protego, and Paxos) were approved by the OCC under eighteen-month preliminary periods. This means the entities have eighteen months from approval to get fully compliant with the federal banking guidelines and expectations before being formally approved. These formalized decisions will either be made in late 2022 or extended for future check-in, as is common practice in the digital assets space (i.e., Bitcoin ETF decisions getting deferred for future review rather than accepted or denied).[10]

NOTES

1. See https://www.makeuseof.com/best-cryptocurrency-payment-gateways/

2. See https://www.bankrate.com/finance/credit-cards/merchants-guide-to-credit-card-processing-fees/ and https://www.investopedia.com/foreign-transaction-fee-vs-currency-conversion-fee-know-the-difference-4768955

3. See https://www.bankrate.com/banking/wire-transfer-fees/

4. See https://cointelegraph.com/news/twitter-and-stripe-roll-out-usdc-payout-program-for-creators-via-polygon

5. See https://dilendorf.com/resources/10-questions-about-bitlicense-from-a-crypto-lawyer.html

6. See https://www.bankingdive.com/news/crypto-exchange-kraken-wyoming-banking-license/585514/

7. See https://news.bitcoin.com/anchorage-obtains-federal-license-to-operate-as-crypto-bank-from-the-occ/ and https://www.occ.gov/news-issuances/news-releases/2021/nr-occ-2021-6.html

8. See https://www.businesswire.com/news/home/20210205005102/en/Protego-Trust-Bank-N.A.-Gets-Conditional-Approval-for-OCC-Charter

9. See https://www.coindesk.com/markets/2021/04/23/paxos-becomes-third-federally-regulated-crypto-bank/ and https://decrypt.co/68838/paxos-gets-federal-bank-charter-from-occ

10. See https://www.regulationtomorrow.com/us/occ-conditionally-approves-bank-charter-for-second-crypto-firm/

CHAPTER 8

SECURITY TOKENS

Security Tokens are digital assets that represent a real-world underlying asset. The digital nature of the token enables token holders to trade with other markets, investors, and asset owners globally.

A security token is simply a blockchain-based *wrapper* encompassing the underlying asset according to a programmable set of rules, guidelines, and parameters. These instructions are baked into each token upon development and may include but are not limited to the following:

- The amount of the underlying asset that each token represents.
- Type of investor allowed (retail, accredited, qualified, institutional).
- Jurisdictions allowed for investors.
- Investment instrument type.
- Distributions (percentage, amount, tiers).
- Lock-Up Periods or trading limits.
- Number of total tokens issued.
- Associated compliance filings.

All of these parameters can be coded into each security token via smart contract and self-governed with limited intermediary actions.

What these smart contracts enable are the automatic execution of the pre-programmed rules (including the parameters listed above). These rules work in tandem with additional technology services to create a healthy and thriving ecosystem to enable the fractionalization of ownership, real-time trading and settlement, global capital access, and reduced execution fees relative to the incumbent markets. Security tokens can encompass nearly all assets and types of assets, including the following:

- Individual Real Estate Properties
- Single Real Estate Portfolio
- Private Investment Funds (PE/VC)
- Revenue-Backed Businesses (Physical and Digital)
- Publicly-Tradable Shares
- Pre-IPO Shares (private, illiquid companies)
- Art and Collectible Investments

As these examples will show, Security Tokens take on fungibility and transferability traits of cryptocurrencies like *BTC* and *ETH* but provide intrinsic value via the underlying asset. *Security Tokens are an upgrade to asset management many people have been waiting for.*

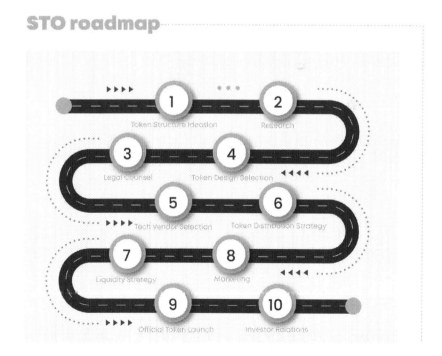

The high-level lifecycle of a security token includes the following stages:

1. Asset Selection
2. Offering Structuring
3. Token Development
4. Primary Token Issuance
5. Secondary Token Trading

Once a security token reaches the final stage of Secondary Trading it can technically exist on the secondary markets for as long as it is in good standing, much like public company shares continue to trade on the Nasdaq or NYSE. Security tokens can be structured in numerous ways to present exit opportunities even after they are being traded. Any of the components covered in this chapter may play a complementary role to the five steps listed above, which can elongate or shorten any given step along the way, ideally while creating value for the security token ecosystem. Because there are hundreds of trillions of dollars' worth of assets, equities, debt instruments, derivatives, and thousands of financial structures, the applications for security tokens are wide-ranging and significant in benefits.

Token Structuring

Security tokens are simply wrappers for automating an investment. Think of it like a digital receipt for your investment in the form of a token. The flexibility of smart contracts means the structure of a security token can take on several forms, including equity, debt, revenue share, profit share, or a blended hybrid approach. Additional utility can also be baked into security token smart contracts to offer loyalty rewards, perks, or access for token holders.

Equity

Equity is the ownership right to an underlying asset, whether it be direct shares in a company, membership interests in a Special Purpose

Vehicle (SPV), or rights to future investment value, and is typically executed in *pro rata* fashion to ensure each investor gets a fair share based on investment terms.

EQUITY INFO

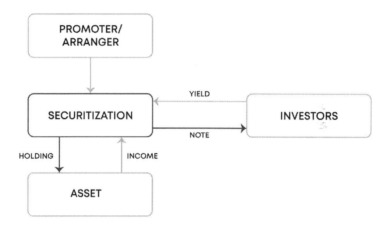

Security tokens can be used to facilitate equity investments into an underlying vehicle. Since security tokens are simply the digital wrapper around the security instrument (equity), investors can hold tokens with the peace of mind that they have the same equity rights and provisions as they would with a traditional structure. The only true difference is the digital nature and custody of these ownership rights.

Example: Enegra ($EGX)

Enegra is a global commodity trading platform based in Malaysia that tokenized 100 percent of its equity on the Ethereum blockchain across 85 million $EGX tokens via Tokeny in 2019. In November 2021, Ene gra migrated its tokens from Ethereum to Polygon in favor of better fees and greater scalability potential. The collective value of the equity was $28 billion in the primary market. A portion of the tokens began trading on the BigONE exchange, and the token is the largest by market cap on the secondary markets to date, coming in at $14 billion per Security Token Market.[1]

Debt

Similarly, security tokens can be developed and coded to represent fixed-income or variable-rate debt offerings. Token issuers can structure their offering to distribute a predetermined rate, automatically distributed on schedule per the smart contract. Additionally, with an API-driven financial data feed, it's feasible to pull in LIBOR data via API to ensure the security token is always representing the proper variable rate in real-time if elected.

REIMAGINING DEBT WITH SECURITY TOKENS

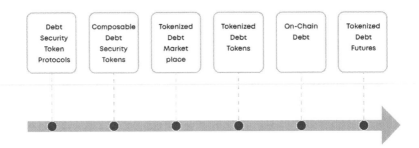

Example: El Salvador Bitcoin-backed Bonds

It was June 2021 when El Salvador announced Bitcoin would be considered legal tender in its jurisdiction.[2] Shortly thereafter, a tokenized Bitcoin bond offering was announced. The ten-year 6.5 percent bond offering would raise funds to purchase $1 billion worth of Bitcoin in an effort to boost the country's treasury of its new official currency, and reduce the circulating supply to external Bitcoin buyers. The bonds were to be issued via a security token on the Liquid Network, which is a bitcoin sidechain supporting tokenization and is the same technology Blockstream utilizes in its $BMN1 offerings mentioned later in this chapter.[3]

EL SALVADOR'S EXPERIMENT WITH BITCOIN AS LEGAL TENDER

MEASURE OF BITCOIN USE

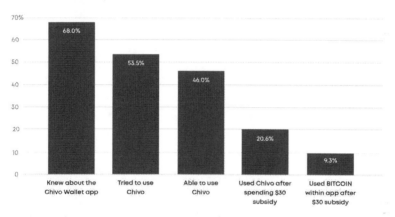

Source: Researchers' calculations using data from a national survey in El Salvador

Revenue Share / Profit Share

Revenue Share and Profit Share structures are unique alternatives to the standard Equity or Debt offering. And they are becoming even more popular within the security token wrapper as both issuers and investors find value in them.

Revenue Share agreements typically come with an exit multiple so investors can calculate their expected returns. Without this ability, the instrument may be considered too unreliable for most asset managers. The benefits of revenue share agreements include the following:

1. Company/asset owners maintain all or more of their owner-ship interests while forgoing a portion of future revenues over the predetermined period.
2. Investors gain access to potentially above-average distributions without needing a liquidity event to return their investment.

The revenue share agreement makes more sense in established, high-growth markets that are beginning to scale operations since company/asset owners may not have enough free capital to commit to fixed-income distributions, but will be able to meet the guidelines after a set period of time or an operational milestone. Investors could gain exposure to a high-growth revenue schedule and a lucrative exit multiple given this, which comes with income distributions not normally found in early-stage equity investments. [4]

REVENUE SHARE

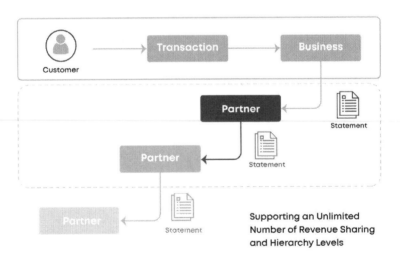

Profit Share agreements fall under a similar umbrella, although they usually entail heavier disclosure guidelines to protect investors and ensure fair profit distribution. For this reason, revenue share agreements are more widely used as private companies don't always wish to reveal their operational status to the general public (and by extension, their competitors), electing instead for "adjusted gross revenue" as the common profitability metric. Nonetheless, security tokens could be programmed to distribute a certain portion of company revenue or profits pro rata to all token holders.

Additionally, given these agreements usually have a well-defined exit multiple to retire the investment instrument, revenue share and/or profit share tokens can be "retired" from the secondary trading markets upon "maturity," which in this case would be the point in time the predetermined multiple is reached. Rather than continuing to trade on speculation, the tokens may actually be "burned" and taken out of circulation upon full and proper repayment to the token holders.

Example: tZERO ($TZROP)

The secondary trading venue tZERO issued its own security token representing Class A shares of preferred stock in 2018. The $TZROP token, amassing $134 million in initial fundraising from accredited investors, entitles investors to 10 percent of adjusted gross revenues through tZERO's operations, mainly consisting of listing and trading fees, on a quarterly basis. Since this was done as an accredited-only private placement, the tokens became tradable and open for retail investors in mid-2019.[5]

The unique feature of this offering is its token-agnostic bet on the security token industry as a whole itself. Owning a $TZROP token could be comparable to owning a piece of the Nasdaq and enjoying a portion of all of the trading revenues generated through it. As the number of security token investors and issuances grow, tZERO will be able to capture an exponential amount of trading fees and grow its own revenue lines out further, which will directly benefit token holders.

Example: Blockstream Mining Note ($BMN1)

Blockstream is a Bitcoin infrastructure firm founded in 2014 that owns and operates one of the largest North American Bitcoin mining facilities. Blockstream has been financing much of their operational expansion through security token offerings known as the Blockstream Mining Note (BMN). BMN is structured as a revenue-sharing note, of which its $BMN1 token has historically been shown to outperform spot Bitcoin itself per a Security Token Market deep-dive report.[6]

Blockstream raised $46 million across eight different tranches of BMN notes,[7] which are fungible with each other, from qualified international investors through STOKR and Bitfinex Securities. BMN1, a specific tranche within the collection, is listed and currently trades internationally on Bitfinex Securities. The Blockstream Mining Note is minted and issued on the Liquid Network, a Bitcoin Layer 2 solution that supports asset tokenization and issuance.

Example: INX ($INX)

As a publicly-registered alternative to tZERO and $TZROP, INX Limited (now known as INX One) issued its own $INX token that amassed an initial investment amount of $85 million across 7,200 investors through its Ethereum-based IPO with TokenSoft.[8] Since INX raised traditional funds earlier, this brings their total funding to around $125 million. Per TokenSoft CEO Mason Borda, "Token holders receive 40 percent of distributions from the company with no voting rights, while equity holders will receive 60 percent of distributions with voting rights." Officially, this is a profit-sharing token and provides distributions with the company's net cash flows. Additionally, INX Limited redistributes profits to an ever-diminishing supply of $INX tokens, as every token that gets used as a utility for reduced commission fees gets transferred to the INX Limited treasury reserve.[9]

SAFE Note

A SAFE is a Simple Agreement for Future Equity. The SAFE structure is a convertible note pioneered by YCombinator that provides investors with the ability to access equity in a company during a future priced round, but not at the time of investment. The SAFE is largely seen as a "pro-company" instrument since any SAFE purchasers are not legally or officially on the cap table until a liquidation event occurs.[10]

SAFEs typically make use of a discount to the priced round at the time of conversion or a valuation cap at which SAFE investors may convert their notes into equity. In some instances, SAFEs may include both a discount and a valuation cap, or even neither, in which case there may be a lock-up period or other guidelines that govern the investors' abilities to convert notes into equity at the market rate. There will sometimes be what's known as a Most Favored Nation (MFN) clause that protects investors and enables them to convert at the best deal offered based on the SAFE note terms.

In the scenario involving tokenization, SAFEs become an even more attractive instrument for both issuers and investors. The future tradability of a security token means investors likely do not have to wait for a liquidity event or a certain valuation to be met before being able to realize gains. They can buy and sell these tokenized SAFEs as they see fit on the secondary markets. Given this, tokenized SAFEs are likely to behave more as "perceived equity" rather than some illiquid alternative investment instrument like the majority of existing SAFEs. Issuers maintain the same ease and protections and investors are granted a path to liquidity should they not wish to hold their investment positions until all terms of the SAFE are met.

In fact, the prominent crowdfunding platform Republic took the SAFE model one step further keeping the emerging crowdfunding market in mind, and solidified the Crowd SAFE.[11] In a Crowd SAFE, the group of investors purchase the instrument in exchange for an opportunity to earn shares or a cash return when the company goes public via IPO, gets acquired, or sells all of its assets. Again, given the tokenized nature of these instruments, the Crowd SAFE can be even more flexible since investors can actively buy and sell positions throughout the lifecycle of the security token rather than returns being contingent on an exit event.

Example: Republic Note ($R/Note)

Built on the Algorand (*ALGO*) blockchain, the Republic Note known as $R/Note is a profit-sharing SAFE offered to investors with the rights to distributions from successful Republic portfolio company exits.[12] Per the PPM from July 2020, Republic planned on issuing these notes over the course of a few years, with around half of the supply being front-loaded in the initial offering.[13] There is a minimum buy-in of $1,000 with a price of $0.12 per note, an initial circulating supply of up to 370 million notes, a max supply of 800 million notes, and the ability to purchase fractional notes.[14]

Dividends will be paid out in $2 million increments (pro rata to investors) based on the portfolio company's performance and activity. Investors essentially get upside in the Republic offerings and listings, which Republic invests directly into without being on the cap tables directly or without even owning equity in Republic itself. This is beneficial to Republic as the issuer, as it may raise capital for expansionary activities or additional investments, and to the investors as they may partake in Republic's vetting and investment processes.

Loyalty Rewards and Perks

Aside from securities, security tokens can be used to facilitate and distribute rewards points, loyalty rewards, perks, or any other type of digital asset. Given the fungible nature of security tokens (i.e., uniformity in value and use across each token in the offering), companies could distribute perks, rewards, and points directly to their users' digital wallets, all automatically programmed and distributed.

Complex Structures

Lastly, token issuers can create a hybrid offering using multiple security instruments or share classes under a *complex structure*. Hybrid examples would typically be executed through separate offerings, such as one equity round and one debt round at concurrent times, or a single offering with multiple tranches in which each tranche represents a different instrument. See the following short examples:

- A Real Estate Developer offers one security token that represents equity in the land and another security token that represents rental cash flows and another security token that represents the debt on the property.
- An eSports Startup has equity investors but needs additional working capital to scale operations: chooses to digitize the current equity investors through security tokens and offer another round of Revenue Share tokens with a 3x Revenue exit multiple.
- An Agnostic Family Office is seeking early liquidity and wants to attract a wide range of investors: chooses a single security token offering with two tranches - the first being an 11 percent debt offering on its Private Credit division and the second being Equity shares in its M&A activities.

Security tokens simply enable more capabilities for already existing financial instruments commonly used by investment bankers and financiers. While the new technology is generally thought of to open up additional ways to raise capital and issue financial products, there's already a very strong value proposition when dealing with complex financial structures.

Take a major real estate investment firm and look at all of its allocations, for example. One investment manager could have exposure to 20+ share classes in a commercial real estate property. This exposure could be spread across equity ownership, debt financing, convertible products, and other agreements with unique covenants. Managing all of this via Excel sheets and an entire analyst team is cumbersome and largely unnecessary. There is little value-add to hiring an additional analyst to keep up with new investments and capital stack changes when the investment manager could better manage these nuances on-chain.

When tokenizing and bringing assets and investments on-chain, asset owners can be sure that any distributions, rights, reporting, and usual tasks are carried out in an automated fashion. Material changes, marks, and updates to an asset will still be initiated by a person (and therefore have a human element), although the life cycle management beyond that will be done by the blockchain ledger itself. When dealing with complex structures involving multiple rounds of financing and covenants and requirements, baking these into a blockchain rather than relying on numerous unlinked Excel sheets and management systems relay efficiencies in the form of cost savings including the following:

- Investor management fee reductions
- Back-office expense reductions
- More timely updates to asset valuations
- Seamless asset-level reporting and data

Mortgage-backed securities, asset-backed securities, and structured products are great examples of complex structures in this regard. Mortgage-Backed Securities (MBS) could have anywhere from a few to a dozen tranches of varying interest rates and yields, prices, risk levels, maturity dates, and other factors that affect their investment profiles. Managing all of these tranches, investors, distributions, and obligations is a bulky procedure. Instead, an MBS issuance could be facilitated on-chain, and therefore have most or all of the tranche data and information properly coded and tied to the underlying blockchain. Actions can become automated from there. As the MBS issuer realizes these benefits, they can then focus on more value creation to the firm (i.e., shift resources from management towards origination) and generate additional gains.[15]

Token Issuance

The current process for issuing tokens varies based on country and jurisdiction. In the United States, security tokens are not compliant simply by being minted and sold on a blockchain. Securities laws require compliance with specific regulations. Most often a *Transfer Agent* is employed to manage the cap table and transfer of ownerships associated with the real underlying asset. The reason for this is that the SEC and FINRA are wary of digital asset hacks and losses, and they're right to be wary. Self-custody in crypto and digital assets is bittersweet as it enables token holders to truly own their assets, but also delegates the "*last line of defense*" to them as well. Even custodians can be hacked or subject to malpractice resulting in the loss of cryptocurrencies, ERC-20 tokens, and NFTs.

Since security tokens are developed following existing securities frameworks and typically in conjunction with a licensed Transfer Agent, security token issuance platforms can "burn" lost or stolen tokens and "mint" or reissue new tokens at the equivalent value. With these developments, security token investors are always protected and not at risk of misplacing a private key and forever losing access to the investment. Some token developers even formulated a more cost-effective method of restoring and saving lost or stolen tokens without fully burning and reissuing tokens. Unlike purchasing a cryptocurrency, security tokens are investment instruments protected by the law and enforced by the SEC and therefore means you are legally entitled to your investment, regardless of whether you misplaced your digital receipt.

Additional designations that benefit security token issuance platforms include *Broker-Dealer* (BD) licenses to legally solicit investors, *Alternative Trading Systems* (ATS) to facilitate secondary trading, and a *Funding Portal Registration* to offer securities to retail investors.

Token Developers and Issuance Platforms

While the blockchains themselves are the foundation upon which security tokens are developed and issued, the blockchains alone cannot yet encompass all of the necessary features associated with securities. For example, the SEC does not yet allow the sole recording of ownership to be done directly on the blockchain. Additionally, most blockchains don't have built-in KYC/AML functionality, so this too must be handled externally.

Fortunately, there are numerous development and issuance platforms that maintain and offer the required licensing or open-ecosystem connectivity to properly and compliantly facilitate security tokens.

Remember, the blockchain of choice is simply the foundation in the pavement in this case, the token developers and issuers draw and organize the roads on top of that.

Securitize

One of the most prominent security token developers, issuance platforms, and now secondary trading venues (*covered later*), Securitize is designed to be an end-to-end solution for those seeking a tokenization solution. As the SEC's first appointed blockchain-based Transfer Agent, Securitize was actually spun out of a tokenized VC fund called SPiCE VC.[16] Now Securitize boasts over 400,000 onboarded investors and users as it carves out its Broker-Dealer/ATS services. Securitize makes use of its DS-Protocol (Digital Securities Protocol) to include all necessary components to a proper security token issuance. With backing from Morgan Stanley's Tactical Value group, Securitize is positioned as one of the most institutional-capable issuance platforms in the market today. Notably, they have raised over $100 Million since 2018 and feature large financial institutions as clients including KKR and Hamilton Lane.[17]

Vertalo

Vertalo is more of an open-ecosystem platform. The firm is a registered Transfer Agent and token developer with its "V-token" protocol, now rebranded as the Vertalo Securities Protocol. As mentioned earlier, Transfer Agents in this industry must have capabilities to burn stolen, lost, or void security tokens and reissue valid tokens to the rightful owner. The SEC calls this "good control location" of securities.

Vertalo actually developed a unique solution that circumvents the full re-issuance of security tokens in some instances by keeping unnecessary or non-critical information off-chain. Post-issuance services like built-in dividends, variable distribution changes, and jurisdictional upgrades can all be modified without a full token re-issuance. This may not seem significant on the surface, but as token uses scale, an issuer must take both development/maintenance expenses and gas fees associated with the chosen blockchain into consideration, and this proprietary solution may prove to solidify Vertalo as a cost-efficient token developer and platform over time.

Tokeny

Prominent overseas security token developer Tokeny has had some marquee headlines in the latter half of 2021 and sits as one of the largest issuance platforms with over $8.5 billion in tokenized assets.[18] As visionaries regarding the scalability of security token issuance, Tokeny partnered with the Ethereum sidechain known as Polygon.[19] What Polygon does is circumvent Ethereum's "mainnet" and instead routes orders to a new layer (categorizing Polygon as a *Layer 2* solution). This can be thought of as taking the side roads rather than sitting in traffic on a main highway. This partnership is baked into Tokeny's proprietary "T-REX" (recently renamed as ERC3643) Token structure.[20] Lastly, Tokeny is backed by the Euronext, a leading pan-European exchange, and therefore caters to European issuers and abides by non-US jurisdictions.

Figure Technologies

Tech conglomerate Figure Technologies developed its own blockchain technology to complement the firm's current and future operations. Provenance blockchain, which can be accessed with the utility token *HASH*, is specially-built for securitizations and transactions of HELOCs, Mortgage-Backed Securities, general fixed income, and similar asset-backed products.[21] In late 2020, Figure was responsible for securitizing and selling the largest HELOC-backed bond in a decade (worth $308 million), all on Provenance.[22] With the approval of an ATS license, Figure is working towards becoming a one-stop-shop for specialty securitization, redemptions, and secondary trading across private equities and private funds.[23]

DigiShares

DigiShares is a white-label service provider that creates and manages the smart contract structuring for security token issuers. As of mid-2022, DigiShares is working towards obtaining its own Transfer Agent license, in addition to becoming an approved Funding Portal for retail-focused capital raises under the Regulation Crowdfund and Regulation A+ placements. Whereas many funding portals compete on fees and commission percentages of raises, DigiShares maintains its white-labeled strategy and favorable fee structure to support earlier stage firms in their quests to raise up to $5 million at a time.

Secondary Trading Venues

The main feature of security tokens that unlocks liquidity across tokenized assets is the secondary trading component. Much like shares of stock can be traded on an exchange, security token buyers and sellers can be matched up on secondary trading venues. This capability provides investors with greater precision throughout the asset management lifecycle, and may serve to reduce the liquidity premium that investors typically pay on illiquid assets such as Limited Partner interests in a venture capital fund, commercial real estate assets, and other investments with traditionally long lock-up periods.[24]

Given the nascent stage of the industry, most US trading venues are classified as *Alternative Trading Systems* (ATS), not national exchanges, and solely rely on their abilities to match orders rather than to manage client assets and books. As more firms obtain Broker-Dealer and ATS licenses, more volume will pile into the secondary trading space and venues could even begin specializing in certain asset classes, or catering towards certain investor bases. In order for a security token to trade on an ATS, they are required to have a transfer agent. The following section covers several of the existing prominent secondary trading venues as well as a couple promising future developments.

Note that certain international offerings trade through decentralized exchanges (DEX) or international marketplaces as they do not fall under the SEC's jurisdiction and guidelines. Comparable international licenses similar to the ATS license in the US include the Multilateral Trading Facility (MTF) License in the UK, Markets in Financial Instruments Directive (MiFID) in the European Union, the Proprietary Trading System (PTS) License in Japan, and Registered Market Operator (RMO) License in Singapore.

tZERO

As arguably the most established Alternative Trading System in the United States, tZERO currently offers four security token assets and 15+ cryptocurrencies. While this number seems low for the go-to venue in the industry, the number of security tokens listed can be seen as a function of the diligence tZERO performs for each newly trading token. When it comes to "practicing what you preach," tZERO issued its own preferred equity share ($TZROP) in 2018, which is one of four tokens currently supported. As of the end of 2022, $TZROP has a market cap of nearly $80 million per Security Token Market, and revenues are poised to improve with more listings in the pipeline.[25]

tZERO is not a primary issuance platform, so it relies on other primary issuers and developers to "plug-in" to its order book. While this means tZERO doesn't necessarily have a competitive advantage when it comes to controlling the entire lifecycle of an asset, it also keeps tZERO acting neutral in the primary issuance phase and presents a wide range of broker-dealer subscribers to add value on the secondary market.

Boston Security Token Exchange (BSTX)

As the first national exchange to be approved by the SEC to use blockchain-based settlements and trades, the Boston Security Token Exchange surpasses the capabilities of competing Alternative Trading Systems (ATS). BSTX is a joint venture between tZERO and the Boston Options Exchange (BOX) to make strides towards the vision of issuing stocks, bonds, ETFs, and security tokens all on one marketplace. ETFs, for instance, can only be issued on national exchanges, not ATSs, which limits that vision under the existing ATS-driven landscape.[26]

To bolster this approval, Intercontinental Exchange (ICE), the parent company to the New York Stock Exchange (NYSE), invested in tZERO itself and appointed its own Chief Strategy Officer David Goone as the CEO of tZERO. Goon will oversee both the ATS operations and growth and the joint venture national exchange to further close the gap between analog and digital capital markets.[27]

INX

As the largest competitor to tZERO, INX is an international marketplace for security tokens and cryptocurrencies. Having launched its own profit-sharing token ($INX) that comes with trading perks like reduced commission fees for token holders, INX and tZERO are often compared based on their token's performance and market cap. $INX is currently one the largest US-based security tokens with a market cap of over $50 million.

Having acquired OpenFinance's ATS license in 2021, INX streamlined itself as both a token developer and a secondary venue, providing it with more surface-level strength than tZERO as a sole secondary venue. Most recently, INX Limited acquired TokenSoft's Transfer Agent in January 2022, thus making it the only 'nose-to-tail' solution that offers digital securities trading 24/7/365 for US issuers and investors.[28]

Securitize Markets

While tZERO and INX are usually pit against each other, Securitize Markets is arguably a more comparable service to INX than tZERO is. Securitize Markets is the secondary trading arm (the ATS) of Securitize, the issuance platform mentioned earlier. The marketplace was launched in late 2021 and seeks to build out its capabilities on Reg A, Reg CF, Reg D, and Reg S.

Whereas tZERO seeks to plug in from other issuance platforms, and therefore enjoys synergies with the ecosystem around it, Securitize

Markets is designed to rely on its own issuance division. By this, it seems like Securitize and INX are more compatible competitors, but without its own security token to "formally" compare, Securitize is sometimes left out of the discussion. Nonetheless, Securitize and its ATS produce high-quality offerings and may even integrate into the ecosystem more as needed.

Oasis Pro Markets

Oasis Pro Markets (OPM) received FINRA approval to operate a Digital Security Broker-Dealer and Alternative Trading System in January 2021. This is notable as it makes OPM a digitally native platform that can accept and list blockchain-based products. While other platforms support what are known as digitally enhanced products, meaning the investment product may exist in traditional form but is also represented as a security token on the blockchain, digitally-native products exist only in digital form. An example would be a new share class in a 1940 Act investment fund only accessible via the blockchain-based offering. OPM acts as a primary issuance broker-dealer and a secondary trading venue, and is backed by the mortgage-backed securities behemoth Redwood Trust and the venture arm of the half-a-trillion dollar global asset manager Mirae Asset Financial Group.[29]

Archax

Archax is a United Kingdom-based firm that has its own primary issuance and brokerage, secondary trading, and custodial arms. Registered as a Multilateral Trading Facility (MTF) in Europe, which can be seen as the equivalent to an Alternative Trading System in the United States, and regulated by the Financial Conduct Authority (FCA), which is England's FINRA equivalent, Archax is capable of helping raise capital for firms, custodying assets, and listing these assets for secondary trading. The firm is backed by asset management giant Abrdn and the Tezos Foundation, hinting at future private equity products built on the Tezos blockchain via Archax.[30]

MERJ

As a Seychelles-based nationally licensed exchange, MERJ is able to offer more than a traditional Broker-Dealer or Alternative Trading System (ATS). MERJ is able to manage a true order book, act as a transfer agent, a custodian, and more all on behalf of the same issuer. Their platform is designed to compete with international financial giants including the New York Stock Exchange, London Stock Exchange Group, Toronto Stock Exchange, and other national exchanges by supporting both digital securities and analog securities alike. They now have dozens of securities listed for trading across 30+ jurisdictions, and work in tandem with Digital Markets for security token issuance and management.

Gemini Galactic Markets

The cryptocurrency giant Gemini also threw its hat in the security token ring with the successful FINRA approval of the Broker-Dealer and Alternative Trading System known as Gemini Galactic Markets in January 2022. The team's statement is as follows: "As the digital asset industry continues to grow, we believe blockchain infrastructure will change the way companies raise money in capital markets, and the ability to provide a regulated venue for the buying and selling of digital assets that are securities will be an important part of the blockchain ecosystem."[31]

Crypto Exchange Investment in Security Token Platforms

As a preluding theme as of late in the digital assets world, many products are being built as security tokens or as compliant offerings. In preparation of a *security token sweep*, meaning crypto products being deemed securities and being encouraged to register or file as such, a number of crypto platforms, exchanges, and companies have been investing in the security token or registered securities space. Coinbase and Binance are two such examples.

Coinbase - InvestaX

Coinbase, while not yet supporting security tokens or tokenized stocks as of the end of 2022, acquired Keystone Capital's broker-dealer license that may one day support securities. One of their publications states, "Ultimately, we can envision a world where we may even work with regulators to tokenize existing types of securities, bringing to this space the benefits of cryptocurrency-based markets — like 24/7 trading, real-time settlement, and chain-of-title. We believe this will democratize access to capital markets for companies and investors alike, lowering costs for all participants and bringing additional transparency and inclusion to the ecosystem."[32]

Ultimately, Coinbase being a publicly-traded company supporting security tokens would be massively bullish for the industry. Rather than directly supporting security tokens, Coinbase elected to invest in InvestaX, a registered securities exchange in Singapore with its own security tokens services in both the centralized marketplace and DeFi realms, in March 2022 to test the waters and to stay competitive with Binance.[33]

Binance - HG Exchange

In late December 2021, Binance Asia announced an 18 percent stake in the Singaporean-licensed private securities exchange, Hg Exchange.[34] Built on the Zilliqa blockchain, HGX facilitates the trading of tokenized private company shares, with plans of expanding into tokenized art, real estate, and other assets. This move signals a change in tides from unregulated cryptocurrencies and utility tokens to compliant and "by the book" digital securities.[35]

Binance Singapore CEO Richard Teng stated, "Crypto and traditional financial offerings continue to converge. Through this investment, we seek to work with HGX in enhancing offerings of products and services supported by blockchain technology." This is potentially even more beneficial news to the security token industry than a Coinbase announcement given Binance's positioning as the largest crypto exchange in the world, reaching $76 billion in daily trading volume in late 2021, more than the next top four exchange volumes combined at the time.[36] Binance's strategic investment in HGX will likely yield stronger security token roots in the Singaporean region, and force US-based marketplaces to compete.[37]

The Primary Issuance Market

The Primary Issuance Market refers to the market in which securities are created and sold to investors for the first time. Not traded. While the secondary trading market may have a collective value of $15 billion at the end of 2022, the entire security token industry must encompass all primary issuance tokens created and represent underlying assets regardless of lock-up periods, tradability, or circulation.

The first step in the scope of the primary issuance market in this case falls under the term "tokenization," which means taking assets that currently have value and securitizing them on the blockchain for 1) storage and management or 2) future tradability. The general life cycle of a security token is as follows:

TOKEN ISSUANCE JOURNEY

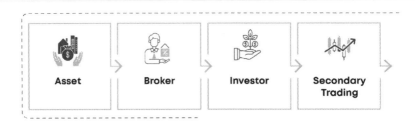

Asset → Broker → Investor → Secondary Trading

1. Securitization
2. Token Development
3. Token Issuance and Offering
4. Secondary Trading

Any actions within the first three steps contribute to the Primary Issuance Market.

Traditionally, company shares are considered to hit the primary market upon IPO when the shares are actually created and offered for the first time via an investment bank (or direct listing). After that point, the shares are subject to a *seasoning period*, or lock-up period, which prevents the shares from being traded for a certain period of time, depending on the fundraising regulations used for the primary issuance.

Following that period, the token is then able to be listed at which point it may trade on various secondary markets, which is when the general public may buy or sell. In the case of security tokens, the primary offering (initial creation) is offered to investors ranging from retail to institutional through a security token issuance portal or broker. These numbers are not always accounted for or even publicly known, but the projects and issuances certainly exist. Security Token Advisors estimates the Primary market to already be worth around $80 billion at the end of 2022. This will likely spill over into the secondary trading pipeline and activate the secondary market cap's ascent.

Keep in mind, security tokens are global and can span all types of assets, both tangible and intangible. This enables the *Total Addressable Market* to include but not be limited to the following (value estimates as of the end of 2022):

- $128 Trillion global bond market.
- $32 Trillion global commercial real estate.
- $5.5 Trillion Mortgage-Backed Securities Industry.
- $5.1 Trillion global insurance market.
- $600+ Billion global Private Equity industry.
- $500 Billion venture-backed Pre-IPO Shares.

Primary issuance / tokenization examples as of 2022 include the following:

→ Enegra: $28 Billion tokenization on the Polygon blockchain.
→ Tokeny: $8.5 Billion of European Real Estate.
→ RedSwan: $2.2 Billion of Commercial Real Estate.
→ El Salvador: $1 billion tokenized Bitcoin Bond via Blockstream.
→ Blockstream: $46 million for its own mining operations.
→ Numerous $100+ million opportunities in real estate, geothermal technology, and renewable energy in the Security Token Advisors pipeline.

Securitizations of products on the blockchain include the following:

→ $15.6 Billion in Centrotrenta Servicing assets.
→ $9 billion in digital mortgages and asset-backed securities on Provenance.
→ $2.8 Billion Central Bank of China government bond.

→ $308 Million Saluda Grade HELOC on Figure's Provenance blockchain.

→ $148 Million Central Bank of Australia government bond (across two tranches).

→ $449 Million Redwood Trust Residential MBS with Liquid Mortgage.

→ $1.3 Billion Bank of Communications Residential MBS on Jucai Chain.

→ $117 Million BBVA Corporate Loans called "Smart Bonds."

The main takeaway from the Primary Issuance Market is that there are a number of steps that go into tokenization before a token's trading. Any momentum forward from securitizing an asset or group of assets on a blockchain, implementing blockchain for data management, and using a blockchain-supportive Transfer Agent are all positive. These are all steps indicative of a future security token issuance as the true value of the aforementioned activities can be fully unlocked via token.

As the $100 billion primary pipeline grows by 2x, 5x, 10x, 100x and beyond, it simply takes the flick of a switch for a blockchain-based asset issuer to develop a token or a pre-existing token to begin trading on the secondary market and contribute to the aggregate tradable market cap as seen on STM.co.[38]

Initial Offering vs. Direct Listing

Understanding the relationship between the primary and secondary markets is important. Primary markets are where securities are created and offered for the first time. These securities then become freely traded and transferred in the secondary markets, usually to a much wider base of investors and participants. The reason for this is because new primary offerings, referred to as initial offerings, are typically targeted toward a specific group of higher-net-worth investors than the average person, and come with a high minimum investment amount. This minimum investment amount ensures each primary investor has significant skin in the game, but of course limits the number of investors who can get in on a primary round. While this trend is being revolutionized through retail-focused private offerings (more on this in Chapter 10), the vast majority of existing capital comes from high-net-worth individuals and organizations.

Once primary rounds are closed and settled with the initial investors, assets can be traded in secondary markets at a certain point in the future (this varies based on the exemption or rule followed for raising capital). Once they're on secondary markets, investors can purchase as many or as few shares of the investment offering as they desire, even as low as a single share in some cases. Given this, securities in the secondary markets tend to expand across the investor base as there's no longer a high-floor minimum investment amount and therefore many retail investors can gain exposure to the offering at varied market prices.

An important distinction that bridges the primary and secondary markets is the offering method: Initial Offering vs. Direct Listing. In traditional markets, an Initial Public Offering is when a company issues new shares to the general public for the first time. The public gets access to ownership in the company as the firm is essentially selling off a piece of itself to the public investors. The shares come from an investment bank and there are usually lock-up periods associated with new investors and key players.

DIRECT LISTING   VS   INITIAL OFFERING

A direct listing occurs when a company's existing investors, employees, and owners sell portions of their shares directly to the public, rather than creating new shares and issuing them. This prevents or reduces ownership dilution as no new shares are being formed and offered. Instead, the amount of shares will be determined by how much ownership the existing investors and employees are willing to offer. In a direct listing, banks are not necessary (but could still be useful) since there is not as much underwriting services needed.[39]

In the security token world, Security Token Offerings (STOs) can be comparable to Initial Public Offerings (IPOs), and tokenizing existing assets are comparable to direct listings. Issuing a new security token offering with the goal of raising capital for the firm is an undertaking that requires similar principles to an IPO. Tokenizing existing assets and offering portions to the crowd is more like a direct offering, and may be less pressure-intensive since the assets already exist.

Marketspace Capital, a $400 million real estate private equity firm in Houston, TX, brought one of their assets to the tZERO ATS via direct listing in 2022. Since the capital was already raised and secured for the firm's Myra Park property prior to this, they were able to tokenize and issue the asset directly to retail investors on the secondary markets. Had this been done through a security token offering, Marketspace Capital would have raised the capital via STO, deployed it into Myra Park, abided by any lock-up rules for primary investors, and issued the tokens on the tZERO marketplace after twelve months (for example). Neither option—direct listing or STO—is right or wrong. The decision comes down to what's best for the issuers and the investors, and security tokens and tokenization can handle both scenarios with scale.[40]

Use Cases - Investments

On a deeper level, the use case for investment products within the security token landscape is very flexible. Since security tokens can wrap any type or stage of asset on a blockchain, there are few limitations as to what investment products will be rolled out via security token. Pending compliance and regulatory requirements, the range of assets that can be tokenized and offered as investment opportunities will likely span across multiple geographic borders, investor profiles, sectors, and market cap sizes. Below are a handful of sample cases that can be implemented by incumbents or by new-age asset managers and issuers.

Real Estate

Real estate is one of the most, if not *the* most, straightforward asset classes for tokenization. A bare-bones use case would be tokenizing a rental property to allow current investors to exit early (if desired) and enable new investors (accredited and retail) to buy in. Assuming a well-oiled property management team is in place, the new investors who are token holders will be completely hands-off and simply receive automated distributions via rental cash flows proportionate to their ownership amount. Tokens can be traded on secondary markets and pricing will fluctuate with supply and demand.

What's unique is that while the token structure is fixed, the real-time terms of the token can change just like a tradable fixed income product. Take the following example:

→ Each token represents a 1/100 share in a rental property valued at $100,000.
→ The annual rental cash flows are $10,000, equating to a 10 percent annual yield.
→ The initial token price was $1,000.

Once the tokens hit the secondary markets, they trade as a function of supply and demand. If demand for the token exceeds selling pressure, then the token price might rise to something like $1,200, which values the property at $120,000. Now, the annual $10,000 yield is only an 8.3 percent yield. This token would be trading at a premium.

If sell pressure is greater than demand, then the token will likely fall in price to something like $800, which values the property at $80,000. Now, the annual $10,000 yield is a 12.5 percent yield. The token would now be trading at a discount.

Investors can create trading strategies based on their own unique goals surrounding growth, income, or value, and can tailor these factors to certain property locations.

Additionally, this concept can be taken deeper into examples like restaurants, night clubs, healthcare facilities, retail stores, and any level of "brick and mortar" operations, otherwise known as commercial real estate or CRE. Not only can the underlying property be tokenized, but the operations can be tokenized and offered as an equity, debt, or revenue sharing agreement to investors.

The appeal of security tokens is their ability to efficiently create these additional layers in the capital stack and bring much-needed precision to markets and industries that have never had the opportunity of doing so. Real estate tokenization is not limited to CRE, providing benefits for REITs, real estate debt, and even residential.

Tokenized ETFs and Investment Baskets

Tokenized ETFs can solve the cross-border barrier that's hindering the ETF industry. While American investors have easy access to the majority of ETFs, foreign investors are not always granted the same access for all funds. This is why certain ETF sponsors will also issue foreign counterparts of funds.[41] These funds hold the same shares of underlying stock, but are structured for whatever the targeted jurisdiction is. Unfortunately, this split based on jurisdictional access into the investment product in turn divides the total available liquidity, something that could be reconnected with tokenization.

Take the *Global X ETFs FinTech ETF* for example. The original FinTech ETF (FINX) currently has *$1.14 billion* in AUM.[42] Its counterpart European fund, called the FinTech UCITS ETF (FINX), has *$2.2 billion* in AUM.[43] The underlying holdings are actually slightly different, although likely have at least 95 percent commonality with each holding being off by mere bps. What's also interesting is the various Authorized Participants across both funds. Authorized Participants are personnel who act as market makers in the ETF space, and serve to "create" and "redeem" shares to keep an ETF in-line with its NAV.

Rather than having these 2 near-identical ETFs operating separately and with separate personnel, a single tokenized ETF would solve the cross-border issue between American and European investors in real-time and would drive the collective fund AUM upwards to *$3.24 billion*. This higher AUM would likely result in improved volumes and act as a positive sign for future investors concerned about liquidity. Additionally, it would potentially combine all Authorized Participants into one fund, thus resulting in a more liquid and properly priced market.

ETFs and security tokens have many similarities as pointed out earlier. Investors prefer the ETF wrapper to previous baskets of funds over time, and security tokens can act as the wrapper for baskets of private assets.[44] The functionality of the "create" and "redeem" mechanism in ETFs is something that can be used for tokenized baskets and tokenized products that contain underlying security tokens. Thematic ETFs faced (and still face) a similar challenge when it came to garnering assets as they were so niche and new, yet a significant hand-ful of thematic funds have proved successful and are now prominent names.[45] As Authorized Participants and market makers enter the secu-rity token space—taking advantage of comparable mechanisms for profit—investors and issuers will feel more confident and see greater success on the secondary markets.

Security Token Fund-of-Funds

The ETF structure and mold can be applied directly to private assets much like it already does to publicly traded stocks, bonds, and alter-natives. As the security token industry matures—defined by more quality assets, widespread primary investor bases, investment bank participation, and active, liquid secondary markets—there will be the opportunity to create funds and baskets of existing security tokens. These baskets could be themed much like a basket of stocks would, with some examples below:

STO FUND OF FUNDS WITH EXAMPLES

General Real Estate Basket
consists of the top 50 real estate security tokens by market capitalization

Commercial Real Estate Basket
consists of the top 10 largest CRE assets

Residential Real Estate Basket
consists of 30 single and multifamily property security tokens

Private Equity & Venture Capital Basket
consists of the top-performing private investment funds

Latin America BaskGeneral Real Estate Basket
consists of the largest security tokens issued out of the Latin American region

Small-Cap Pre-IPO Shares
consists of private company security tokens under $50 million in market cap / valuation

- General Real Estate Basket: Consists of the top 50 real estate security tokens by market capitalization.
- Commercial Real Estate Basket: Consists of the top 10 largest CRE assets.
- Residential Real Estate Basket: Consists of 30 single and multifamily property security tokens.
- Private Equity and Venture Capital Basket: Consists of the top-performing private investment funds.
- Latin America Basket: Consists of the largest security tokens issued out of the Latin American region.
- Small-Cap Pre-IPO Shares: Consists of private company security tokens under $50 million in market cap/valuation.

These baskets can be curated based on metrics ranging from market cap size to industry or sector to geographical locations. These baskets will also themselves be structured as security tokens, thus creating a fund-of-funds approach in certain instances, such as the security token that holds other tokenized PE/VC funds. This concept can be instituted at the time of writing as existing private equity and venture capital security tokens on the secondary markets include Blockchain Capital ($BCAP), SPiCE VC ($SPICE), Protos ($PRTS), 22x ($22X), and others in the primary issuance phase including digital share classes in the Hamilton Lane Private Assets Fund (PAF), tokenized interests in the KKR Health Care Strategic Growth Fund II (HCSGII), and Cosimo X ($COSX).[46]

Since the first four investment funds tokens are currently trading on secondary marketplaces, the argument could be made that an issuer could purchase X amount of tokens in each one, wrap that bundle in a security token, and issue the security token so the general investor base may gain access to all four funds rather than betting on just one or diluting capital across all four for the desired exposure.

As the individual four tokens see greater liquidity and trading volume, the basket token (which acts as the fund-of-funds here) will likely see a differing value to the calculated weighted sum market value of its underlying holdings. As it so happens in the ETF markets, market makers could come in with arbitrage strategies between then fund-of-funds and its underlying four tokens which will 1) enable the arbitrageur to profit off of pricing differentials between the fund and individuals and 2) bring the price of the fund and the four individuals closer to each other, acting as a balancing mechanism to ensure the value of the fund properly reflects its holdings.

Private Investment Funds

Much like Blockchain Capital and SPiCE VC did with their $BCAP and $SPiCE tokens, investment managers can tokenize their fund's Limited Partner interest and enable early exits, access to a wider investor base, and more precise and tailored approaches to investment management. As of March 15, 2021, after commentary and suggestions from *Security Token Group* and other involved parties, the SEC officially raised the Regulation CF (Crowdfunding) limits from $1.07 million to $5 million, and Regulation A+ from $50 million to $75 million.[47]

These amendments are pretty clear indicators of the shifting investment landscape, especially in the private sector. Crowdfunding platforms like SeedInvest and Wefunder are strong current beneficiaries of this progress, but there is a deeper root that stands to benefit even more heavily, including Private Investment Funds and Special Purpose Vehicles through security token capabilities.

With firms like Allocations and Digital SPV enabling a streamlined SPV and micro-fund creation process, investment managers do not have to run the gauntlet and pay up for the typical legal fees associated with a private equity or venture capital fund. That's not to say these elements don't still exist because they do. Expenses are simply compressing and packages are becoming more all-encompassing. The next step in this initiative is reaching a wider investor base through placements like Reg CF, Reg A, and Reg D, rather than the traditional method of tapping into one's direct network, which usually consists of the same cohort of ultra high net worth investors.

Just like the precision security tokens can bring to real estate and brick-and-mortar businesses, security tokens can improve the capital stack associated with private fund investments, including but not limited to the following:

→ Reduced liquidity premium for investors looking to exit early.
→ Automated periodic distributions or collections, such as Carried Interest and Capital Calls.
→ Easily coded, non-manual investment instruments for a blend of equity and debt.
→ Agostic across different types of investments such as Metaverse Funds, DeFi Funds, and traditional funds.

Pre-IPO Shares

Stemming from Pre-IPO marketplaces like SecondMarket (now Nasdaq Private Market), EquityZen, SharesPost, and ThElephant, the Pre-IPO industry is huge. Think of all the VC-backed companies and dollars poured into them during the 2010s.[48] EquityZen estimates a collective market cap of *$1.2 trillion* across private companies supported on its marketplace alone.[49] The real kicker is that "Pre-IPO shares" aren't limited to early or growth-stage companies. The category encompasses Pre-Seed, Seed, Series A, Series B, Series C, Series D, and so on through Series H or however long a firm decides to stay private. Stripe is a prime example in its ninth round of funding.[50]

As these shares both *1)* exist for angel investors, venture capitalists, and private equity firms and *2)* vest for employees from early stage to growth stage to late stage, they typically stay locked up until a true exit, usually when the company is acquired or goes public via IPO. As companies choose to stay private longer due to favorable financing terms, employees and investors are forced to delay the liquidity event that would unlock all of their vested capital.

The security token industry phrase *"go public while staying private"* could not be more applicable to this scenario. Rather than locking employees and investors up out of tradition, tokenized shares can trade freely in the market without affecting company operations, management, and growth.

It simply allows early liquidity for existing shares while allowing other investors to invest prior to an IPO. This is especially powerful for retail and non-institutional investors who have never truly had the opportunity to participate in growth before a company goes public, which has often been considered the highest-return asset class of all time (outside of crypto).

Use Cases - Infrastructure and Operations

What makes security tokens a potentially superior form of collateral relative to a general cryptocurrency is the intrinsic value associated with the underlying asset. Many staking pools and lending protocols require over-collateralization to hedge against massive volatility of the utility tokens like *AAVE, UNI,* and other ERC-20s. Many of these cases require a 150 percent over-collateralization rate, and we've even seen cases on MakerDAO that imply coverage rates as high as 172 percent.

In theory, a piece of real estate should not fluctuate the same way a utility cryptocurrency would, and therefore the security token representing that real estate should not be treated the same as a utility token. In the future, this could alleviate the overcollateralization guidelines that govern many DeFi protocols, and bring the Loan-to-Value (LTV) ratio up to more usable and feasible levels (i.e., even fifty–fifty).

On an institutional level, collateral management is most commonly used by banks, broker-dealers, investment firms, asset managers, and other associated parties to reduce risk and improve their own credit profiles and leverage their assets. This is especially applicable to parties partaking in various credit and debt investments, as it would make sense to reduce exposure to certain investments like higher-yield and/ or unsecured bonds.

Parties are able to reduce their risk to products on their balance sheets through collateral management processes. For instance, a firm might be holding onto a 14 percent coupon corporate bond that's lowly rated by Moody's or Fitch. They could sell a small portion off and/or exchange a portion of that bond with another institution in a credit swap. This would essentially dilute Firm A's position in the bond while adding, presumably, a higher quality product to its own balance sheet, and therefore improving its own credit profile.

Interestingly, on the note of credit profiles and ratings, while many assume digital assets of any sort are "risky," security tokens sometimes prove to be the contrarian indicator. Bonds issued on the blockchain sometimes receive higher or improved ratings from traditional agencies like Fitch, Moody's, and Morningstar who tout the real-time valuation benefits and transparency of blockchain-based assets as a positive.

Rather than certain assets remaining opaque to investors as seen in the analog financial services world, blockchain may add an extra layer of surveillance that reduces asymmetrical information between issuers, investors, and rating agencies, which may prove to be helpful to regulators too. In short, two identical assets may be rated differently if one is managed the "old-fashioned way" while the other runs on Ethereum (or any blockchain), and this difference likely skews in favor of the blockchain-based asset. Below are a few examples of blockchain-based assets that were rated by major agencies:[51]

- European Investment Bank (EIB) — Digital Bond Issuance (Fitch AAA Rating)
- Societe Generale — Obligations de Financement de l'Habitat (Fitch AAA Rating, Moody's Aaa Rating).
- FAT Brands — $40 Million Ethereum-based Bonds (Morningstar BB and B).

Rather than limiting the practice of collateral management and asset ratings to debt, tokenization can unlock assets of all kinds with equivalent efficiencies as transferring cash between banks. Traditionally, cash, treasuries, and other government and high-quality debt products are the most common assets used in collateral management because they are the most liquid and reliable. Still, the process of sending cash wires or trading/pledging treasuries from Bank A to Bank B in order to meet liquidity requirements, reserve ratios, and credit covenants takes longer than it should in a digital world.

OLD WALL STREET PROBLEMS

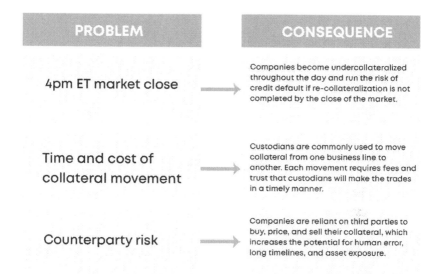

PROBLEM	CONSEQUENCE
4pm ET market close	Companies become undercollateralized throughout the day and run the risk of credit default if re-collateralization is not completed by the close of the market.
Time and cost of collateral movement	Custodians are commonly used to move collateral from one business line to another. Each movement requires fees and trust that custodians will make the trades in a timely manner.
Counterparty risk	Companies are reliant on third parties to buy, price, and sell their collateral, which increases the potential for human error, long timelines, and asset exposure.

This is where the digital assets investment firm Arca pioneered a tokenization-powered method of collateral management through the Arca Treasury Fund ($ArCoin).[52] Tokenized treasuries can be sent in a matter of minutes (or seconds) and can be used for parties involved to precisely manage their books, records, and desired transactions. The price of the $ArCoin token has been quite stable at $1.00 NAV through Arca's management of the fund that holds the treasury assets, and therefore the price risk is quite low. Given that, this can be used on a greater scale for collateral and credit management, and will probably find other significant use cases within the financial services infrastructure.

While this product and similar ones will be a priority for integration, the future financial services landscape for collateral management practices may even include tokenized real estate, tokenized private shares, tokenized private investment fund interests, tokenized corporate debt, and more. Since these assets are typically illiquid and difficult to move, they are rarely (if ever) used in the pledging and management process, and may unlock billions of dollars worth of assets for the involved parties.

In fact, JP Morgan Chase launched its own blockchain initiative directed at its repurchase agreements (repo) business, which falls in a similar field as treasury and collateral management. Repurchase agreements, more commonly referred to as repos, are very short-term loans in which one party sells an asset to another party while agreeing to buy it back at a slightly higher price in a predetermined time frame. The lender (the asset seller) gains cash and liquidity necessary to continue performing short-term business operations under proper reserve ratio and liquidity guidelines and the lender (the asset buyer) makes money on the spread of its buying price and its future agreed upon selling price.

The SEC estimates that the repo market had $4.1 trillion locked up in it at the point of September 2021. Increasing repo markets are usually a signal that banks and securities providers and dealers are borrowing with greater volume, as the purpose of the repo market is to create a functional system between these securities operators to ensure regulations and guidelines are met. The simplest way to do that, as of now, is to enable these players to work together and make low margin profits on high volume asset-backed loans.

JP Morgan's blockchain-based repo business flew somewhat under the radar until June 2021 when Goldman Sachs announced its first transaction through the platform. Swapping a tokenized US Treasury bond for an undisclosed amount of *JPM Coin*, the bank's internal stablecoin, Goldman Sachs got a glimpse of the revolutionary transparency blockchain-based transactions ushers in. The whole program is powered by JP Morgan's proprietary blockchain platform called Onyx.

Goldman Sachs Managing Director Mathew McDermott noted that for the first time ever the exact amount of time the banks took to complete the transaction was quantifiable. This initial transaction was quoted at three hours and five minutes precisely, meaning the origination of the repurchase agreement, the transfer from Goldman Sachs to JP Morgan, and the closing of the agreement took exactly three hours and five minutes. This newfound precision is crucial as repo transactions typically charge interest *by the minute.*

Previously, parties involved in repo transactions had to do their best to check each other and ensure fair charging and timelines, and there would be little way to actually verify the exact amount of time a bank was holding another's bank's assets on its books. The traditional record-keeping method was akin to lawyers charging billable hours in increments based on integrity. Rather than basing this multi-trillion-dollar market on integrity, big banks and securities dealers can now base it on smart contracts and erase any doubt or double-entry record-keeping between multiple parties.

After launching in October 2020 and achieving its first trades in December 2020, the repo platform built up enough steam to reach over $1 billion worth of transactions on a daily basis around this time of June 2021, and eclipsed the $300 billion mark in aggregate blockchain-based repo transactions in May 2022. Existing clients and users include Goldman Sachs, BNP Paribas, and BNY Mellon, among many others.[53]

Security Token History

While other securities like fund vehicles Blockchain Capital ($BCAP) and SPiCE VC ($SPICE) were previously working on security tokens, one of the first-ever security token offerings for private company stock was facilitated by Security Token Group's co-founder Herwig Konings. Amidst the Initial Coin Offering (ICO) boom in 2017/2018, Herwig was approached by a facial recognition firm known as Kairos, which was looking for his help in structuring a digital asset for fundraising purposes. Thanks to Herwig's background in compliance and crowdfunding, he recognized the enormous legal liability Initial Coin Offerings would hold in the eyes of the Securities and Exchange Commission (SEC) and took a step back.

Upon further consideration, Herwig was determined to set out and find the necessary legal and tech partners he could bring together in order to make this happen for Kairos, and to do it in an SEC compliant and regulated manner. After successfully structuring a dual-featured security token and utility token, Kairos issued this to the general market and raised $12 million to fund its business expansion.

This was the birth of something special. Herwig saw the writing on the wall and recognized the complexity and fragmentation of the digital assets industry—especially as it applies to regulated and compliant offerings. From there, Security Token Advisors was born under the Security Token Group umbrella to provide the highest-quality advisory and consulting services to clients. The firm has since evolved into an advisory service for both clients themselves and industry participants and organizations, with the ultimate goal of iterating and facilitating a well-oiled security token ecosystem to foster the adoption of security tokens worldwide.

NOTES

1. See https://tokeny.com/28-billion-company-migrates-its-security-tokens -from-ethereum-to-polygon/ and https://stomarket.com/

2. See https://foreignpolicy.com/2021/09/17/el-salvador-bitcoin-law-farce

3. See https://www.ledgerinsights.com/el-salvador-bitcoin-bond-great-promotion-for-security-tokens/

4. See https://startupdefinition.com/hockey-stick-curve/

5. See https://www.coindesk.com/markets/2019/02/15/tzero-is-live-but-volume-is-light-and-its-tokens-price-is-down-sharply/ and https://www.businesswire.com/news/home/20190812005400/en/%C 2%A0tZERO-Security-Tokens-Now-Tradable-by-Non-Accredited-Investors

6. See https://docsend.com/view/hqgdg6f8c8xeixin

7. See https://blog.blockstream.com/blockstream-mining-note-tranche-8-now-live-on-bitfinex-securities/

8. See https://www.coindesk.com/markets/2021/05/03/inx-closes-its-ethereum-based-ipo-with-85m-in-proceeds/

9. See https://www.inx.co/securities/the-inx-token

10. See https://www.upcounsel.com/safe-notes

11. See https://republic.com/learn/investors/crowdsafe and https://capbase. com/most-favored-nation-mfn-clause-in-startup-investing-what-it-is-and-how-it-works/ .

12. See https://republic.com/note

13. See https://uploads.republic.com/p/documents/attachments/original /000/000/254/254-1594945304-4c6bae7df13762fd39503252779f 9a96ceb74e75.pdf

14. See https://republic.com/help/category/republic-note

15. See https://corporatefinanceinstitute.com/resources/fixed-income/ bond-tranches/

16. See https://www.finextra.com/pressarticle/79561/securitize-becomes-an-sec-registered-transfer-agent and https://spicevc.com/

17. See https://securitize.io/press-releases/series-b

18. See https://tokeny.com/we-celebrated-tokenys-4th-birthday/

19. See https://tokeny.com/tokeny-has-solved-the-problem-of-gas-fees/

20. See https://tokeny.com/security-tokens-conditional-transfer/

21. See https://www.provenance.io/

22. See https://www.bloomberg.com/news/articles/2020-09-03/former-sofi-ceo-cagney-sells-biggest-heloc-backed-bond-in-decade

23. See https://www.businesswire.com/news/home/20210921005392/en/Figure-Completes-First-Digital-Securities-Transaction-Using-Real-time-Marketplace

24. See https://corporatefinanceinstitute.com/resources/equities/liquidity-premium/

25. See https://stomarket.com/

26. See https://www.businesswire.com/news/home/20220128005108/en/tZERO%E2%80%99s-BSTX-Joint-Venture-Receives-Approval-as-National-Securities-Exchange-Facility

27. See https://www.businesswire.com/news/home/20220222006084/en/tZERO-Accelerates-Leadership-in-Digital-Innovation-with-the-Appointment-of-ICE-Executive-David-Goone-as-New-Chief-Executive-Officer-and-Strategic-Funding-Round-Led-by-Intercontinental-Exchange

28. See https://finance.yahoo.com/news/inx-limited-acquires-tokensofts-transfer-140000531.html

29. See https://ghost.staging.oasispromarkets.com/blog/oasis-pro-markets-llc-receives-u-s-regulatory-approval-for-its-digital-security-alternative-trading-system-ats-2/

30. See https://www.archax.com/ and https://a-teaminsight.com/blog/archax-raises-28-5m-in-series-a-funding/?brand=tti

31. See https://www.gemini.com/blog/gemini-galactic-markets-approved-for-finra-membership-and-broker-dealer

32. See https://www.investopedia.com/news/why-coinbase-bought-brokerdealer/

33. See https://www.businesswire.com/news/home/20220316005446/en/InvestaX-Secures-Funding-From-Major-Crypto-Investment-and-Capital-Markets-Firms

34. See https://www.theblockcrypto.com/post/126761/binance-to-acquire-18-stake-singapore-hg-exchange

35. See https://www.theblock.co/post/126761/binance-to-acquire-18-stake-singapore-hg-exchange

36. See https://www.wsj.com/articles/binance-became-the-biggest-cryp tocurrency-exchange-without-licenses-or-headquarters-thats-coming-to-an-end-11636640029

37. See https://www.wsj.com/articles/binance-became-the-biggest-cryptocurrency-exchange-without-licenses-or-headquarters-thats-coming-to-an-end-11636640029

38. See https://stomarket.com/

39. See https://corporatefinanceinstitute.com/resources/knowledge/finance/direct-listing/

40. See https://www.globest.com/2021/10/19/marketspace-capital-uses-blockchain-to-tokenize-a-multifamily-project/

41. See https://smartasset.com/investing/invest-ucits-funds

42. See https://www.globalxetfs.com/funds/finx/

43. See https://globalxetfs.eu/funds/finx/

44. See https://www.globalxetfs.com/etfs-vs-actively-managed-mutual-funds-and-the-popularity-of-index-investing/

45. See https://www.globalxetfs.com/explore/

46. See https://stomarket.com/

47. See https://www.crowdfundinsider.com/2021/03/173206-as-reg-cf-funding-cap-jumps-to-5-million-first-issuers-take-advantage-of-the-increased-funding-amount/ and https://www.bassberrysecuritieslawexchange.com/patchwork-exempt-offering-framework-reg-a

48. See https://news.crunchbase.com/news/global-2020-funding-and-exit/

49. See https://equityzen.com/

50. See https://www.crunchbase.com/funding_round/stripe-series-h--52ea4a6a

51. See https://www.fitchratings.com/research/sovereigns/fitch-assigns-european-investment-bank-proposed-digital-bond-issuance-aaa-rating-28-04-2021, https://www.fitchratings.com/research/banks/sg-covered-bonds-issued-settled-with-blockchain-tech nology-21-05-2020, https://www.oecd.org/finance/The-Tokenisation-of-Assets-and-Potential-Implications-for-Financial-Markets.pdf, and https://www.financemagnates.com/cryptocurrency/news/dbrs-morningstar-grants-1st-ever-ethereum-security-rating/

52. See https://arcoin.arcalabs.com/blog-posts/the-first-blockchain-transferred-fund

53. See https://www.linkedin.com/posts/the-blockworks-group_jpmorgan-powered-blockchain-platform-has-activity-6934449133311168513-SUXL?utm_source=linkedin_share&utm_medium=member_desktop_web, https://www.sec.gov/files/mmfs-and-the-repo-market-021721.pdf, https://www.bloomberg.com/news/articles/2021-06-22/goldman-sachs-begins-trading-on-jpmorgan-repo-blockchain-network, and https://www.ft.com/content/f23c990a-913d-4613-8014-f61d35b6e09d

CHAPTER 9

DECENTRALIZED AUTONOMOUS ORGANIZATION (DAOS)

The first ever Decentralized Autonomous Organization (DAO) was actually named "The DAO." Formed in April 2016, The DAO caught fire on the Ethereum blockchain and raised $150 million from 11,000 investors, or members, within a month's time. This symbolized the largest crowdfunding vehicle ever, at that point in time. The DAO raised its funds via Initial Coin Offering, one of the first of its kind.

The function of The DAO was to serve as a member-driven or investor-driven Venture Capital fund. Members who own tokens in The DAO can vote on investment decisions, and therefore have hands-on access to the fund's choices. In essence, it shifts power from VC fund managers over to the crowd. However, these utility tokens were not registered securities or investment products with any financial regulatory bodies, and therefore investors had limited or no protections or guidance aside from what The DAO founders were unofficially providing.[1]

THE DAO HACK

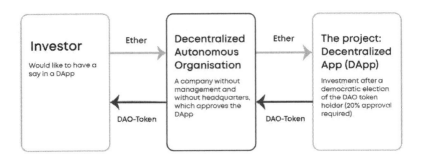

The DAO made headlines just a month later in June 2016 when it was hacked via smart contract errors that allowed the fund to be drained of its assets. This is widely known for being the driving force behind the Ethereum Hard Fork of 2016, where the blockchain was 'rolled back' to before the hack occurred to return assets back to investors. This led to the split between Ethereum Classic and the Ethereum used today. While detrimental to the project and investors, The DAO still goes down in history as the first Decentralized Autonomous Organization. Funding hundreds of millions of dollars from the crowd itself rather than a curated network of Limited Partners and arms-length investors, was a remarkable feat that established the basis of digital assets and the resulting evolution in capital markets.

What is the motivation behind a DAO in general? Cointelegraph states it eloquently: "The main advantage of DAOs is that they offer a solution to the principal-agent dilemma. This dilemma is a conflict in priorities between a person or group (the principal) and those making decisions and acting on their behalf (the agent)."[2]

As the line between principals and agents blurs through the DAO model, where members may all directly contribute and participate in upside accordingly, members become more fully aligned to the DAOs mission, perhaps even more aligned than a typical employee at a company would be.

DAO mechanics have been an extremely influential piece to the digital assets universe as the sentiment of a DAO is very well aligned with the rest of the 'crypto' thesis, which is the democratization of access to something. The idea that organizations, companies, and groups can be reformed in a decentralized manner rather than centralized is the key facet. DAOs aim to do to organizations what DeFi has been doing to financial services. The key features of a DAO are as follows:

- Governance
- Rewards and Payouts
- Token Issuance Models and Lock-Ups

Just like the term "organization" is widespread and all-encompassing, the term DAO can be applied to a multitude of types of groups and organizations, not solely investment vehicles or companies. The following are some examples of DAO categories:[3]

DAO TYPES

- *Operating Systems*: Whitelabel framework services that enable the formation of DAOs (Orca, Colony, XDAO).
- *Protocol DAOs*: DeFi projects and decentralized applications that operate as DAOs (Aave, Uniswap, Maker, Compound).
- *Investment DAOs*: Pool capital from members to deploy into various DeFi applications to generate returns (BitDAO, MANTRA DAO, The Lau).
- *Grants DAOs*: Pool capital from members to deploy into various digital assets infrastructure ventures to improve the ecosystem (MolochDAO, Balancer Grants DAO).
- *Collector DAOs*: Syndicate capital for the purchase and collecting of art, memorabilia, or any collectible items (Flamingo, ConstitutionDAO)
- *Social DAOs*: Decentralized social media and networking platforms (Friends with Benefits, Seed Club, Krause DAO).
- *Service DAOs*: Recruiting and talent acquisition agencies for Web 3.0 (DaoHaus, Metaverse DAO).
- *Media DAOs*: Decentralized news and media aggregator (Mirror, Contento DAO).

Since members typically have some sort of governance and voting rights, the future of DAOs are largely driven by members and their associated voting and decision-making powers. While it's standard to make decisions based on the majority or supermajority vote, it is important to remember the history of digital assets, namely, the schism that forked Bitcoin and led to the birth of Bitcoin Cash, and another schism that led to the birth of Bitcoin SV. Even without the majority of member votes, if a DAO is undergoing a very significant structural change or decision and the vote is split 60/40, for example, it is still possible that the 40 percent group decides to cut loose and pursue its side of the vision separately.

This schism could also lead to a hard fork that would result in two different DAOs under the same initial mission, which may signal a weakening of the DAO, slow or halt progress, or even cause legal challenges now that the organization is split into multiple entities. These problems may be exacerbated by any initial or early members, as was seen through the disagreements between Roger Ver and Craig Wright on Bitcoin. When comparing a DAO structure to a company structure, this fork cannot always be completed seamlessly like a utility token since it inherently forms two competing and separate organizations.

DAO Governance Structures

Keeping those risks in mind, it is important to also understand what the typical governing structures of DAOs are like, and where developments have been evolving. DOAs originally subscribed to the general format of "one vote per token" whereby investors' and members' voting power were equal to their pro rata ownership of the DAO's circulating tokens. As this structure revealed some limitations, DAO organizers began evaluating other more equitable and feasible strategies, although those two terms are not always compatible.

The original model gave power to whoever could afford more tokens. It did not favor merit or contributions over dollars, and led to frustration and misalignment among DAO members as large token holders and syndicates could simply sway the project in their preferred directions. These 'decentralized organizations' were acting more like they were centralized around a few large parties, thus eroding the true purpose and value proposition of a DAO.

Another model was centered around the early board of advisors and lead developers holding a controlling portion of the voting token supply, and leaving minority shares to be divided up and distributed among investors and other DAO members. This essentially gave the lead developers power in unity to move the project as they saw fit, while still considering the members' desires. This was more democratic since the lead developers could be split in their decisions with each other, and so the vote and future decisions would then come down to the other members, while also having the DAO act as a focus group of sorts regarding major decisions.

Beyond that structure, the 'tiering structure' came to be to improve on the original model of 'one vote per token' in a more democratic model. Under this, investors would fall into tiers based on their holdings, and votes would be distributed and dispersed among the tiers.

This essentially provides greater representation for the lesser-value token holders and prevents them from being silenced or drowned out by the larger token holders.

TOKEN VOTING & GOVERNANCE

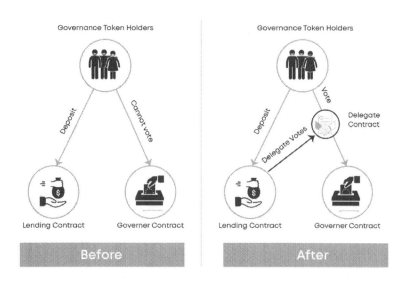

To revisit the Principal-Agent concept from earlier, one notable thought arises: Not every member is made to be a principal. When too many members are enabled to make decisions or contribute to the decision-making process, organizations may find themselves at a standstill. This standstill may be even more severe or slow than can be overcome through a Board of Advisors or a smaller group of decision makers. Without saying there is only one correct way of structuring a DAO and its associated decision-making and governance rights, it's worth noting that not all DAOs and their purposes are created equal. For example, A structure that works for a Collector DAO may not be best suited for an Investment DAO.

DAO Formation

Use the typical company structure as a starting point for DAOs. A company will incorporate or file as an LLC in a certain state (or jurisdiction, if outside the US), appoint a Board of Directors or executive board members, establish Articles of Incorporation and additional bylaws, and operate as an organization under the guidance of the aforementioned leaders. Operations for typical firms are centralized since orders, developments, and associated activities stem directly from the leadership committee. Employees answer to the higher-ups according to a hierarchy (in most cases, but not all) and typically have more narrow job descriptions and duties as one moves down the ladder toward the entry-level rung.

Under a DAO, the organization is designed to be more flexible and open as employees, or members, are free to contribute to aspects that they believe they add value to. Work is done in groups and tasks are handled in priority order as the majority of the DAO sees fit. Rather than relying on manager or employer review in order to receive compensation, smart contracts may distribute funds as certain tasks in the agenda are successfully completed over time. A general DAO structuring process is as follows:[4]

DAO FORMATION

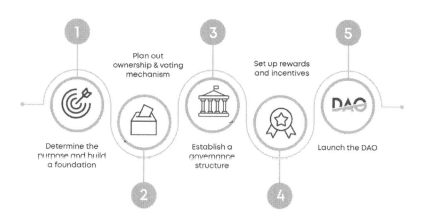

1. Decide on governance structure and the necessary smart contracts.
2. File any Articles of Incorporation, whitepaper, or related and/ or substitute organization documents.
3. Develop the smart contracts on desired blockchain.
4. Issue the token to raise capital from public investors, who become members in the DAO.
5. Implement and commence the operation of the DAO, including any communication, reporting, and voting to the members.

In July 2021, the American CryptoFed DAO in Wyoming became the first legally recognized DAO in the United States. Wyoming had previously passed a legislative order that recognizes a DAO as a distinctive form of an LLC, thereby enabling DAOs to operate as legitimate companies if formed accordingly in the state of Wyoming. Secretary of State Edward Buchanon stated, "Wyoming has a reputation for being on the leading edge of business technology, beginning in 1977 with the recognition of LLCs. We are proud to continue this innovation by offering legal protections to Decentralized Autonomous Organizations. I congratulate American CryptoFed DAO, LLC, the first legally recognized DAO filed in Wyoming with the Secretary of State's Office."[5]

The American CryptoFed's mission is to establish and sustain an economic system with zero inflation and zero transaction costs. Under the leadership of CEO Marian Orr, the organization makes use of the 'Ducat' algorithmic stablecoin and the 'Locke' governance token to develop and sustain this desired ecosystem. Within this two-token economy, Ducat has no fixed supply as an algorithmic stablecoin and will adhere to the pre-programmed guidance to maintain a stable price, while Locke has a fixed maximum supply of 10 trillion tokens available to DAO participants and contributors.[6]

The DAO is governed purely by its governance tokens according to the Token Safe Harbor Proposal 2.0 written and filed by SEC Commissioner Hester Peirce, who is unofficially known as 'Crypto Mom' for her pro-digital assets vision. This proposal highlights key facets for decentralized yet legitimate operations including token allocation limits on the initial development teams, development and progress reporting to the SEC every 6 months for three years, and analysis on the extent of decentralization and organization maturity.[7]

Perhaps to show that he practices what he preaches, Orr went on to say, "In time, my role as CEO will vanish, as all governance token holders will be voting on governance matters without the influence of an executive team."[8]

Up to this point in time, Wyoming had been breaking down barriers for digital assets access and services as it passed two banking charters, officially known as Special-Purpose Depository Institutions (SPDI), to the cryptocurrency exchange Kraken and the niche merchant bank Avanti.[9] These banks are usually referred to as 'crypto banks,' although the SPDI designation is not limited to digital assets, but rather is used for unique banking situations. As of mid-2022, only three companies (Anchorage, Protego, and Paxos) have received federal bank charters that supersede individual state charters for digital assets activity, making the two aforementioned state bank charters even more scarce.[10]

Regarding the DAO formation progress, it is important to keep in mind that the fundamentals of a corporation, LLC, or other structure do not go by the wayside even if an organization is formed as a DAO. Members of the DAO may still be liable or targeted in lawsuits or financially driven legal action, just as company employees, directors, and associated individuals may be liable in certain circumstances. The management of these possible lawsuits and organizational issues is a major barrier and challenge that will likely not be crossed in the next couple of years, if not already seen on a smaller scale. It will be important to follow legislation and decentralized organization legal rulings closely as these next several years may be the basis of precedents for decades to come.

Aside from legal recourse, the following statement from Andrew Lee, an Attorney at Foley & Lardner LLP, posits an interesting question surrounding physical, manual actions that are sometimes necessary. He stated, "It would be interesting if a DAO could authorize one of its members to sign documents on its behalf, which at some point would have to happen. But unless it's on an approved-proposal specific basis, this would lean toward centralization rather than decentralization."[11]

Even in a decentralized structure, there are certain decisions and actions that need to be *fulfilled*, not just *voted on*, such as the following questions:

- What if a DAO receives delivery of physical items and needs a representative to sign off on packages?
- Or an investment DAO perhaps deploys capital into a venture that requires a whitelisted point of contact with proper compliance protocols like KYC/AML?
- Or a supply chain DAO that requires humans to interact with machinery upon the final steps?

These problems have not yet been solved with decentralization, and while these examples may not be the focus of existing DAOs, one cannot ignore the question and the possible dilemmas that may arise without studying and developing possible solutions.

Longest Ongoing DAO - MakerDAO

MakerDAO is the official longest-standing DAO in existence with its primary focus being decentralized lending and collateralization. Given its decentralized governance and core functions, it is vaguely seen as a decentralized banking application, although it's important to understand it is not backed or regulated by FDIC or related depository institutions. A brief look into the core functions are as follows:

- Decentralized Banking: Any user with enough collateral can mint DAI stablecoin and receive a loan without traditional credit and/or borrower checks, as MakerDAO is a pure collateralization machine.

- Savings Account: Any user can deposit DAI stablecoin and earn yield on those deposits per supply and demand within MakerDAO's ecosystem.
- Monetary Policy: As users deposit collateral into MakerDAO, a greater number of DAI stablecoin may be minted, thus increasing the supply of DAI.

Despite being decentralized, MakerDao generates revenue much like any for-profit organization through the fees it collects. In MakerDAO's case, it generates revenues through interest collection from borrowers at varying rates based on supply and demand of its user base. In April 2022, MakerDao was generating 2.25 percent on $9 billion of outstanding DAI which equates to an annualized revenue of $200 million.

This $200 million and any future earnings are used to pay DAO contributors, including the users who actually work for the DAO and provide technical, functional, and risk management upkeep on behalf of the community. Nonetheless, the governance capabilities of Maker-DAO ensure certain incentive mechanisms to larger role-playing users based on the voting capabilities of the general ecosystem.[12]

DAOs and Real-World Assets (RWA)

The idea of Real-World Assets (RWA) is bringing existing traditional assets on-chain in order to interact with the decentralized finance ecosystem. Since DAOs are designed to be on-chain organizations, combining real-world assets with decentralized group decision-making could be a powerful initiative. One group working on this is Balcony DAO, a Web 3.0 investment bank seeking to fractionalize real estate for investment while enabling buyers to lead the charge.

Balcony DAO's inaugural project is a $13 million condominium building along the shore in Long Branch, New Jersey. Balcony DAO will issue these as Non Fungible Tokens (NFTs), which serve as the legal wrappers of each property, containing the property deed, title, mortgage, air rights, and other property-level data. Eventually, buyers will be able to make use of the NFTs within the DeFi ecosystem for

lending, collateralization, and swapping purposes, none of which owners could do with the assets in traditional form.[13]

Even the always-pioneering Maker DAO began accepting other
assets to complement ETH as collateral for its loans. One such case is
with French investment bank, Societe Generale. The bank submitted
a proposal for Maker to accept Ethereum-based bonds the bank previously issued as collateral to borrow $20 million in DAI. This is an
interesting proposal as it would 1) enable a prominent investment bank
to draw funding from a decentralized source in a proof-of-concept,
and 2) enable Maker to diversify its own vault funds backing DAI,
possibly reducing the risk profile of DAI.[14]

Maker eventually leaned into the proposal and accepted it, with its
users voting to extend a $30 million credit limit in DAI to Societe Gen-
erale with 40 million Euros in the form of Societe Generale on-chain
bonds as collateral. Societe Generale withdrew $7 million of that $30
million credit line in January 2023.[15] This is the basis of Real-World
Assets (RWA); bringing existing or traditional assets onto the blockchain (on-chain) to make use of them in the broader DeFi ecosystem.

NOTES

1. See https://www.gemini.com/cryptopedia/the-dao-hack-makerdao #section-origins-of-the-dao

2. See https://cointelegraph.com/ethereum-for-beginners/what-is-a-decentralized-autonomous-organization-and-how-does-a-dao-work

3. See https://economictimes.indiatimes.com/markets/cryptocurrency/dao-explained-types-key-characteristics-flipsides/articleshow/89040222.cms

4. See https://www.jdsupra.com/legalnews/5-things-to-consider-when-creating-a-dao-5888423/

5. See https://www.prnewswire.com/news-releases/the-american-cryptofed-dao-is-legally-recognized-by-the-state-of-wyoming-as-the-first-decentralized-autonomous-organization-dao-in-the-united-states-301325384.html

6. See https://www.americancryptofed.org/

7. See https://www.jdsupra.com/legalnews/the-return-of-the-token-safe-harbor-4114830/

8. See https://www.prnewswire.com/news-releases/the-american-cryptofed-dao-is-legally-recognized-by-the-state-of-wyoming-as-the-first-decentralized-autonomous-organization-dao-in-the-united-states-301325384.html

9. See https://www.natlawreview.com/article/wyoming-issues-second-crypto-bank-charter

10. See https://www.coindesk.com/markets/2021/04/23/paxos-becomes-third-federally-regulated-crypto-bank/

11. See https://www.businessofbusiness.com/articles/dao-lawsuit-sued-litigation-accountability/

12. See https://thedefireport.substack.com/p/makerdao?s=r

13. See https://decrypt.co/videos/live-events/cPCAx4xG/balcony-dao-is-fractionalizing-investment-in-a-new-jersey-building-as-an-nft and https://www.balconydao.com/

14. See https://www.coindesk.com/business/2021/09/30/societe-generale-applies-for-20m-makerdao-loan-using-bond-token-collateral/

15. See https://blockworks.co/news/societe-generale-withdraws-makerdao-vault

CHAPTER 10

NON-FUNGIBLE TOKENS (NFTS)

The Non-Fungible Token (NFT) swept the world by storm from late 2020 through mid-2021, solidifying itself as a legitimate vertical within digital assets. With an aggregate market capitalization of $10 billion as of April 2022 (close to its all-time high), NFTs and NFT collections garnered the interest from some 2.2 million people across the globe.[1] Ushered in under the guise of *NBA TopShot* and strengthened through the popularity and high-ticket sales across the *CryptoPunks* and *Bored Ape Yacht Club* collections, the NFT proved that not all digital assets are fungible and identical, asserting a certain uniqueness of items within this class of assets.

NON-FUNGIBLE TOKENS

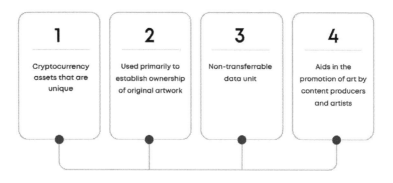

1	2	3	4
Cryptocurrency assets that are unique	Used primarily to establish ownership of original artwork	Non-transferrable data unit	Aids in the promotion of art by content producers and artists

An NFT builds on the same principles of utility tokens and smart contacts, as covered earlier. Certain data, guidelines, and features can be programmed into the digital wrapper that is an NFT, and these features may be unique to each individual NFT so that no two Non-Fungible Tokens are alike. Rather than exchanging one *BTC* for one *BTC*, which is a kind-for-kind swap (the definition of fungible), most NFTs cannot simply be swapped as identicals since they have their own qualities and features. These features can sometimes be visible to the naked eye, such as the various designs in the *Bored Ape Yacht Club* art collection, while others may only be uncovered through the *metadata*, which is the data and parameters that are coded into the smart contacts. Examples of metadata include names of individual songs, music albums cover art, and even physical item descriptions that back the digital assets itself. Any information can be programmed as metadata. These may not be as easily visible and discerning as a piece of digital artwork, but nonetheless they make each NFT unique from one another, which is the purpose behind NFTs.

The technical structure of an NFT relies on the one key concept that the NFT lives on the blockchain. An NFT is originated on the blockchain and all history of transactions and metadata descriptions can be found through the ledger. Each item can be differentiated, tracked, and verified by following the "paper trail" back to the origination of the NFT, and thereby verifying ownership of the associated asset.[2]

This blockchain-based origination is what reduces or even prevents fraud among the digital economy. Even if two NFTs (pieces of art, for example) have the same surface level qualities, colors, features, and designations, digging down to the blockchain will reveal which technical tag these pieces have. These technical tags are most commonly described as Mint Numbers, especially in large-scale collections. It's possible that multiple pieces in a single collection share features and even have multiple copies of the same features, but the differentiating factor is the precise mint number of the NFT.[3] This also prevents scammers from easily duplicating high profile NFTs as it can always be verified on the blockchain if it is real or fake.

For instance, a collection of one thousand pieces of art could have five pieces sharing 100 percent of the same features. These items are still differentiated by their mint numbers, which could range from anywhere from 1 through 1,000. The earlier minted ones may be seen as more valuable than the later mints, much like NFTs with rarer features may be worth more than the more common-featured NFTs in the collection. This principle is most typically applied to art NFTs, although can and most likely will be rolled out into other use cases for NFTs, some of which are covered below.

Perhaps the most attention-grabbing feature of NFTs is the ability to code royalties into these digital tokens. Royalties are one of the strongest value drivers to an NFT creator as it establishes the ability to monetize a token or a collection in perpetuity. Many NFT mints have anywhere from 2–10 percent royalties coded in, which means the original creator receives that amount on all re-sales of the NFT going forward. As previously mentioned, ownership and mint status can be tracked all the way back to the original creator on the blockchain so the creator is receiving their rightful royalty amounts on all re-sales. This is one of the most powerful features that shifts the leverage into the hands of the creators and away from the hands of the studios, galleries, and incumbent creative organizations. Much like DAOs stand to democratize organizations, NFTs stand to democratize rewards on creativity.

Art Collection NFTs

The most popular and early-adopted type of NFT is the Digital Art NFT. In fact, NFTs accounted for 16 percent of the global art market by value in 2021, an extremely sizable number for an asset type that was created only four years prior. Art sales in 2021 totaled $17.4 billion, divided up as $2.8 billion from Ethereum-based NFTs and $14.6 billion from traditional art. These numbers and associated volumes forced incumbents like Christie's, Sotheby's, and Phillips to get involved, and those 3 organizations sold $150 million, $100 million, and $6.2 million worth of NFTs, respectively.[4]

The royalty feature of art collections is powerful enough to fuel operations and growth of the creating individuals or organizations behind them, much like a Venture Capitalist's management fees are enough to support operational expenses. Take the very popular *Bored Ape Yacht Club* NFT collection. Originated and minted by Yuga Labs in April 2021, the *Bored Ape Yacht Club* collection consists of 10,000 unique digital graphics of apes, each with their own features (gold chains, sunglasses, facial expressions, marks, and so on) and associated rarities. The combination of features is what differentiates each *Bored Ape* from the other, and a greater blend of rare features likely commands a higher valuation relative to the more common-featured items in the collection.[5]

All 10,000 individual *Bored Apes* have a 2.5 percent royalty coded in that goes back to Yuga Labs on every resale. As the velocity of *Bored Apes* on the secondary trading markets increases, so does the earnings potential for Yuga Labs. Combine an increasing average sale price with a greater amount of volume and it's understandable to see Yuga Labs' top line revenue on an upwards trajectory.

Across a seven-day period at the end of 2022, the average *Bored Ape* was priced at $92,000 (around 80 *ETH*) and generated over $23 million in sales on the secondary markets. While Yuga Labs doesn't keep most of the $23 million (since the NFTs are being traded in a peer-to-peer manner amongst users), it does receive 2.5 percent on that volume, or $575,000 of a week's worth of royalty revenue.[6]

Annualized, that is nearly $30 million worth of revenue through royalties alone, excluding any other expansionary work or projects Yuga Labs is developing. This same principle can be applied to individual creators alike, not just organizations. Even on a smaller scale, artists and creators can gain access to newfound revenue channels through digital royalties that have never been offered or have been extremely limited through traditional art channels such as galleries and museums. That same year, Yuga Labs received a $450M investment from Andreessen Horowitz (the Venture Capital firm behind Coinbase, Airbnb, Lyft, Twitter, and many others), valuing the company at a unicorn valuation of $4 Billion dollars.[7]

Music Collection NFTs

Another parallel use case for NFTs is seen in the music industry. Typically, music labels and groups own the vast majority of their signed artists' works and associated earnings. Artists may do well after ramping up their catalogs of work, although for however well an individual artist is doing, the label and record company are typically doing even better. Much like was seen in art galleries such as Sotheby's and Christie's, music groups must begin deciding how to implement NFT capabilities for their artists in order to stay competitive or risk losing talent to the purely independent world.

Examples of NFT uses in this industry included morning tokens on an individual song, album, or label itself, and providing early access or exclusive access to these, revenue sharing agreements, or exclusive events and perks from the artists themselves. These would be available only to token holders and not to the general public, although the general public obviously has access to purchase the NFTs and gain this exclusivity. Music artists such as Meek Mill, Tory Lanez, and Dyl have all released NFT songs that enable their purchasers with exclusive or early access to these pieces.

Beyond that, platforms like Royal and Glozal have been creating solutions to shift the focus away from major record labels and groups and into the hands of creators themselves with a more beneficial earnings structure. Glozal, based in Miami, FL, developed an SEC-compliant music platform that allows artists to release music to their fans that can be played and listened to directly on the platform itself, rather than relying on an existing service like Spotify or Apple Music.[8]

Royal, which was developed by the EDM artist 3LAU, is an NFT marketplace where fans can take ownership stakes in their favorite songs. Investors will share in the financial upside through royalties, and these royalties are theorized to grow in accordance with popularity of the songs. When asked about the vision, founder Justin Blau stated, "When we open up the platform to all artists, Royal would enable you to tokenize and monetize a completed musical work. Let's say you made five songs. You can tokenize those songs and assign ownership to your fans. Those fans can pay for these tokens. Let's say you have 100 limited editions of each of those five songs, and you sell them each for $100. You're a small artist. You can sell any percentage of ownership in that music to your fans and generate about $10,000 per track."[9]

It's worth noting that when revenue sharing, profit sharing, and most other forms of financial upside come into the mix, this usually triggers a securities designation. Most NFTs are minted without legal structuring or representation, an approach that is not recommended for items and collections providing some direct financial upside to the buyers and users.

Gaming NFTs

When it comes to utility and purpose, Gaming NFTs are a great case to see these digital items in action. Some of the most popular video games such as Call of Duty, Fortnite, and the NBA 2k series revolve around customizing and upgrading your gameplay, whether that's through wardrobe upgrades, skins, new maps and locations, skills, exclusive invite events, and a range of other perks. However, in most gaming systems up until this Web 3.0 era, players could not take their in-game perks elsewhere or trade them to others in an open market. They were limited to the immediate gaming interface in which they earned or bought these upgrades. In other words, there was not a robust or feasible marketplace to trade or sell these achievements, which could well be valued in real currency.

A solution for this challenge was presented through NFTs, as in-game items and perks could actually be issued as NFTs and used in other gaming venues where applicable, or even brought over to a marketplace like OpenSea for free trade. The goal of this is to shift power into the hands of the individual gamers rather than the game developers. Yet again, this is parallel to shifting the power from art galleries to artists and from music labels to musicians. The theme of democratization is heavy in most digital asset verticals but is especially apparent in NFTs.

One of the most popular NFT-native games in 2021 was Axie Infinity developed by Sky Mavis in March 2018. Each character, known as an Axie, is an NFT. The game setting is an expansive virtual plot of land, known as a Metaverse, where players collect and breed digital pets that can then be used to compete in card games against one another. Since the Axies are NFTs, each newly-bred Axie may have rarer properties than other Axies in the gaming metaverse. These properties may be aesthetic or functional, and contribute to the valuation of each individual Axie.

Axies were originally only traded on the Axie Marketplace but have since adopted the OpenSea standard to reach a larger audience of buyers and sellers under one umbrella. In addition to the NFTs that represent characters themselves, Axie Infinity also has the utility token *AXS*. The *AXS* token is used to access and navigate around the Axie Infinity metaverse, much like the *ETH* token enables users to access the Ethereum ecosystem. Players can be rewarded in *AXS* for contributing and playing within the Axie Infinity gaming realm, marking the strong beginning of the digital "play-to-earn" era. Additionally, as a true utility token, *AXS* holders gain governance capability through voting rights and future airdrops that will benefit the ecosystem.[10]

The term metaverse is widespread and simply designates any virtual universe whereby users can purchase plots of land, develop them, and make use of them in an interconnected fashion. While gaming is one of the strongest value-drivers and catalysts for metaverse usage, there are open-ended metaverses like Decentraland and The Sandbox, where users can build retail shops, eCommerce storefronts, and other virtual services like concerts and shows in a decentralized fashion. These parcels of land are typically represented as NFTs and trade in the same manner an Axie NFT would. Lastly, metaverses like Decentraland and The Sandbox have their own utility tokens to focus on the governance and accessibility of the metaverses themselves.

Real World Item NFTs

Arguably one of the most revolutionary uses for NFTs comes in the form of real-world items and assets. The vast majority of ownership and legal documents are held in paper form or scanned to a computer system that still relies on human interaction. Think of a club membership card, the pink slip to a car, insurance documents and licenses, and even Intellectual Property rights. These can all be digitized and stored on the blockchain—and since each pink slip or car deed or patent is unique, an NFT is the most suitable form of digital asset.

The benefit to digitization like this can be seen through the sale of a home. Rather than manually relying on a real estate agent and an escrow servicer, a home seller can post the necessary documents up in a designated smart contract that verifies when funds are transferred from the buyer to the escrow account. Upon such verification, the smart contract can release the documents (deed, inspection, legal agreements, and so on) and finalize the transaction. Propy currently does this as it streamlines the property purchasing process in the following ways:[11]

1. Aggregating data from the MLS (Multiple Listing Service).
2. Generating legal documents such as purchase and sale agreements and sending signable copies to each party involved.
3. Organizing the title agent and associated steps such as signing the title agreement and establishing the escrow account.
4. Accepting payment in fiat currency or cryptocurrency, which then gets deposited to the Propy smart contract for this transaction.
5. Recording the official deed transfer from seller to buyer on the blockchain and updating the property records accordingly in an immutable fashion.

3 CASES OF NFT USAGE IN REAL ESTATE

Understanding this will be helpful in drawing lines to other real-world uses for NFTs. Supply-chain management, for instance, is reliant on tracking the various parts that come through a supply chain from start to finish, and this process is not always as streamlined as it may seem. Rather than relying on barcodes that may need to be re-marked or restamped as an item changes warehouses, these items can have associated NFTs minted and embedded through a platform revamp, which would cut down on middlemen interaction throughout the process and ensure that items are the same ones as they are designated to be from the start since NFTs are immutable and will not be modified mid-process.

This will likely lead to expense savings and a higher bottom line for companies themselves, while also potentially decreasing the timelines of production and therefore improving efficiency as measured by both time and money. Furthermore, customers could benefit from the increased transparency to know where their product (especially for produce) came from. Any industry still relying on paper accounts and records is inherently relying on human interaction for the bulk of its processes. Those processes can and likely will be streamlined on the backs of NFTs and associated smart contract systems, which goes way beyond digital art, music, and gaming, as it has the power to integrate with a multitude of industry types.

NFT Valuation and Transacting

The floor price is a commonly-used term when valuing or assessing an NFT or NFT collection. The floor price is defined as the lowest asking price for an NFT in the collection and is oftentimes used to compare 1) items in a collection against each other and 2) one collection against another collection. An increasing floor price may signal that the collection is gaining value and trending upwards, as NFT owners are no longer willing to sell for less than that floor price amount. Conversely, a decreasing floor price may be a signal that the collection is overhyped, losing social value, or was simply priced too high for the market, and is now in price discovery mode until it finds traction.

NFT FLOOR PRICE & VALUATION

The floor price is defined as the lowest asking price for an NFT in the collection, and is oftentimes used to compare...

Items in a collection against each other

One collection against another collection

For instance, it was common to compare the *Bored Ape Yacht Club* collection with the *CryptoPunks* collection through the floor price metric. The *CryptoPunks* collection was created in 2017 by Larva Labs and reigned as the highest-value collection for roughly four years. In December 2021, however, the *Bored Ape Yacht Club* floor price officially eclipsed and surpassed the *CryptoPunks* floor price at around 53 *ETH* on NFT marketplace OpenSea, signaling a change in sentiment and market preference shift from *CryptoPunks* to *Bored Apes*. It was determined that investors and buyers would rather hold *Bored Apes* than *CryptoPunks*, and therefore marked a higher price on the *Bored Ape* collection.[12]

Still, the floor price is only indicative of the lowest sell offer and does not consider the average sales price or the most valuable NFT in the collection. It is possible that one NFT collection has a lower floor price yet a higher average sales price than another if the majority of sales are happening at a much higher price than the floor. This typically will not last for long as savvy investors and buyers/sellers will take advantage of this mispricing, much like arbitrageurs may take advantage of mispricing in crypto and equities markets. Nonetheless, the floor price alone may be a misleading metric and should not be the sole basis of an investment thesis or signal to buy. Looking at volume trends and the average sale price within a collection will provide more color to the picture, as does understanding the utility and perks associated with items in a collection, if any.

NOTES

1. See https://coinmarketcap.com/nft/

2. See https://www.gemini.com/cryptopedia/what-is-a-non-fungible-token-nft-crypto#section-what-are-non-fungible-tokens

3. See https://thetoppscompany.helpshift.com/hc/en/17-topps-nfts/faq/991-what-is-a-mint-number-and-what-does-it-mean/?han=1&hpn=1&p=web

4. See https://ocula.com/magazine/art-news/nfts-now-constitute-16-percent-of-the-art-market/

5. See https://www.benzinga.com/money/how-does-bored-ape-yacht-club-bayc-make-money/

6. See https://www.nft-stats.com/collection/boredapeyachtclub

7. See https://techcrunch.com/2022/03/22/bored-apes-nft-startup-yuga-labs-raises-at-monster-4-billion-valuation/amp/

8. See https://www.einnews.com/pr_news/567021923/glozal-creator-of-the-first-nft-music-player-will-be-unveiling-their-flagship-project-playone-on-april-1-in-miami

9. See https://www.protocol.com/fintech/royal-nft-music-3lau

10. See https://www.gemini.com/cryptopedia/axie-infinity-game-axie-marketplace-axie-nft#section-a-gaming-metaverse-with-earning-potential

11. See https://propy.com/browse/what-is-propy-how-does-propy-work/

12. See https://decrypt.co/89060/bored-ape-yacht-club-nfts-flip-cryptopunks-floor-price-in-ethereum

CHAPTER 11

REGULATIONS

Most digital assets, at the time of publishing, are not registered with the SEC or other regulatory bodies. The majority take on the form of an ICO, an NFT, a DAO token, or simply another utility token. Nonetheless, there exists a strong thesis and possibility that the SEC and regulatory bodies will require future digital asset offerings to register as true securities, much like stock and bond issuers have to register new offerings of certain criteria. It is still not out of the question for these regulatory agencies to find a way to enforce securities law on existing digital asset projects. Should that happen, there would be a major wave of digital assets that become registered and relisted as security tokens, as described in Chapter 7.

The Howey Test

One of the common arguments for cryptocurrency projects being unregistered securities stems from the Howey Test, which is the precedent set in the court of law that is now used to determine what is an investment contract. The Howey Test states that there is an investment contract in scenarios where money is invested in a common enterprise with the expectation of profits derived from the work and efforts of others. Remember these prongs as this is the very test used in the US and by most other countries (by following what the US does) used to enable a token to flourish or be doomed. Imagine a coin used by millions designed to be accessible by anyone with a wallet that supports the technology. Suddenly, regulators say it must be registered like a stock, follow numerous compliance requirements including knowing who the holder is, alongside a new set of rules about how it can trade. This is the very debate around Bitcoin and Ethereum (and virtually every coin that is issued) that scares market participants due to the possible ramifications. Though the regulators in the US have left Bitcoin alone and admitting it is too decentralized to be governed, they have not said the same about any other blockchain-powered coin.[1]

Howey test Prongs graphic

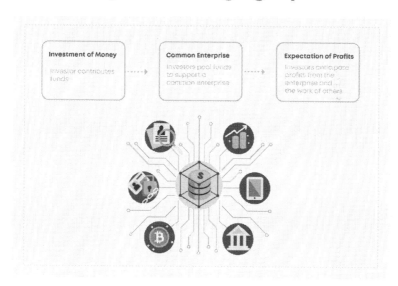

As touched upon in the Initial Coin Offering (ICO) section, the vast majority of these tokens were being marketed as unregistered securities. Issuers would mint and offer these coins to the general public either 1) after already raising venture capital funding or 2) as the venture capital funding itself from the crowd. Investors would largely buy these ICOs for what they believed was a cheaper price in relation to the future digital assets market growth that was strengthening all throughout 2017.

While some projects indeed had merit and a strong thesis (and investors are free to purchase what they like), most projects and associated tokens were being purchased by investors with the intention of flipping them for profits in the short term. Many investors were not simply buying new coin offerings for the utility they offered, such as decentralized data storage or smart contract development services, but rather under the expectation of future profit and gains. In some cases, the utility was just a promise and had not even been built yet. This investment construct checks one of the boxes used under the Howey Test classifying most of these ICOs as unregistered securities.

The argument many token issuers would have to make a case for is that they were simply a gift because there was no investment of money or it was a product and no expectation of profit from the purchaser. The latter was considered a gray area because the token could be used as part of the functioning blockchain network and therefore wasn't being purchased as an investment as much as for speculation.

To counter this, the SEC typically focused on the fact there was a common enterprise (a central party controlling the operation) and were providing the efforts as a third-party to increase the value of the coin. The result was that most ICO projects indeed fell under this framework where they 1) accepted crypto or money in exchange for the coin, 2) had publicly stated plans to improve the value of the coin and/ or network, and 3) typically were being run by a management team or core group of people (meaning a common enterprise) and third-party efforts as they were the de facto 'promoter' of the coin.

The unregistered security factor is, in some sense, more important for investors than for issuers, as the investors are usually the ones in need of some protections and guidance. Since these ICOs were unregistered, the issuers and project creators were free to do what they saw fit with the funds raised from token purchasers. In some cases this meant deploying capital into development of the blockchain project promised, while in others it meant operating under unverified and unaudited practices or even shutting the project down and disappearing with investors' funds.

In a more recent case closed in March 2022, the founders of Bitqyck sold investors a dream of getting in on the "next bitcoin," playing into investors' regrets of missing out on the monstrous returns Bitcoin showed over the course of its inception. The Bitqyck ICO raised $24 million from 13,000 investors in 2016 under the "get rich quick" guise promising exposure to Bitcoin and cryptocurrency mining activities and other revenue-generating lines. Nonetheless, the two founders retained 100 percent of the common shares in the entity, leaving investors with simple utility tokens and the unenforced promise of upside in the firm's activities.

These founders were convicted of tax evasion in March 2022, although the real issue is the lack of investor protection and reimbursement. Unfortunately, these stories are a dime a dozen and had many variations throughout the ICO boom of 2017 and 2018. As more of these projects came under SEC and Department of Justice scrutiny, it became clear how digital assets investors would benefit from the same or similar protections and regulations as typically securities, or at least those acting as securities, as many ICO projects were. Below is coverage on some of the most prominent cases in the industry regarding securities law and designation.[2]

SEC V Telegram Outcome

The largest ICO prosecution in history by the SEC was the case against the company behind the popular messenger app, Telegram. On October 11, 2019, the SEC filed a complaint that Telegram was illegally selling securities under the guise of cryptocurrency they called Grams, of which they sold over 2.9 billion Grams to 171 people according to the SEC. What were 2.9 billion Grams worth? Roughly $1.2 Billion dollars flooded into this ICO given the popularity and user base of Telegram, most investors assuming the coin would pump in value through the usage in the native messenger app used by millions of people around the world.

Telegram is an Israel-based company, but since they included American citizens in their sale, the law came down on them. In March 2020, the U.S. District Court for the Southern District of New York issued a preliminary injunction barring the delivery of Grams and finding the SEC had shown a substantial likelihood of proving Telegram's sales were part of a larger scheme to unlawfully distribute the Grams to the secondary public market. It is likely the Howey Test was used to demonstrate to the court they were indeed illegal securities sales. After just three months, the entire ICO was forced to shut down after Telegram, Inc. settled with the SEC with a fine of nearly $20 Million USD and being required to return *all* of the money to purchasers. This signaled the end of the ICO era as it showed the industry, no matter how big or far away, how trying to skirt securities laws will result in the ultimate price.[3]

XRP Lawsuit and Decision

Ripple Labs, the organization behind *XRP*, was sued by the SEC in December 2020 for the failure to register $1.4 billion worth of *XRP* as securities. This was one of the most prominent and grand-scale lawsuits in the digital assets industry to date, as it would likely set a precedent for other digital assets products in regard to securities law and their overlap.

The official claim is that *XRP* was issued to investors and used to finance the Ripple platform for retailer and commercial money transfer and facilitation. The SEC determined that *XRP*, the coin, passed the Howey Test and fell into the security classification as investors would anticipate future returns and growth on *XRP* as the operations and traction of Ripple expanded upon the successful offering of XRP to the public.

Ripple's rebuttals included claiming the platform was initially funded through venture capital financing, not an ICO or token offering, and that *XRP* is simply the transaction coin associated with Ripple's operations, not an investment product or token.

As of the end of 2022, this case was still ongoing. The important takeaway here is that the settlement of SEC v. Ripple will possibly set a precedent for future cases of similar nature, namely, platform tokens and exchange tokens that carry themselves in a parallel fashion.

While never officially being investigated to the extent of Ripple, Ethereum and its 2014 $18 million *ETH* ICO have come up in conversation regarding the security-or-not-security debate. The Ripple outcome may have a bigger effect than intended, as any spillover effects could come onto Ethereum in the future, although this is speculative at best.[4]

Adding onto these cases and possibilities, SEC Chairman Gary Gensler suggested all centralized cryptocurrency exchanges should register as securities markets in the future. To do so would require a Broker-Dealer (BD) license and additional reporting and surveillance when it comes to market manipulation, order book auditing, and other execution customs. This would likely go hand-in-hand with the need for an Alternative Trading System (ATS) license to facilitate trades between buyers and sellers, or even National Exchange designation to act in full principal capacity, enabling each exchange to trade its own book of assets with clients while ideally providing more efficient pricing.

Recall from the security token chapter how several cryptocurrency exchanges like Coinbase, Gemini, and Binance either acquired a BD/ATS license, launched their own, or invested in companies with securities capabilities. If these actions are any indicator, it is likely the SEC's goal of turning all digital asset exchanges into registered Broker-Dealers may be on the horizon. As of the time of publication, no decision has been made regarding the case.[5]

The Rise and Fall of FTX and Its Founder Sam-Bankman Fried

In 2019, most of the major cryptocurrency exchange platforms such as Coinbase, Binance, Gemini, and Kraken had already been established and were dominating the industry. Then a twenty-something crypto entrepreneur by the name of Sam-Bankman Fried (or "SBF" to most) launched a new platform, stemming from 'The Futures Exchange' called FTX. Seemingly out of nowhere, the platform was adopted by more than a million users and as a result of the success he was worth billions of dollars before even turning thirty. What appeared to be the industry's newest celebrity ambassador, hailing from Stanford parents and being touted as a hustler for always sleeping in the office on a beanbag in order to get back to work as quickly as possible, ended up causing billions of dollars in harm and removed any progress the industry had made in recovering its image from the ICO scandals.

What is playing out in court over the course of 2023 is a criminal case against SBF while the company itself goes through bankruptcy. October 2022 saw a complete collapse of the exchange over the course of 72 hours. Though not much can be said with true accuracy or much validity, it turns out SBF was responsible for manipulating crypto markets using the Venture Capital funds he had raised alongside co-mingling customer funds to do what he pleased. From buying up real-estate in the Bahamas and investing hundreds of millions of dollars in startups to hiding large losses and attacking specific cryptocurrencies and markets, SBF used his status as an industry idol to his full advantage.

The unraveling occurred after Binance alerted the community about FTX's potential solvency issues by pulling out of a deal via Twitter. The value of most of FTX's balance sheet had been washed with a cryptocurrency FTX had created and sold called FTT. The speculation led to a bank run on FTX (people wanted to withdraw as quickly as possible under the assumption there wasn't enough available for everyone to do so), thereby causing the collapse of the value of the FTT token as well. The inevitable breakdown revealed SBF was having serious business troubles that led him to engage in fraudulent practices. Not only was this yet another multi-billion-dollar blow to the crypto industry after Terra Luna's collapse, but it also appears SBF may have been linked to that specific downfall as well.[6]

Private Placements and Exemption Filings

In order to issue digital assets as securities, the most commonly used strategy is to look at private placement and SEC exemptions or filings. Private placements enable investment issuers to raise capital from very targeted groups of people, both in the United States and internationally, without listing an asset on a stock exchange or similar entity.

FINRA details how private placements in 2019 raised over $1.5 trillion, versus just $1.2 trillion through registered public offerings. The annual volume of private placements exceeded $105 billion in 2020 and $115 billion in 2021, likely shifting the outstanding number to nearly two trillion dollars. For reference, US stock markets (NYSE, Nasdaq, and OTC markets) totaled $43 trillion as of May 2022. These numbers may dwarf the private placement market in terms of active offerings but can be misleading given the capital raise differences between new offerings.[7]

The private placement market may be a precursor to publicly listed stocks. Private placements are exactly that—private. These filings are made so companies can raise private capital from a range of retail, accredited, institutional, and qualified investors without registering as a public company with the SEC. Eventually, the goal of many private companies is to exit via an Initial Public Offering (IPO) or an acquisition by another private or public company.

Therefore, the total size of the stock markets increases as more and more companies flow from private-to-public. This inherently adds more companies to the stock markets and provides additional capital that feeds into the aggregate size.

One limitation to private placements is the lack of liquidity and tradability among investments. Usually, private investments are considered long-term (7–10 years or even more) as companies have been raising funds into the Series D, Series E, and even Series F range toward the latter half of the 2010s, and therefore staying private longer. For early investors, this means their investments cannot be liquidated until the company goes the IPO route or is acquired, which symbolizes the exit event and enables investors to realize any potential gains.

Digital assets come into play to unlock these liquidity features before a traditional exit event like an IPO or acquisition. As explained in the Security Token chapter, it is possible for issuing organizations to compliantly make use of digital assets for fundraising purposes. These issuances are typically done through private placements that can be filed on new ventures or on existing assets (along the lines of the Security Token Offering versus Direct Listing comparison).

For some historical context on private placements, the JOBS Act of 2012 was the inflection point. Standing for "Jumpstart Our Business Startups Act," The JOBS Act provided additional framework for private placements and registration exemptions, which was seen as a loosening of SEC requirements on small businesses. Specifically, it limits the reporting requirements of companies that generate less than $1 billion in annual revenue, enables the marketing and solicitation of securities in certain instances, and increases the range of crowdfunding vehicles and mechanisms. In short, the JOBS Act is meant to make it easier and more accessible for smaller businesses, startups, and entities to raise capital outside the traditional methods.[8]

The reason private placements are classified as SEC exemptions is due to the fact that filing these types of offerings is done in place of full SEC registrations, such as the listing of a stock on the Nasdaq or the secondary sale of an existing publicly registered company, per the Securities Act of 1933. Private placements are typically more cost effective than full SEC registrations due to the reduced reporting and audit requirements, as well as ongoing maintenance and fees. Naturally, this reduced reporting comes with its own risks investors or prospective investors must take into consideration, but guidelines are nonetheless set and provided for issuers. The most common private placements are the following:

Regulation Exemptions

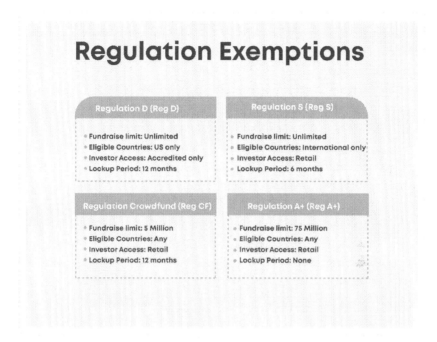

- Regulation D (Reg D)
- Regulation S (Reg S)
- Regulation Crowdfund (Reg CF)
- Regulation A+ (Reg A+)

Regulation D (Reg D)

Regulation D, commonly known as *Reg D*, is an exemption enabling a securities issuer to primarily target US accredited investors. Reg D filings have no minimum or maximum capital raise amounts, and have perhaps the simplest reporting requirements. Issuers simply need to file a Form D with the SEC within fifteen business days of the securities offering going live. Form D usually indicates the entity involved, the desired fundraise amount, the investment instrument, and any risk disclosures. Minimal or no audits are required as these securities are offered primarily to accredited investors, who by definition are deemed to be more sophisticated and capable of performing proper due diligence on investment opportunities. Reg D offerings have twelve-month lockup periods in which the securities cannot be moved or transferred to another entity or party.

Within Reg D offerings are two key subsets: 506(b) and 506(c). Reg D 506(b) offerings are the gold standard for private market exemptions, representing over 90 percent of all such activity. The rule enables issuers to raise unlimited amounts of capital from accredited investors and can also support up to thirty-five non-accredited investors (retail investors) who must have an established pre-existing relationship with the issuer.

The accredited investor verification is done on an issuer-to-investor basis under 506(b), meaning investors self-report their accreditation status. Reporting requirements are the standard, limited scope if the offering solely has accredited investors, but quickly becomes more cumbersome and detailed with the involvement of non-accredited investors. Any offering including non-accredited investors can expect an increased level of SEC scrutiny. Additionally, there is no public solicitation or marketing of the investment opportunity under a Reg D 506(b) placement, essentially limiting the offering to a closed network of accredited and potentially non-accredited investors.

The other Reg D type, 506(c) is limited solely to accredited investors and may under no circumstances involve any non-accredited investors. The issuer may market its brand and its offering across the internet, via email, on television commercials, social media, and a variety of paper marketing avenues. The issuer must take reasonable steps to verify that each and every investor is accredited. Issuers can rely on third-party verification services like InvestReady to reduce their liability and expenses associated with verifying accreditation status. InvestReady was started by Herwig Konings (one of the authors of this book) in 2013 to support online investments with software allowing issuers to meet this verification requirement.

In summary, Reg D encompasses a wide range of wealth through US-accredited investors. The Reg D 506(b) designation may be useful for issuers who already have a personal or tangential network of accredited investors and potentially have a handful of personally connected non-accredited investors who wish to gain access to the deal.

On the other hand, the Reg D 506(c) designation is beneficial for issuers looking to tap into new audiences or utilize widespread marketing, advertising, and solicitation methods. Reporting requirements are limited to what the issuer decides to share with investors, making the 506(c) filing one of the more practical and straightforward go-to-market options, if not almost a requirement for security token offerings.[9]

Regulation S (Reg S)

The Reg D exemption focused on US-Accredited investors, with no reference to international investors. Reg S offerings are geared solely to international investors and simply require following the rules of Regulation S. From there, issuers are free to raise capital from international investors as far as the SEC is concerned. Reg S offerings have six-month lockup periods in which the securities cannot be moved or transferred to another entity or party.

The SEC's goal is to protect US-based investors. They are not patrolling practices for international capital raising. Issuers should still be diligent and apprised of international capital raising laws to ensure they are also complying with the jurisdictions from which they may be taking capital as jurisdictions will likely have their own version of the SEC and accompanying rules.

In short, the SEC is established to protect US-based investors no matter where the issuing entity resides. The issuer can be based in any of the seven continents, but if it targets even one US investor, the SEC will be involved and require either registration with the SEC or filing a private exemption. On the other hand, an issuer can be based in the US and target investors in other countries simply by filing Form S and alerting the SEC of the intended capital raise from non-US investors.

It is common for Reg D 506(c) and Reg S to be used simultaneously to raise capital from both US accredited investors and international investors while maintaining full marketing capabilities (pending international securities governing body regulations and guidelines, of course).[10]

Regulation Crowdfund (Reg CF)

As the first retail-oriented private placement introduced in this chapter, Reg CF was designed in an effort to match the popularity of crowdfunding platforms like Kickstarter and Indiegogo. These platforms offered perks and non-financial rewards to people who donated to companies and organizations listed on the platform. In a little over a decade, Kickstarter helped over 200,000 organizations raise an aggregate $6.2 billion, which is remarkable considering the donors received no financial upside in projects to which they contributed.

These crowdfunding efforts set the foundation for equity crowdfunding, which actually does provide contributors with financial upside in organizations, thereby making them investors. Since Reg CF offerings do indeed target retail investors, the SEC requires more stringent requirements to issuers than Reg D and Reg S guidelines.

First, Reg CF offerings must be handled and managed by a FINRA approved Funding Portal or Broker-Dealer. As of 2022, there are around seventy approved Funding Portals, with some of the more popular examples being Republic, SeedInvest, StartEngine, and Wefunder.

Second, issuers must file the Form C, which is more detailed and demanding than Forms D or S. Under Reg CF, issuers are able to raise either up to $1.07 million or $5 million in a 12-month period. These caps vary with the audit capabilities and desires of the issuing entity. If the entity wishes to raise the full $5 million, it will need to have 2 years of audited financials and ongoing reporting. If not, the entity can raise up to $1.07 million with limited or "soft" audits and ongoing financial reporting.

One of the authors of this book, Herwig Konings, directly contributed market feedback provided to the SEC regarding improvements to this exemption, specifically in regard to raising the limit from $1.07M to $5M. For anyone curious about the '.07', this was increased from the original $1M to account for inflation.

Issuers are able to advertise the brand and the fact that they are making use of a crowdfund, although investment terms can only be displayed and disclosed on the designated Funding Portal itself, rather than in widespread marketing materials.

Lastly, Reg CF offerings have a 12-month lockup period in which the securities cannot be moved or transferred to another entity or party. Prior to the offering actually going live, the issuer can take advantage of what's officially known as the "Test the Waters" period. During this period, issuers can market the offering to their network and get a sense of how it will be received before following through with the filing and issuance process. Investment terms should not be marketed during the Test the Waters phase, and issuers must be careful to comply with SEC guidelines.

Regulation CF has helped raise over $1 Billion for small businesses since its inception in 2015. Being designed for a mass audience, this exemption is popular for security token issuers.[11]

Regulation A+ (Reg A+)

Sometimes referred to as the "Mini-IPO," Reg A+ offerings represent the highest fundraising limits directed at retail investors, essentially taking Reg CF offerings to another level. Initiated by filing Form 1-A, there are two tiers in the Reg A+ selection process: Tier 1 and Tier 2.

Tier 1 Reg A+ offerings may raise up to $20 million in a 12-month period from retail, accredited, and institutional investors. The reporting requirements are similar to a Reg CF, including 'bad actor' background checks, multiple-year audits, and ongoing financial reporting and disclosures.

Tier 2 Reg A+ offerings may raise up to $75 million in a 12-month period from the same target investor audience. Tier 2 offerings come with the same requirements as Tier 1 offerings, with an added limitation on the amount a retail investor can contribute, either via a fixed dollar amount or a maximum portion of annual income.

Given the size and the potential widespread pool of thousands of investors involved in a Reg A+, it earned the nickname "Mini-IPO" and positioned itself as the bridge between private and public retail investors. Exodus, a blockchain wallet company, successfully raised the full $75M amount via a security token offering.[12]

Initial Public Offering (IPO): S-1

Compare these private placements to a full Initial Public Offering via S-1 filing. The S-1 is the full offering filing document required by the SEC to issue public securities. The S-1 contains details about the company, its business model, the existing investor base, the offering type and amount, and any underwriting and investor syndication information, among other points.

The S-1 filing is more extensive than a Regulation A+ filing, and legal fees typically expand with the additional requirements. For smaller companies, the fees may not make financial sense. Instead, many microcap or small-cap firms would likely be better off leveraging the private placement and security token combination to still achieve the liquidity and offering goals that motivate a company's stock listing.

International Issuer IPO in the United States: F-1

In terms of true public filings, security token issuance platform and Alternative Trading System INX issued its own security token via F-1, as the firm was acting as a foreign issuer to the US-based public markets. An F-1 is another example of a full public filing and prospectus. INX was able to raise $85 million across 7,200 retail, accredited, and institutional investors in this tokenized public offering, which surpasses the $75 million limit under Regulation A+ offerings and stands as one of the largest security token offerings to date.[13]

Keep in mind that these filings are for the investment offering specifically. They are quite powerful on their own, as shown by the hundreds of billions in capital raised through private placements, but also have their own limitations. Liquidity and asset management are two of the key limitations blockchain-based securities strive to solve.

When referring to liquidity, the easy answer is secondary trading capabilities for investors to fluidly buy and sell positions on some sort of marketplace. This is the most commonly cited liquidity solution in most securities or tradable assets. On the blockchain, investors are also able to maintain peer-to-peer swaps through internal bulletin boards (populated with other existing investors) or even tap into DeFi mechanisms such as Aave, Compound, or Uniswap.

Regarding asset management, the concept that blockchain-based securities can be fungible and precise is the key piece to the puzzle. Investors no longer need to hold onto the entire portfolio of a private placement investment when they can take multiple practices into account such as liquidity, asset lending, collateralization, and other potential yield-generating activities as explored in the DeFi chapter.

The private placement guidelines are the key to opening up the security token industry and will serve to blend traditional financial markets with digital asset markets. It's become evident that certain digital assets act like securities but call themselves utilities or have multi-pronged uses that cross over into the securities designation. As the SEC and governing bodies examine these developments, expect the usage of private placements in digital assets to increase. As this chapter has demonstrated, the guidelines for private securities sales are indeed evident, and issuers are free to use these placements in tandem with a coin or token to initiate a compliant token sale to the public (or to the target investor audience). Gone are the days of the ICO. Instead, these are the days of registered token offerings. The authors of this book may be biased, but given how security tokens offer legitimate financial opportunities backed by real-world assets, along with investor protections, we believe the security token will be the ultimate application of tokenization.

NOTES

1. See https://www.investopedia.com/terms/h/howey-test.asp

2. See https://www.justice.gov/usao-ndtx/pr/founders-crypto-ico-sentenced-combined-8-years-prison-tax-evasion-after-raising-24

3. See https://www.sec.gov/news/press-release/2020-146

4. See https://www.protocol.com/fintech/ripple-sec-xrp-lawsuit-trial, https://www.hartdavidcarson.com/news/sec-ripple-lawsuit/, and https://www.investopedia.com/terms/i/initial-coin-offering-ico.asp

5. See https://www.investopedia.com/news/how-sec-regs-will-change-cryptocurrency-markets/ and https://www.investopedia.com/articles/03/012403.asp

6. See https://www.investopedia.com/ftx-exchange-5200842 and https://www.nytimes.com/2022/12/07/business/ftx-sbf-crypto-market-investigation.html

7. See https://www.securianam.com/content/securianAM/en/insights/articles/private-placement-investing.html, https://www.slcmanagement.com/us/en/insights/all-insights/q4-2021-investment-grade-private-credit-market-update/, https://siblisresearch.com/data/us-stock-market-value/, and https://www.finra.org/investors/insights/private-placements-explained

8. See https://www.investopedia.com/terms/j/jumpstart-our-business-startups-act-jobs.asp and https://jobsactlawyers.com/

9. See https://www.upcounsel.com/form-d, https://www.investopedia.com/terms/r/regulationd.asp, and https://crowdfundingattorney.com/2017/03/06/whats-the-difference-between-rule-506c-and-rule-506b-in-crowdfunding/

10. See https://www.securitieslawyer101.com/2013/regulation-s/

11. See https://www.investopedia.com/best-alternatives-to-kickstarter-5081260, https://www.seedinvest.com/how-it-works/regulation-cf, and https://www.crowdfundinsider.com/2022/04/189954-reg-cf-the-number-of-funding-portals-stabilizes-as-industry-expects-more-growth/

12. See https://www.sec.gov/education/smallbusiness/exemptofferings/rega and https://www.seedinvest.com/how-it-works/regulation-a

13. See https://www.jdsupra.com/legalnews/first-ever-sec-registered-digital-token-7084681/

CHAPTER 12

DIGITAL ASSET HYBRIDS

After discussing the various classifications of digital assets, it's important to understand how these types are not mutually exclusive. In some cases, a single digital asset can fall under multiple classifications, or a project will encompass different types of digital assets in the complete vision. This chapter explores conceptual and active examples of what we'll call *hybrid digital assets*.

Examples of hybrid digital assets include the following:

- DAOs acting as investment funds, and therefore should be issuing compliant security tokens that may double as utility or governance tokens.
- NFTs offering profit-sharing or revenue-sharing agreements to owners, usually structured as royalties.
- NFTs acting as invitations or accessibility tokens to exclusive events and groups.

Exchange tokens may be some of the lowest-hanging fruit of hybrid digital assets the general cryptocurrency world knows. Examples include Binance Coin (*BNB*) of Binance and Cronos (*CRO*) of Crypto. com. As covered on the Security Token Show and by The Motley Fool,[1] these tokens, which were originally issued via Initial Exchange Offering (IEO), a unique form of ICO, show signs of representing the value of these exchanges.

Whereas decentralized exchanges like Uniswap and SushiSwap are quite clear that utility coin holders share in transaction fees since users are the ones facilitating these trades by providing liquidity, centralized exchanges are set up as more traditional vehicles. Investment into these parties is usually only done via private or venture capital investment, something that is difficult for retail investors to access. Instead, the issuance of these exchange tokens is a bit misleading as it gives retail and ordinary investors the impression they are purchasing upside participation in the exchanges themselves.

There are also features like staking, which provides yield to stakers for providing liquidity and facilitating operations across various networks. In the case of exchanges, staking likely allows the exchange to either 1) lend funds to investors or 2) partake in expansionary activities. Gaining yield on staking under this premise is all too similar to dividend payments or compensation for expansionary activity, which is usually protected under securities law as any company that issues dividends and financial compensation would be.

Additional unique digital asset cases that span multiple categories are shown as follows.

Investment DAOs - FlamingoDAO

The primary goal of DAOs is to allow members and participants to vote on and contribute to the direction and mission of the organization. This is done through the purchase and usage of a utility token granting governance rights and other perks usually in the form of a one-vote-per-token structure.

When the mission of a DAO is geared toward novelty actions related to things like events, concerts, shows and movies, gaming, or web development, this model works well. Users are incentivized and the outcome is an action. When the mission is related to investments, however, then the question of securities law and guidelines comes into play.

A popular investment DAO called FlamingoDAO found its claim to fame in the action of turning a $10 million NFT portfolio in October 2020 into a $1 billion dollar value by February 2022, largely through the purchase of *CryptoPunks* and other top-tier collections—215 *CryptoPunks* and 22 *Bored Apes*, specifically. FlamingoDAO, which operates via weekly Zoom meetings for its members, is governed by the collective group in decision-making when it comes to buying, selling, holding, or swapping of Punks and other items with the goal of capital appreciation and investment gains. It is one of the first and most prominent leaderless investment organizations and a trailblazer for doing so.

Interestingly enough the DAO is limited to a maximum of 100 members at any given time. This was a wise structure as it enables the organization to categorize itself as a group rather than an investment organization, and therefore circumvent SEC oversight, filings, and rules. Nonetheless, should this model be spun out to a larger audience, one of three routes will likely be taken:

1. The DAO registers with the SEC under traditional filing, likely with added oversight, reporting, and limitations given the group-think approach.
2. The DAO issues security tokens under a private placement and simply abides by whichever filing requirements are dictated.
3. The DAO sets up shop internationally and takes steps to avoid any and all US investors, or risk interference from the SEC.

INVESTMENT CLUB

Interestingly enough, the DAO is limited to a maximum of 100 members at any given time. This was a wise structure as it enables the organization to categorize itself as a group rather than an investment organization, and therefore circumvent SEC oversight, filings, and rules. Nonetheless, should this model be spun out to a larger audience, one of three routes will likely be taken:

1
The DAO registers with the SEC under traditional filing, likely with added oversight, reporting, and limitations given the group-think approach.

2
The DAO issues security tokens under a private placement, and simply abides by whichever filing requirements are dictated.

3
The DAO sets up shop internationally and takes steps to avoid any and all US investors or risks interference from the SEC.

These are the guidelines set forth that can straightforwardly organize a true, registered investment DAO that is both 1) compliant and 2) member-governed, making it a hybrid of the security token and DAO model. In fact, it's come to the attention of firms like Security Token Advisors that several DAOs are working on issuing security tokens to give members proper ownership, perks, and protections from an investment and operational standpoint.[2]

Music NFTs and Securities

As mentioned in the NFT chapter, music is a popular and growing use case for NFTs. Since the NFT thesis is one of "shifting power back to the creator," it makes sense that musicians, producers, and engineers may benefit from selling pieces of music (songs, albums, concert rights, etc.) to their fan bases as an NFT. Two popular forums for doing so are Royal and Opulous.

Royal (Royal.io) is a music NFT marketplace founded by the EDM artist Justin Blau (3LAU). NFTs are representative of individual songs and enable buyers to earn royalties as the songs gain popularity and listens. The platform raised a $55 million Series A funding round in November 2021 led by Andreessen Horowitz with music-native contributors including Nas and The Chainsmokers. In short, the platform enables fans to listen to and participate in the upside associated with some of their favorite artists and pieces of work. It creates an investment opportunity in the music industry for the very fans from which the industry derives value.

Nas, in addition to being an investor, was the first artist to launch an NFT on Royal in January 2021 when he auctioned off rights to his songs "Rare" and "Ultra Black." The NFTs ranged in price tiers from $50 to $10,000 based on the size of the royalty (earnings share) across the 1,110 tokens for "Rare" and 760 tokens for "Ultra Black," thus creating investable opportunities for fans of all sizes.[3]

Nas music
NFT

Nas auctioned off rights to his songs "Rare" and "Ultra Black."
The NFTs ranged in price

$50 → $10,000

based on the size of the royalty

In addition to Royal, the music NFT platform Opulous sold out an NFT offering for the British rapper Ard Adz in April 2022. The "Patek Myself" single release was structured as what's being called an S-NFT or Security NFT. The approach is to take a securities angle when it comes to music NFTs on its platform, although because these products offer upside in third-party performance, they will likely pass the Howey Test for securities.

Officially structured as a crowdfund (Reg CF) on the funding portal WeFunder, *Patek Myself LLC*, which owns 50 percent of the Master rights to the "Patek Myself" single, received $65,000 in pledges for a max offering size of $50,000. As mentioned in the regulations chapter, this is allowed in the Test-the-Waters phase of a Reg CF, and the concept is proven here through this Opulous offering.

Since the LLC owns half of the masters to the single itself, the LLC can be sold off to investors who then get pro rata shares in that 50 percent of the financial performance of the "Patek Myself" single. Opulosu took the compliant approach, recognizing this ensures the company and its investors are abiding by securities law, even within an NFT wrapper. This is a great case of a hybrid NFT and security token offering.

To properly facilitate the securities side of the equation, Opulous announced Securitize as its Transfer Agent for this and future offerings. Securitize will legally be able to transfer shares of ownership (NFTs) and make distributions to investors on behalf of Opulous since Securitize is an SEC-registered Transfer Agent.[4]

It will be interesting to see how this structure affects other music (and non-music) NFTs or platforms that promise token holders potential financial upside in the form of profit-sharing wrapped under the royalty description. Should SEC enforcement enter the NFT space, digital Transfer Agents will be well-positioned to take advantage of these platforms that now demand compliant securities services.

Fractional NFTs

As with the Royal and Opulous examples above, a parallel case exists in the world of art NFTs. Fractional (Fractional.Art) is a company that enables community ownership of an NFT across collections ranging from top-tier names to scattered offerings. The goal is that since people cannot always afford the full price of an NFT (a *Bored Ape*, for example, would cost six-figures or more), the market could become more accessible through fractional NFTs. This essentially takes a single NFT and breaks it into multiple pieces or representations, and buyers can collectively own the NFT by purchasing smaller fractions of it.

Some argue that fractionalization of an NFT can help liquidity since sellers do not need to sell the entire asset but rather could find traction selling smaller bits of the asset at lower prices (and vice versa for buyers). Fractional would acquire and verify each NFT on its platform before creating fractions of each one for its users to trade.

While there may be possible utility in fractional NFTs, including for in-game items, event access, or even for future airdrops, the main driver of purchasing a fractional NFT is for future asset appreciation. Shared ownership of an inherently unique asset, however, is somewhat of an oxymoron.

Building off this concept, Rally Rd took things one step further. Not only do they acquire, verify, and fractionalize NFTs, but they offer each NFT as a Reg A+ equity offering to investors. This symbolizes that 1) fractional NFTs are largely for investment purposes and should be treated as such and 2) companies can indeed operate in compliance with SEC guidelines. Rally's product flow is as follows:

1. Rally sources, verifies, and acquires the most sought-after NFT items,
2. turns each of these items or collections into a company, usually via LLC,
3. opens an initial offering on Rally's platform through a Reg A+ or other private placement, and
4. after a 90-day lock-up period, investors can sell shares in-app or through Bid-Ask trading with a registered Broker-Dealer.

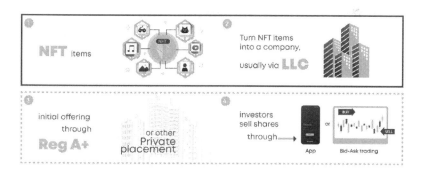

Rally Fractional NFT Ownership

Rally's product flow is as follows:

It should be noted that Fractional is a blockchain-native company and Rally is not, meaning transactions on Fractional may happen on-chain while Rally transactions are off-chain since each NFT is held in an LLC or similar entity. These are not quite apples-to-apples, although they certainly play in the same field. Yet again, the Fractional and Rally parallel is another example of hybrid digital assets as the market sees the NFT and securities realms blend.[5]

Decentralized Security Token Exchange

Security tokens have begun taking advantage of the decentralized benefits cryptocurrency users have been enjoying through the likes of Uniswap, SushiSwap, and other DEXes. IX Swap is the first known and active security token decentralized exchange making use of a similar order matching mechanism as the aforementioned DEX examples. Based in Singapore and owned by the securities exchange InvestaX, IX Swap is building a future where security tokens can trade globally yet compliantly the same way ERC-20 tokens can be swapped in a peer-to-peer manner.

IX Swap has its own utility token, *IXS*, that incentivizes users to stake and earn 50 percent on trading fees through IX Swap, much like one could stake *UNI* and partake in the trading fees. Whereas Uniswap works with ERC-20 tokens for compatibility purposes, IX Swap is able to work with any security tokens sharing the same custodian as IX Swap, which is Fireblocks as of May 2022. This means that as new security tokens utilizing Fireblocks as a custodian are released to market or as existing tokens migrate to Fireblocks, the range of supported assets for IX Swap increases.

Since security tokens are seen as the more centralized digital asset class, given the compliance necessities, this is an important step in getting the "crypto crowd" comfortable with security tokens and making this class more accessible. As digital asset investors realize gains on cryptocurrencies and utility tokens, they may have a desire to rotate some of those funds into other asset classes. Luckily, security tokens are asset-agnostic and can take on a range of assets such as real estate, venture capital funds, private company shares, and other real assets. Being able to simply swap *ETH* or another digital asset for a real estate security token or something similar will be very powerful from a portfolio construction perspective and is where the future of portfolio allocation is headed.

Additionally, if Uniswap is seen as a bet on the decentralized trading markets, IX Swap can be seen as a bet on the decentralized securities markets. Not only could users partake in upsides associated with trade fees on a crypto DEX, but they could also take advantage of trading trends in the global securities market that currently dwarfs the cryptocurrency market at $120 trillion in global equity market cap versus the aggregate crypto market cap at $1.3 trillion to end 2022.[6]

Automated Market Maker and Lending with Security Tokens

Strengthening the bridge between security tokens and DeFi solutions, RealT, the highest-volume issuer of security tokens to date, has formed a white-label partnership with Aave to offer staking, borrowing, and lending services to security tokens of all kinds. Much like IX Swap has done with decentralized trading, RealT's RMM (Real Market Maker) seeks to provide the decentralized lending and borrowing benefits DeFi users have popularized.

During the beta launch in April 2022, RealT curated $4 million of deposits for liquidity pools on RealT assets in the form of Real-Tokens, which represent individual properties RealT owns, manages, and offers to investors. Depositors into liquidity pools receive ArmmmTokens representing the deposit plus any accrued interest and yield, based on Aave's "aTokens" structure. The current collateralization ratio is 50 percent on RMM so investors must essentially keep double the amount of collateral on hand as the loan itself. This ratio should, ideally, increase as the platform is built out and as more capital flows into security tokens since these assets should be more stable than non-asset-backed tokens and therefore should provide investors with greater Loan-to-Value ratios such as 80 percent.

Beyond the beta version limited to RealT assets, RMM is the first major on-chain step in allowing investors to gain liquidity on their assets without having to sell. As this concept is proven with execution, it will be rolled out to such a wide variety of assets that it may even rival Aave's existing network of ERC-20 tokens and similar digital assets. It will also likely find a place in hedge funds and yield strategies as savvy investors can extend their search for yield from real assets.[7]

Kairos Dual-Listing Utility and Security Token

As one of the earlier hybrid digital assets to market, facial recognition software company Kairos issued the industry's first dual token offering in late 2017. Under the advising of Herwig Konings, the token gave investors access to equity in the company via a Security Token and a bonus 1-for-1 on the Utility Token, which happens to be a form of biometric access via blockchain using their proprietary facial recognition technology.

KAIROS DUAL TOKEN

As one of the earlier hybrid digital assets to market, facial recognition software company Kairos issued the industry's first dual token offering in late 2017.

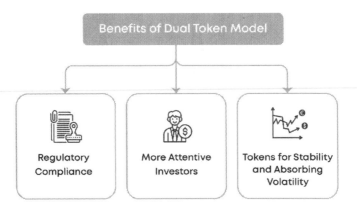

Benefits of Dual Token Model

Regulatory Compliance

More Attentive Investors

Tokens for Stability and Absorbing Volatility

Rather than using the venture capital network to fill a Series B round, Kairos decided to target the global investor capital base and needed a strategy to access this new pool of investors. The utility token was used to garner attention and catch the eyes of those following blockchain-related projects, whereas the security token was the actual investment vehicle. By pairing both together in a dual offering, Kairos expanded its frontier of possible investors while maintaining compliance with securities guidelines.

While looking to raise just $500,000 as a test, the demand for the Kairos offering was oversubscribed and closed at nearly $12 million in aggregate funding, some of which is held in treasury by the company while the rest is in circulation.[8]

NOTES

1. See https://www.fool.com/cryptocurrency/2022/04/28/why-exchange-tokens-bnb-cro-ftt-are-like-stocks/ and https://www.youtube.com/watch?v=YbMhrnNny04&t=874s

2. See https://www.forbes.com/sites/jeffkauflin/2022/02/03/daos-arent-a-fad-theyre-a-platform/?sh=6292528619d0 and https://www.coindesk.com/markets/2022/02/10/flamingodaos-nft-portfolio-is-now-worth-1b/

3. See https://hypebeast.com/2022/1/nas-royal-streaming-royalty-rights-nft and https://www.lexology.com/library/detail.aspx?g=92d81306-ca86-47ca-b570-34ad16483039

4. See https://opulous.medium.com/youve-secured-an-s-nft-what-s-next-d7bcfc6d3363 and https://opulous.medium.com/opulous-partners-with-securitize-to-accelerate-s-nft-adoption-6345b28d3397

5. See https://fractional.art/ and https://rallyrd.com/

6. See https://ixswap.io/ and https://www.sifma.org/resources/research/insights-global-equity-markets-primer/

7. See https://realt.co/understanding-the-technical-mechanisms-realted-to-rmm/

8. See https://blog.stomarket.com/the-dual-token-offering-a-new-standard-for-icos-37ad6a0b9231

CHAPTER 13

FUTURE MARKET OUTLOOK AND TRENDS

The future of capital markets may very well be determined by developments in the emerging forms of hybrid digital assets discussed in the previous chapter. It would be unreasonable to say fractional NFTs and investment DAOs are the be-all-end-all regarding the global capital markets landscape, although the success of such projects may act as proofs-of-concept for interested institutions. While cryptocurrency and DeFi initiatives were originally formed under the guise of avoiding or circumventing traditional institutions, those institutions still drive capital markets forward. Therefore, the future of capital markets lies in combining the best digital asset projects with institutional use cases and drivers.

This is easier said than done since what may be beneficial to institutions is not always directly accessible by retail investors or clients. There is not always a product side to a new development as there is with existing retail DeFi (i.e., staking for yield), but there may be operational efficiencies to be found.

Institutions will likely always need to follow compliance procedures that retail investors do not. The reason is simple: *Institutions are fiduciaries to their clients, and have a responsibility to act in their best financial interest.* Part of fiduciary duty is to ensure proper security, safety, and compliance when it comes to client assets and decisions, which makes diving head-first into DeFi a tough sell.

Instead, institutions are more likely to take the compliant digital asset route of tokenized assets and security tokens. By tokenizing existing assets and onboarding books or business to the blockchain, institutions begin leveling the playing field in terms of transparency and accountability that was previously always manually handled. The value drivers for institutions tokenizing assets include the multiple product-level initiatives described in this book, but also even more significant operational-level developments.

For example, RealT's RMM shows how tokenized assets can tap into the same technology and procedures as digital assets for decentralized borrowing and lending. This would be a great product-level addition to any hedge fund, credit fund, or alternative asset manager looking to expand strategies and capitalize on varying yield opportunities. Institutions would be required to tokenize their assets in order to participate, which is where the tokenization incentive lies.

In fact, Ondo Finance took this concept to an institutional level with its tokenized money market and treasury products in early 2023. Ondo essentially purchases BlackRock and PIMCO money market, treasury, and yield ETFs, storing those traditional shares in a Special Purpose Vehicle (SPV), tokenizing the SPV, and issuing Ethereum-based tokens representing interests in those funds. The motivation here, which is a recurring theme in the industry, is enabling stablecoin holders (a $100+ billion market at the end of 2022) to rotate into traditional yield-generating products fully on-chain. Ondo's first live product, the Ondo Short-Term US Government Bond Fund ($OUSG), accrued roughly $70 million in total value locked (TVL) within a few months of launch and accepts minimum investment subscriptions of $100,000 via USD Coin (USDC).

To make use of the real-world asset benefits, Ondo Finance also launched Flux Finance, a platform that enables investors to collateralize and borrow against their Ondo fund holdings fully on-chain. This is a remarkable initiative to show how traditional and even institutional investors can bring clients into digital assets by holding traditional yield-generating products and offering collateralization services fully on-chain. The playbook involves Ondo Finance as the investment fund manager, Coinbase Custody holding the stablecoins, Clear Street acting as both the prime broker and qualified custodian of the securities, NAV Consulting as the fund administrator, and Richey May as the auditor.[1]

On an operational level, look to Arca's $ArCoin mentioned in the *Chapter 8: Security Tokens*. ArCoin can be used as a near-seamless collateral and treasury management facilitator for institutions who have actively been managing these facets manually for decades or longer. The efficiencies provided by $ArCoin include real-time settlement and round-the-clock transactions rather than being confined to only standard banking hours. This could be critical to the credit profiles and execution of these processes, as many institutions are at the mercy of banking hours regarding transaction settlement.[2]

JP Morgan is perhaps the most active in regards to institutional tokenization to date. With roughly $3 trillion in assets under management, the bank has opened three separate tokenization-driven initiatives through its Onyx division:[3]

- A tokenized repo marketplace.
- *Tokenized Collateral Network* (TCN).
- *Project Guardian*, a joint pilot program with the Monetary Authority of Singapore (MAS), DBS, and Marketnode.

Beyond blockchain-based repos, which were covered in *Chapter 8: Security Tokens*, is the concept of institutional borrowing and lending via tokenized collateral. Companies like BlackRock, KKR, Black-Rock, and State Street (all of which publicly support and/or make use of security tokens) are unlikely to deploy assets directly into Aave, Compound, or other DeFi lending services given the sheer size and security needs of these institutions. The fully on-chain public aspect is something of a limiting factor in this case. Instead, there has to be a midground between the DeFi technology and the backing and management of a traditional institution. This can be found in JP Morgan's TCN or *Tokenized Collateral Network*.

The TCN completed its first real-time frictionless transfer of collateral assets in late May 2022 when it tokenized shares of a BlackRock money market fund and used them as collateral with a counterparty of the bank. This was done for collateral management purposes, and essentially proved the concept of instantaneous collateral posting and transfer.

Ultimately, this transaction and the TCN network is just a wider build-out of the repo network designed under Onyx, using the technology and life-cycle flow for a wider range of underlying products, and the bank has plans to expand this execution to not only repos and money market funds, but also to equities, fixed income, and other alternative asset types. Should JP Morgan move forward in this direction, which it likely will, then real estate, private company shares, public company shares, structured products, mortgage-backed securities, receivables, and more could be tokenized and used as real-time collateral across the bank's different lines of business.[4]

After the TCN proof-of-concept, JP Morgan announced a joint project with the Monetary Authority of Singapore (MAS is the republic's central banking authority) in collaboration with DBS (a roughly $250 billion bank in Singapore) and Marketnode (a digital assets infrastructure company). Project Guardian, as the initiative is named, will be dedicated to exploring tokenization and DeFi in regard to *wholesale funding*.[5]

Wholesale funding is an umbrella term referring to a group of different credit types in a single basket, transaction, or division. Wholesale funding is done on an institutional level to include commercial funding types such as federal funds, brokered deposits, and foreign deposits. This blend of credit sources is meant to diversify the institution's financiers and therefore mitigate risk. Wholesale funding is a strategy usually implemented during times of turbulence or distress. Interestingly, wholesale funding became a focus of this group of collaborators in May 2022 as Project Guardian was seeking use cases in the digital assets world to facilitate more efficient transactions.

The program began with the exploration of liquidity pools consisting of tokenized bonds representing wholesale funding products to be used in facilitating borrowing and lending across a public blockchain. It culminated in an asset swap of tokenized Singapore Dollars and tokenized Japanese Yen on Aave Arc, a permissioned service within

Aave, marking one of, if not the first, institutional initiatives to successfully be completed on a public blockchain.[6]

While this is revolutionary for the world of public blockchains, many new banks and institutions getting comfortable with the technology will likely work on the private or permissioned blockchain side, so as to have greater control and command of the processes. As happens in the background of many JP Morgan TCN transactions, tokenized assets are swapped not into US dollars, as that would require the same existing fiat rails, but rather into *JPM Coin*, which is the bank's internal digital dollar. By settling all blockchain-based transactions, swaps, and trades in *JPM Coin*, parties are always dealing with like-kind assets. This means the flow of asset transactions can eventually evolve as described below:

1. Asset to dollar to new asset (processing and settlement time between the initial asset to dollar sale and between the dollar to asset purchase).
2. Tokenized asset to *JPM Coin* to new tokenized asset (instantaneous processing and settlement of the asset to *JPM Coin* swap, and again from *JPM Coin* to new asset).
3. Tokenized asset to tokenized asset (because tokenized assets are already priced in *JPM Coin* and run on the same rails, assets can be swapped immediately for each other without having to settle in *JPM Coin* first).

The third scenario listed above is where the industry is headed, as any efficiencies and time savings will likely yield significant dollar savings to the banks and institutions through faster client and trade servicing. If tokenized assets and *JPM Coin* are built on the same blockchain or on interoperable networks and rails, they can be swapped for each other in the proper ratio (i.e., $1 per *JPM Coin*). If the value of a *JPM Coin* is constant at $1 and all tokenized assets are valued in *JPM Coin*, the future is swapping two tokenized assets for each other in proper ratios without even settling in *JPM Coin* first, much like investors simply swap ERC-20 tokens for each other in Uniswap without settling in *ETH* first.

This is the type of future Arca had in mind through the creation and operational use case of $ArCoin. It's something banks can work on individually and internally, as with *JPM Coin*, or with a built-out product as with $ArCoin or tokenized money market funds such as Franklin Templeton's OnChain US Government Money Fund ($FOBXX). The key piece is ensuring any involved products live on equivalent blockchain rails so they can be seamlessly and directly swapped.

To visualize, assume there is a tokenized slice of a private equity fund that's valued at $10 million across 10,000 tokens. Rather than selling these tokens for cash and reinvesting into a money market fund generating 4.5 percent annually, a fully digital loop will enable the asset owner to swap a portion of the private equity interests directly into the OnChain US Government Money Fund, for example, assuming they're on compatible blockchain rails. This reduces certain intermediaries, fees, and timing delays, ultimately opening up the true capabilities of cost savings and efficiencies, which will improve institutional bottom lines and may even provide spillover savings to clients.

Being done at scale, Goldman Sachs and BNY Mellon completed the first security lending deal on the HQLAx blockchain. HQLAx, which stands for "High Quality Liquid Assets Exchange," has been working toward becoming the distributed ledger for securities finance and repo markets, aiming to serve large banks and institutions to bring efficiencies to their existing capital markets operations. In this inaugural transaction, hundreds of millions of dollars of agency securities were tokenized by HQLAx on the Corda enterprise blockchain and held at the original custodian.

Typically, these securities take days to settle, and this process sometimes causes a bottleneck in the full range of capabilities institutions could be exercising with the securities since they must remain compliant from a balance sheet standpoint. Instead, as the tokenized securities are held in one custodian rather than physically changing hands, HQLAx's services provide cost savings and speed to banks, which in turn provides greater precision and increased profitability.[7]

In terms of programmable money, there is also a possible future in which tokenized deposits and assets serve a greater function than the stablecoins described earlier in this book. The weaknesses of sta-blecoins were revealed in the stories about de-pegs, false or inaccurate audits, and even the loose definitions and usage of "cash and cash equivalents." Since security tokens are built to be compliant to securi-ties standards, these guidelines likely supersede the guidelines by which fiat-backed stablecoins abide. Something interesting and significant to keep in mind in the years ahead are punishments and enforcement for misleading or under-collateralized stablecoins. The punishment for a securities mishap is rarely just a slap on the wrist and instead comes with fiduciary repercussions which affect not only the immediate com-pany or leadership involved but also any facets of a business in which the leadership may have a hand.

Given this, it's feasible to say a tokenized US dollar provides greater transparency and legitimacy of backing than something like *USDC*, which is audited on a monthly basis. Such examples could include deposit tokens, which JP Morgan covered in depth, the Regulated Liability Network (RLN) with a range of banks and depository insti-tutions backing a stablecoin alternative, or USDF, an FDIC-insured deposit built on the Provenance Blockchain and supported by a dozen commercial banks.[8]

Large asset managers are even exploring the use of traditional financial products on-chain as improved substitutes for stablecoins. Franklin Templeton's OnChain US Government Money Fund was already mentioned; it is a product that garnered roughly $225 million of assets in two years, with much of that growth coming while interest rates were on the rise. The reason for this flow is simple: Stablecoin holders were typically not generating reliable or secure yield and chose to rotate into an on-chain product generating upwards of 4.5 percent in early 2023. The fund now has the potential to displace stablecoins in certain investor portfolios and position itself aptly.[9]

Similarly, WisdomTree Prime, the digital arm of the $82 billion ETF sponsor WIsdomTree Asset Management, received SEC approval for ten blockchain-based 1940 Act funds. Working with Securrency Transfers (the transfer agent of Securrency, an SEC-registered digital broker-dealer and alternative trading system) and on the Stellar block-chain, WisdomTree likely sees a similar future whereby investors will crave traditional products useable in digital asset ecosystems such as collateralization services and lending pools. The products may even be used by institutional partners and clients for real-time treasury and collateral management, as covered in *Chapter 8: Security Tokens*. The majority of WisdomTree's approved products are money market and treasury funds, although there are more unique products like an S&P Twitter Sentiment fund and inflation-protected securities.[10]

Regarding institutional vs. retail-level products and uses, consider the ETF vs. Mutual Fund battle that's been going on over the past two decades. Mutual funds were the original king. They became the investment vehicles upon which many large players relied for targeted exposure to certain indexes, benchmarks, sectors, or general strategies (i.e., capital appreciation, yield, and total return). Since there were such diligent backend management fees and required resources, mutual fund issuers weren't really concerned with addressing any transactions less than seven figures in size. Salespeople were there to cater to institutions and big buyers, not to the average person.

When push came to shove and issuers realized there was a whole pocket of retail capital waiting to be deployed in some comparable fund, they looked to a structure that would allow this, which led to Exchange-Traded Funds (ETFs). The ETF provided intraday liquidity and lower buy-ins since they listed and traded actively on a national stock exchange. There was little need for personalized management and reporting as there was in mutual funds, where investors could buy-in and redeem shares that then affected the price of the mutual fund and its NAV the following day. This manual process of calculating, reporting, and distributing was a strong factor in the mutual fund industry's affinity towards institutions rather than retail investors.

With the ETF, trades were settled intraday between 9:30 am and 4:00 pm EST, much like any share of stock. Retail investors could buy as many or as few shares of an ETF as they wished, with little marginal labor on the issuer's end. Just as importantly, these ETFs tracked similar benchmarks to comparable mutual funds, meaning the retail investors finally had comparable exposure as institutions. It wasn't a perfect one-to-one match as ETFs usually came with certain guidelines in regard to the holdings allocation, amounts and usage of leverage, rebalancing periods, and related nuances, but it was certainly an improvement over zero access.

These days, the global mutual fund industry is valued at $60 trillion while the global ETF market is valued at $10 trillion—up from just $200 billion in 2003. Of that, nearly $20 trillion of the mutual fund market size and just over $5 trillion of the ETF market size comes from the United States, meaning the US accounts for *half* of the global ETF markets versus *one-third* of the global mutual fund markets. The security token market cap is now in the tens of billions of dollars range even though security tokens have the potential and credibility to encompass not only the collective $70 trillion in assets between mutual funds and ETFs, but also the trillions of dollars of private and illiquid assets currently in capital markets. The security token will likely do to most financial products what ETFs did to mutual funds.[11]

Similarly, just as ETFs made products more tradable and liquid through centralized brokers, security tokens will take this process to another level through integration with centralized brokers and decentralized protocols, platforms, and exchanges. The IX Swap and Ondo Finance initiatives described earlier encompass just the tip of the iceberg. Certain broker-dealers and ATSs in the industry are working on solutions to either whitelist partnerships with decentralized services like Aave and Uniswap, or are developing their own to provide the dual ability to trade tokenized assets either on the ATS or on decentralized exchanges under one umbrella. This gives users the option of trading via order book or via liquidity pool, and may even present multiple strategies for trading firms and asset managers.

This likelihood of a crossover between traditional institutions and the DeFi world is highlighted and accentuated through moves like Tesla's use of MakerDAO to finance a $7.8 million real estate deal. Announced on March 30, 2022, this event was a great "meeting of the minds" as MakerDAO had been embracing real-world assets at the same time Tesla was exploring alternative financing for a new repair and collision center. Working with RWA Co. (who assists loan originators and asset managers in accessing Maker Vaults) and 6s Capital (a firm launched in 2020 designed to facilitate Maker loans in response to the poor availability of traditional credit during the COVID-19 pandemic), Tesla successfully secured the loan and added institutional funds to the MakerDAO vaults, thus diversifying the collateral of the vault from strictly retail to include both retail and institutional.[12]

That certainly will not be the last story of its kind. The end of 2022 showed a number of institutions making their real-world asset cases:[13]

- UBS and its $370 million digital bond dual-listed on SIX Swiss and SIX Digital exchanges.
- ABN AMRO issuing a digital corporate bond subscribed to by existing traditional equity holders.
- Siemens issuing a $64 million on the Polygon blockchain to be used in other Ethereum-based DeFi applications.

As digital asset infrastructure continues to find traction and expand user bases, tides will naturally rise from retail projects to institutional-grade projects. Institutions have already begun getting comfortable and familiar with tokenization through traditional financial products that are brought on-chain, and the next step is to begin making use of these on-chain products in applications like lending and swapping. Pending success stories at this stage, more novel, unique cases will potentially flow from asset managers and hedge funds looking to stretch the ability of tokenization, presumably with value-adds to their own business operations, and truly establish tokenization as the technology that underpins the future (and present) of capital markets.

NOTES

1. See https://coinmarketcap.com/view/stablecoin/, https://ondo.finance/ousg, and https://fluxfinance.com/

2. See https://arcoin.arcalabs.com/blog-posts/the-first-blockchain-transferred-fund

3. See https://www.advratings.com/companies/jpmorgan-chase

4. See https://www.ledgerinsights.com/jp-morgan-uses-blockchain-for-collateral-settlement/

5. See https://www.coindesk.com/business/2022/05/31/singapore-to-look-at-crypto-use-cases-with-dbs-jpmorgan-and-marketnode/

6. See https://www.ledgerinsights.com/jp-morgan-dbs-sbi-digital-asset-complete-defi-tokenization-trials-on-public-blockchain/

7. See https://www.ledgerinsights.com/bny-mellon-goldman-execute-first-security-lending-deal-on-hqla%E1%B5%A1-blockchain-platform/

8. See https://regulatedliabilitynetwork.org/, https://www.jpmorgan.com/onyx/documents/deposit-tokens.pdf, and https://usdfconsortium.com/

9. See https://www.franklintempleton.com/investments/options/money-market-funds/products/29386/SINGLCLASS/franklin-on-chain-u-s-government-money-fund/FOBXX

10. See https://cointelegraph.com/news/sec-approves-9-more-wisdomtree-blockchain-enabled-funds and https://www.wisdomtree.com/investments/blog/2022/12/14/our-next-wave-of-digital-fund-launches

11. See https://www.globenewswire.com/news-release/2021/02/04/2170089/0/en/Global-mutual-fund-assets-market-to-generate-101-2-trillion-by-2027-Allied-Market-Research.html, https://etfgi.com/news/press-releases/2022/01/etfgi-reports-global-etfs-industry-ended-2021-record-us1027-trillion, https://www.amazon.com/Bond-King-Market-Built-Empire/dp/1250120845, https://www.statista.com/statistics/295632/etf-us-net-assets/, and https://www.mordorintelligence.com/industry-reports/us-mutual-funds-industry

12. See https://thedefireport.substack.com/p/makerdao?s=r and https://www.yahoo.com/video/tesla-taps-makerdao-powered-lender-170830750.html

13. See https://www.ubs.com/global/en/media/display-page-ndp/en-20221103-digital-bond.html, https://stm.co/articles/blog/abn-amro-issues-first-tokenized-corporate-bond/, and https://www.coindesk.com/business/2023/02/14/siemens-issues-blockchain-based-euro-denominated-bond-on-polygon-blockchain/

CHAPTER 14

SECURITY TOKEN INDUSTRY TOOLS AND RESOURCES

Security tokens are expansive as they draw on information from any of the verticals described throughout this book and likely more as the industry continues building out. They are complex structures drawing from multiple data sources, including asset audits, trading statistics, and regulatory documents, among other industry-specific sources.

To form a holistic ecosystem, data points stemming from each step in the securitization and tokenization process are welcomed. The goal of this chapter is to highlight the most important data providers and infrastructure networks in the industry as of the time of publication. The more these firms can figure out how to work together, the more likely the industry will progress and gain traction. Expect the following services to be consistent contributors in the coming years to the ever-growing *$32.3 billion* in global financial data spend.[1]

Security Token Market as a Source of Data

As all institutional stock trading platforms rely on data providers like Bloomberg, Thomson Reuters, and Refinitiv, the digital assets markets rely on proper data aggregation to facilitate trades among the many marketplaces. Security Token Market is the go-to data source when it comes to security tokens, much like CoinMarketCap reigns supreme for cryptocurrencies. Tracking more than 200 tokenized assets across a dozen live marketplaces worldwide, STM is agnostic and serves to connect the dots of a fragmented industry.

Given the global real-time nature of security tokens, a trustworthy and reputable site is necessary to bring investors and issuers together, especially as exchanges and trading venues continue to build out and cater to various audiences, including retail investors, institutional asset managers, certain industries such as real estate tokens or pre-IPO company tokens, and varying geographic locations. Security Token Market is the leading brand in the industry, with a highly engaged audience numbering in the tens of thousands of visitors from more than 150 countries each month.

In addition to full data packages including tokenized Real Estate data on both the primary and secondary markets, tokenized stock data, and Arbitrage opportunities, Security Token Market acts as an industry influencer with its numerous media platforms, including the industry-revered Security Token Show. The Security Token Market Twitter account (@stomarket) is the cultural epicenter of the security token industry, delivering high-quality research and validation for the industry, positive support and recognition for developing projects and communities, and attentive engagement within its own community. This commitment to public branding results in hundreds of thousands of recurring impressions across its published content, thought leadership, and collaborative efforts with industry behemoths each month. Leading CEOs, institutions, investors, authors, and professors consistently engage with the firm's daily content.

In order for the full vision of tokenized funds, fund-of-funds, and even singular products to truly come to fruition and rival traditional exchange-traded products, tools like indexes, benchmarks, and derivatives are a must. The most likely solution is to use a data provider or valuation agency of a security token's underlying asset to act as a frequent valuation benchmark. This benchmark can then be matched up against the security token on secondary markets and exchanges, tracked, and displayed by Security Token Market for investors to reference.

This will not only create proper indexing for investors to understand and compare returns, but will also enable the creation of strategies to trade security tokens against their fair market values. For instance, if a token is trading at $50 but the benchmark valuation prints at $55, it can be assumed the token is trading at a discount. A savvy investor or trader may purchase additional tokens at $50 with the assumption that the price will converge on the $55 valuation, thereby providing the investor with a capital gain opportunity.

This type of benchmark functionality can be extremely beneficial for illiquid assets like real estate and private funds, as insight into the holdings are otherwise difficult to read. Having a transparent valuation service that essentially prints benchmarks will bring greater confidence and capabilities to the security token markets, which will unlock the markets and allow them to flourish more than they would *sans* publicly accessible benchmarks. This service and capability can be developed by firms such as data oracle Inveniam.

Inveniam

With more than $25 billion in onboarded assets as of Q2 2022 (up from $1 billion in November 2021), Inveniam is carving a lane for itself as the global blockchain-based oracle for assets of all kinds in both the private and public markets. Essentially, Inveniam's operating system accepts documents ranging from valuations and appraisals to audits to rent rolls to balance sheets and more for assets onboarded to its platform. It documents and credentials these data documents on a blockchain like Ethereum, Avalanche, or Accumulate.

This enables asset owners, investors, and associated parties such as auditors and valuation agencies to seamlessly view and understand the flow of records over time, thus providing efficiencies to cumbersome processes such as annual appraisals and assessments. With this foundation in place, Inveniam can also leverage its proprietary artificial intelligence programming to observe external and third-party inputs to help value certain assets. For example, a commercial real estate property onboarded to Inveniam will have all the proper documents in place for itself, while also generating a monthly or periodic valuation based on factors such as the surrounding neighborhood valuations, traffic, trends, and comparable sales. This brings a more frequent and transparent valuation to the asset, ensuring it is always "sale ready" at the fair market value.

Inveniam's proprietary technology and patents also enable asset owners to improve their accounting categorization from Level 3 assets to Level 2 assets.

- Level 2 Asset: Blends observable and unobservable inputs, allowing for *mark-to-market* functionality.
- Level 3 Asset: Mainly unobservable inputs, which are the most illiquid and least transparent type of asset.

With Level 1 assets being the most liquid and publicly observable, such as stocks, bonds, and treasuries, Level 2 assets are a blend of publicly observable and unobservable inputs, such as mortgage-backed securities. The mortgage-backed security can be traded much like a stock, but the underlying value is more opaque as there are a number of unseen or unmeasurable factors affecting their value. For example, investors may see the value of an MBS on a secondary exchange but may not have access to the valuation of every single underlying mortgage and/or asset details of the properties backing those mortgages. This creates a blend of observable inputs (trading price) and unobservable inputs (individual mortgage-level details), which is what makes it a Level 2 asset.

When assets such as real estate properties, private investment funds, and private credit are onboarded to Inveniam, the firm works with the proper valuation services and auditors to verify enough details to shift these assets from mostly illiquid and unobservable Level 3 assets to Level 2 assets. In turn, this provides the ability for the Level 2 assets to be marked to market and achieve more frequent valuations and liquidity opportunities.[2]

The benefits of the transition from Level 3 to Level 2 include improved financing rates, more frequent valuations, lower capital reserve requirements, and higher asset ratings (if applicable). Since Inveniam manages assets on-chain via blockchain technology, the transparency between asset owners, investors, and third parties typically makes lenders, buyers, and sellers more comfortable, thus enabling overall better terms. Moreover, the mark-to-market benefits mean lenders and owners can manage or exit a position with greater precision and a more cushioned backstop, which contributes to more favorable financing terms and asset quality rating.

Rather than buying one's *own* data from a data service as in the Web 2.0 world (where a centralized firm like Amazon, Dropbox, or iCloud owns all onboarded or uploaded data), Inveniam allows asset owners and authorized parties to own their own data. They're free to resell, monetize, or work with the data however they deem fit. This is the forward-looking Web 3.0 thesis.

The demand for Inveniam's services will likely grow exponentially in the coming years as investment managers and property owners compete to differentiate themselves and begin operating in the FinTech field, especially as LPs demand greater automation of operational processes to reduce expenses. The standard property and portfolio management process is becoming bland, and while returns are returns, competition for capital from external investors requires a vision of the future, not one rooted in the past.[3]

What Inveniam can do for these portfolio managers and property owners is absorb all data from Valuation/Appraisal, Audit, and peripheral factors that may contribute to the valuation of each asset. It allows double-sided transparency through its proprietary and patented technology so that both asset owners and investors could potentially gain access to real-time *Fair Market Value* metrics and relevant data. Most importantly, Inveniam shifts the ownership of data from third parties back to the asset owners themselves, enabling another avenue of monetization, reduced expenses, and operational efficiencies.

Ovenue

Ovenue[TM] ("Avenue for Revenue") is a deep technology platform that also bridges the gap between real-world assets and DeFi. Using its own proprietary AI-based valuation engine in conjunction with its blockchain-based solutions, Ovenue offers a technology protocol for real-world asset valuation, tokenization, and monetization. The journey for an asset owner is as follows:

- Identification: Owners select their desired asset(s) to onboard, both tangible and intangible.
- Valuation: Valuation software enables asset owners to generate a Fair Market Value based on historical and predictive metrics to enhance the fidelity and usability of real-world asset valuation.
- Isolation: Asset owners may separate their assets into Special Purpose Vehicles (SPVs) for legal cleanliness.
- Tokenization: Assets are converted into asset-backed tokens, creating a digital twin of the asset on the blockchain.
- Monetization: Assets can be listed in an open marketplace or a private Web 3.0 commerce storefront for sales or collateralization through Ovenue Finance or through compatible DeFi applications.

Ovenue's platform can be used for a unique asset range including intangible assets and intellectual property like contracts, franchise agreements, copyright, trademarked brands, receivables, royalty deals, commodities and natural resources, venture capital and private equity, real estate, infrastructure, fixed income, and more.

At the end of 2022, Ovenue has over USD 400 million of Tokenized Assets Valued (TAV) on its marketplace and platform, including luxury condos, reforestation rights, published novel rights, consultation agreements and franchising rights.[4]

Ovenue offers a very unique solution that could also complement an issuer raising capital via security token offers (STO) if the asset owner chooses to do so. Should the asset owner wish to raise fresh capital via Security Token under Reg CF, Reg D, or Reg A, for example, they can issue a security token offering while also still leveraging Ovenue's services on tangible and intangible assets for either 1) additional or bridge financing, or 2) transparency into its asset(s) valuation, which may prove to strengthen the pitch to investors throughout the capital raise.

Tokenization Resources

Relevance of on-chain asset tokenization in 'crypto winter'

In 2022, one of the leading marketplaces for security tokens in Singapore called ADDX teamed up with Boston Consulting Group to do the research on tokenization. Some compelling results included 10 percent of the entire securities industry being tokenized by the year 2030.[5]

State of Security Tokens

One of the authors, Peter Gaffney, has been writing an annual state of the market report since 2021. It provides details on exactly what has happened in the security token industry, including the rise of security tokens in 2021, their growth in 2022, and their adoption by Wall Street in 2023. These reports can be found at https://reports.STM.co or at https://securitytokenadvisors.com.

Office Hours with Gary Gensler

During his tenure as Chairman of the SEC, Gary Gensler began releasing what can be described as explainer videos about financial markets. Some of these videos are clearly addressed to the crypto industry with the aim of general investor protection through education. It's worth noting that the Chairman previously taught a class on blockchain at the Massachusetts Institute of Technology. The videos range from warnings about celebrity-promoted investment offerings to explaining lending crypto platforms, along with other general market information. Learn more at https://www.sec.gov/news/sec-videos/office-hours-gary-gensler.

General Crypto Educational Tools and Publications

Podcasts

Podcasts are a great way to learn more information about the industry by hearing from industry experts on current events and concepts that are relevant to the current market cycles.

- The Security Token Show: https://www.youtube.com/@ SecurityTokenMarket/videos
- Bankless Podcast: https://www.youtube.com/@Bankless
- The Money Movement: https://www.youtube.com/@TheMoneyMovement
- What Bitcoin Did: https://www.whatbitcoindid.com/
- On the Brink with Castle Island: https:// onthebrink-podcast.com/

Industry Publications

News and media platforms cover the top headlines in the market, and it is crucial to find reputable companies that focus on unbiased coverage. The best way to stay informed is to consult multiple sources of information.

- Blockchain.com
- BlockWorks.co
- CoinDesk.com
- CoinTelegraph.com
- Crypto.com
- Securities.io
- TheBlock.co
- Crowdfundinsider.com
- Decrypt.co

Research Terminals

Headlines can provide perspective, but the data tells the full story. Use research terminals to better understand how the markets are moving and make your own conclusions.

- STM.co
- IntoTheBlock.com
- Messari.io

- DelphiDigital.io
- Arcana.io
- CoinMarketCap.com
- CoinGecko.com
- Dune.com

Industry Associations

A company cannot service an entire industry on its own. Instead, collective networks of synergistic businesses offer complementary services to build an ecosystem that properly delivers value across the lifecycle of an asset.

- STA Success Network: success.securitytokenadvisors.com
- Japan Security Token Association: https://securitytoken.or.jp/en
- The Blockchain Association: https://theblockchainassociation.org/

Book Recommendations

Published authors lend expertise and academic authority to this industry, and create a pathway for institutions to build a framework for developing the next generation of innovators.

- *Digital Finance* by Baxter Hines.
- *The STO Financial Revolution: How Security Tokens Change Businesses Forever* - 3rd Edition by Alex Nascimento.
- *Bitcoin Billionaires: A True Story of Genius, Betrayal and Redemption* by Ben Mezrich.

Finally, though not a book, we highly recommend you read the Original Bitcoin Whitepaper by Satoshi Nakamoto.[6]

NOTES

1. See https://www.prnewswire.com/news-releases/global-spend-on-financial-market-data-totals-a-record-33-2-billion-in-2020--rising-5-9-on-demand-for-pricing-reference-and-portfolio-management-data---new-burton-taylor-report-301264995.html

2. See https://www.plantemoran.com/explore-our-thinking/insight/2015/05/thats-not-fair-or-is-it-fair-value-explained

3. See https://www.linkedin.com/feed/update/urn:li:activity:6846530626993057794/

4. See https://ovenue.com/ and https://blog.securitytokenadvisors.com/security-token-advisors-infrastructure-client-and-vendor-ovenue-brings-real-world-asset-valuation-c2983740aa25

5. See https://web-assets.bcg.com/1e/a2/5b5f2b7e42dfad2cb3113a291222/on-chain-asset-tokenization.pdf

6. See https://www.bitcoin.com/satoshi-archive/whitepaper/

GLOSSARY OF TERMS

2017 ICO Era: Time period describing the 2017 bull market and the rise and fall of the popular Initial Coin Offering (ICO) token sales. In a public offering, companies were able to raise funds via ICO to build technology solutions and sold a digital token to represent shares. These tokens were often spent inside games and apps, but relied on strict supply and demand principles to drive value to holders. Due to the popularity of these offerings, billions were invested into these assets, and many investors received exponential gains in a matter of days, weeks, or months after investing. Due to the difficulty in creating economically productive networks, many of these tokens failed to perform positively on the secondary market, and developed a negative reputation for attracting speculators and dubious actors seeking to take advantage of unknowing customers. In time, regulatory bodies and enforcement agencies began to prosecute bad actors, and the hype began to subside by early 2018.

2019 Defi Summer: Time period describing the 2019 bull market and the evolution of smart contract technology, specifically on the Ethereum network. In what was described by David Hoffman of Bankless as a "Money Game," developers and mathematicians began building smart contract solutions that facilitated many of the world's banking activities through crypto testnets. Collateralized lending, shareholder governance, derivative trading, mass securitization, rehypothecation, market making, liquidity mining, and exchange platforms were all developed using immutable, self-executing code. Most of these platforms aimed to provide decentralized services, allowing for auditable code and pro rata governance through a token or decentralized autonomous organization.

2021 NFT Era: Time period describing the 2021 bull market and the mass adoption of nonfungible tokens (NFTs) by public audiences. With record high inflation around the world during the economic fallout from the COVID-19 pandemic, the crypto market saw many all-time highs, including Bitcoin reaching a peak of more than $68,000. The speculative market was spearheaded by digital art traded on platforms such as Opensea, topping $17B in volume in 2021. The NFT technology blossomed into many use cases in verifying identity, authenticity, and building authorized access to unique content and opportunities. This technology is still being used and optimized across many industries seeking to store identification metadata on blockchains.

51% Attack: In a Proof-of-Work system, consensus is reached through a 'majority rules' system, meaning decisions are codified through approval from a majority of the processing power being contributed to the network. In this way, if an adverse party gained control of a majority (51 percent or more) of the processing power of the entire network, either through brute force scaling or a denial of service (DDoS) attack, then that party has full control over the decisions inside of the network, and therefore could seize assets, make core changes, or even shut down the entire operation. This has consistently been an existential threat to PoW mechanisms because as technology improves exponentially, so do existential threats through quantum computing, energy constraints, or DDoS attacks, all of which present real risks to miners and investors.

Aave (*AAVE*): The Aave platform is a decentralized smart contract protocol built to allow users to receive collateralized loans on their assets. Using its native *AAVE* token, users can elect to govern the yields and general protocol operation. Without leveraging credit history as a factor for interest rates, Aave requires overcollateralized loans, where users must deposit a higher nominal (base) value of asset than what is received in a loan. Aave traditionally quotes loans in *ETH* terms, regardless of the currency being used as leverage.

Accredited Investor: An investor, either an individual or entity, that is eligible to invest in generally most private placements and are treated differently from retail investors known as non-accredited investors. As defined by the SEC, an accredited investor in the United States is an individual who qualifies a specified income or wealth threshold. As for wealth thresholds, an individual must have a net worth of at least $1 million, excluding their primary residence. The income test requires the individual to be making income over $200,000 per year in each of the prior two years, with an expectation for this to continue in the future. In combination with a spouse or partner, the investor must make $300,000 in combined income. If a corporation seeks accreditation, it must have either $5 million in investment assets, or all equity holders in the entity must be accredited. Other means of accreditation for individuals and corporations include financial sophistication, including certain broker-dealer licensure and professional criteria. Roughly 10 percent of Americans qualify as accredited investors and less than 1 percent of the population participates in the private exemptions designated to them.

Accrued Interest: Uncollected interest from a fixed income or yield-bearing instrument, which is represented as the aggregate of coupon payments yet to be distributed by the issuer. It consists of a base yield and any additional variable interest, whether through additional profits or returns over the holding period.

Accumulate: The act of increasing holdings in a specific asset class. *Accumulation* results in increased *exposure* to the asset class, presenting a higher profit or loss on investment following a change in price.

ACH Transfer: Electronic money transfer using the bank-to-bank Automated Clearing House (ACH) Network. Unlike a wire transfer, using an ACH transfer is often free due to the ACH Network's batch processing, where many individual transactions can be completed in one swift transfer between Nacha, the intermediary operating the ACH Network, and each customer's respective bank.

Aggregator: Digital assets protocols have unique liquidity pools that power the trading activity for the underlying platform. *Aggregators* integrate across pools to capture the best prices by 'skimming off the top' of each platform to reduce *slippage* in any given pool. This process can be optimized with algorithmic trading contracts or by increasing the number of pools and subsequent liquidity of an asset.

Airdrop: With enhanced transparency for wallet addresses that own every token in an economy, issuers are able to reward their largest holders and most active users by programmatically releasing new or additional tokens via smart contracts. Similar to an automated stock dividend, airdrops can range from NFTs to utility tokens or even governance tokens for a network. Popularized by companies like Uniswap, which released its $UNI governance token to any user of the viral Decentralized Exchange prior to a specified *snapshot* date, or *Bored Ape Yacht Club* via their *APE* token, these tokens were gifted to wallets and could then be purchased or sold on a secondary market.

Algorithm: Mathematical formulas built to verify and execute a set of rules or processes set forth by a function or protocol. Algorithms are calculations often solved by computer programs, either processed directly through a node's processor (in a Proof-of-Work system) or in cloud-based computing systems.

Algorithmic Stablecoin: A crypto asset backed by a complex system of smart contracts and financial engineering, designed to maintain a stable price, often pegged to a traditional fiat currency, like the US Dollar, Japanese Yen, or Chinese Yuan. While many algorithms have been developed, they are much more vulnerable to collapse due to no true asset backing the price. With the only value provided to investors being a stable price, a deviation from the pegged price often results in a *death spiral*, an economic phenomenon detailing the collapse of an asset's value through a vicious cycle of negative reinforcement, as seen famously by TerraLuna's *UST* stablecoin collapse in 2022.

Algorithmic Trading: Process of using automated trading programs to analyze multivariable data to buy and sell assets on a liquid market. Unlike traditional trading, where an investor researches an investment opportunity themselves, algorithmic trading processes many investments at the same time and can execute many investment strategies concurrently. Algorithmic trading allows investment firms to capitalize on small movements in the market by increasing the amount of trades they are able to make in a given time period. Algorithmic trading facilitates the *high-frequency trading* environment seen in the trading markets today.

Allocation: A defined budget to be spent or invested by a company or individual.

All-Time High: The highest price at which an asset has ever been priced on a secondary market.

All-Time Low: The lowest price at which an asset has ever been priced on a secondary market.

Alpha Coefficient: Term used to measure the investment return of an asset compared to the average returns of the market.

Altcoin: Generally used as a descriptive term for any cryptocurrency that is not Bitcoin. Originally coined during the ICO Era of 2017.

Alternative Trading System (ATS): Regulatory standard established by the United States, acting as a requirement to enable a licensed broker-dealer to trade securities on a secondary market. ATS systems traditionally use an *order book* to provide liquidity to investors on their platforms. The ATS license is not an exchange, and is generally considered the 'lite' version of National Exchange licenses held by firms like the New York Stock Exchange, NASDAQ, or CBOE.

American CryptoFed DAO: The first legally recognized DAO in the United States on July 4, 2021.

Amortizing: Distribution of debt in equal payments across the full term of a loan. Amortization also be applied in accounting for factoring in depreciation of assets.

Anchorage Digital: Anchorage Digital is a digital asset custodian and infrastructure provider for cryptocurrency assets and products. It is notable for its landmark approval as the first federally chartered cryptocurrency bank, for which it received licensed approval by the Office of the Comptroller of the Currency in 2021.

Angel Investor: An individual accredited investor who specializes in investing in early-stage companies and backing entrepreneurs, often in exchange for equity in the company. These investors typically are investing their own money, but may also participate in a *syndicate* of investors, allowing them to acquire a larger stake in a business as a group.

Annual Percentage Rate (APR): The interest rate to be paid on a loan or debt offering factored over a full year. Some interest rates are described in daily, monthly, or quarterly terms, so *APR* standardizes the yield for more effective comparison.

Annual Percentage Yield (APY): The interest rate received on an investment with consistent cash flows factored over a full year. Some interest rates are described in daily, monthly, or quarterly terms, so *APY* standardizes the yield for more effective comparison.

Application Programing Interface (API): Set of functions built to allow outside parties to access data and information. Used by companies to connect its backend databases with new data sources and with customers and applications.

Apple ($AAPL): American multinational technology company that creates consumer technology like computers, cell phones, and accessories. $AAPL stock represents one of the largest stocks by market capitalization on the NASDAQ.

Arbitrage: The act of simultaneously purchasing and selling a share of an asset or derivative on a secondary market in order to capitalize on the difference in price between liquidity pools. Arbitrage trades represent 'risk-free' trades, if executed properly, as trades are structured to minimize exposure to the underlying asset as much as possible. In an ideal scenario, both the *buy* and the *sell* occur at the same time, netting an investor with profit from the *spread* between the two trades.

Arbitrum: Arbitrum is an Ethereum scaling solution that uses optimistic roll-ups to operate with the goal of scaling the Ethereum network to 40,000 transactions-per-second capabilities at a price of mere cents per transaction given its bundling and batching mechanism.

Arca Treasury Fund ($ArCoin): Tokenized treasury fund created by digital asset manager Arca. The price of the $ArCoin token is pegged at $1.00, consisting of a basket of treasury assets managed by the fund, which pays investors a variable yield each year. $ArCoin pioneered the token redemption model, allowing for shareholders to retire old shares for a redemption price.

Artificial Intelligence: Field of technology centered around building computational systems to perform tasks requiring advanced comprehension, correlation, pattern-recognition, and other abstract processing. The field has expanded dramatically in recent years as machine learning, neural networks, and artificial general intelligence have all become separate fields of study with wide-reaching applications worldwide.

Asset: Any valuable thing that can represent hard assets or digital assets across any ecosystem.

Assets Under Management (AUM): Measure of the total market value of the financial assets held in an individual, fund, or institutional portfolio. It's an important metric used to compare the relative size of assets managers, irrespective of industry, jurisdiction, or management fees.

Atomic Swap: The process of automatically swapping two digital assets using smart contracts in a peer-to-peer network without the oversight of a third party.

Auction: Public sale of an asset or property to the highest bidder.

Automated Market Maker (AMM): Programmatic or algorithmically enforced platforms built to enable trading of assets in an ecosystem. Unique pricing functions allow the AMM to evaluate the depth of a liquidity pool, and adjust the market price accordingly to incentivize buying or selling of an asset in high demand. *Liquidity pools* power the trading pairs inside of the smart contract applications, which allow users to contribute resources to the trading pair to ease the friction of exchange for other users, and are paid a portion of the transaction fees inside of the platform as a reward.

Automated Portfolio Manager: Programmatic or algorithmically enforced trading strategies built to enforce a trading thesis to deliver returns to investors. Long sets of back-tested data are used to test the logic of the algorithms and determine the projected forward-looking returns for investors depositing money into the system. Larger investment totals allow for more complex investment decisions, which leverage options, derivatives, and futures products to hedge risk and time market trades based on micro adjustments in the market.

Automation: Using technologies such as smart contracts and programming to automatically execute tasks without the need for human oversight. Automation allows for quicker speeds and lower costs.

Avalanche (*AVAX*): A Layer 1 blockchain and smart contract platform. Built on an Ethereum Virtual Machine (EVM), the blockchain can take advantage of smart contracts built on solidity while leveraging a separate consensus mechanism to support faster and cheaper transactions than Ethereum. The Avalanche solution consists of separate blockchains for different needs, called subnets, that allow multivariable on-chain networks to coexist without competing for resources. *AVAX* represents the blockchain's native transactional currency, which was sold using the Reg D and Reg S private securities fundraising exemptions.

Backtesting: The process of testing an algorithmic model by using historical data to measure results in a test environment. This sequence allows for manual tweaks and improvements to be made before the production version is implemented in real-time trading scenarios.

Backward Compatibility: Technology that can be connected and integrated with previous versions, allowing for interoperability between generations and cross-platform coordination.

Badger Finance (*BADGER*): BadgerDAO is a decentralized organization that governs the Badger Finance protocol, which acts as an aggregated market maker across staking pools. Staking and lending the *BADGER* governance token across the protocol's vaults allows for users to capitalize on additional interest on their holdings.

Bahamian Sand Dollar: One of the first Central Bank Digital Currencies (CBDC) issued by an internationally-recognized country. The Bahamian Sand Dollar token (BSD) is backed 1:1 to the Bahamian dollar (BSD), which is and has been pegged to the US dollar.

Balancer (*BAL*): Balancer is a DeFi platform that leverages automated portfolio management and automated market making to create liquidity in the crypto economy. Balancer's many pools rebalances passive investment portfolios of different baskets of assets. Balancer led innovation in multi-asset liquidity pools, allowing liquidity providers to diversify their exposure across a set of digital assets, thereby decreasing the risk of impermanent loss in the portfolio. The native *BAL* tokens are used to pay yields and staking rewards while acting as a governance token for the protocol, allowing shareholders to vote on yields and behaviors across the smart contract network.

Bandwidth: The maximum throughput in a system. Traditionally used to describe the maximum rate of data that can be transmitted in a network.

Bank: A regulated institution licensed to store money on behalf of others and profit on lending out those funds to other investors. Using fractionalized reserve strategies, licensed banks must keep a certain portion of their total funds in accessible cash accounts to limit their exposure to insolvency. Many cryptocurrency exchanges and lending institutions perform banking services, and many are not currently regulated entities, which puts investor money at risk. This is one of the main focuses around regulatory crackdowns in the industry.

Bank Run: A financial event where customers try to retrieve their assets all at the same time from a bank or financial institution due to a scare caused by public news or private rumors questioning whether those assets are safe and available.

Base Currency: The first of two assets in a trading pair, used to determine the market price of a *quoted currency*, often represented by only a few of the most common and liquid currencies for proper comparison across asset classes and trading platforms.

Bear Market: Term used to describe cool downs and sell offs in the economy. Bear markets lead to increased selling pressure in the market, which in turn causes asset prices to depreciate and thinner liquidity. *Bear market* exists to describe the opposite trading scenario as a *bull market*, where there is high demand.

Beta Coefficient: Term used to measure the volatility of an asset compared to the average risk of the market.

Bid-Ask Spread: The difference in value between the highest price at which a buyer is willing to purchase an asset and the lowest price a seller is willing to accept for an asset. Market makers profit off the spread by adjusting the difference between the bid price and the ask price to account for the risk of being stuck with illiquid shares. Traditionally, the more liquid an asset is on a secondary market, the 'shorter' the spread is because market makers are not taking as much risk to resell the asset. Bid/ask spreads exist in centralized order books as well and need to be calculated manually because market makers do not exist in these models. The midpoint between the Bid/Ask spread is often referred to as the *Market Price*.

Binance (*BNB*): International cryptocurrency exchange founded in 2017 that became the largest exchange in terms of daily trading volume. The platform lists over 600 tokens, including tokenized stock derivatives, stablecoins, and cryptocurrencies, and leverages its native *BNB* token to act as a base trading pair for all assets on the platform. Binance launched its own blockchain, Binance Smart Chain, which acts as the distributed ledger used to track transactions and smart contract applications inside of the Binance ecosystem

Bitcoin (*BTC*): The first cryptocurrency created by Satoshi Nakamoto, detailed in the Bitcoin Whitepaper in 2008. Bitcoin uses a Proof-of-Work consensus mechanism to reward miners with BTC rewards in exchange for validating transactions through a SHA-256 hash function. Bitcoin is a permissionless, immutable, and transparent payment system, meaning any user can transact with the network as long as they have a connection to the network and a *BTC* wallet. Bitcoin is the largest digital asset by market capitalization, and acts as the 'digital gold' of the Web3 movement.

Bitcoin Cash (*BCH*): A hard fork of the Bitcoin Blockchain pioneered by Roger Ver and Craig Wright in 2017 with a goal to create a more scalable transactional system while leveraging the security and trustworthiness of the Bitcoin blockchain. This offshoot Bitcoin product had limited developer and investor support, and later experienced its own hard fork, splitting between *BCH* and *BSV* in late 2018.

Bitfinex: Cryptocurrency exchange owned and operated by iFinex Inc. registered in the British Virgin Islands. Bitfinex has been a central player in cryptocurrency exchange since 2013. The exchange has faced some regulatory challenges, including lawsuits from regulators focused on monitoring and regulating global monetary exchange.

Blacklist: A list of individuals, companies, or wallet addresses prohibited from accessing or transacting within a smart contract system. Often used as fraud protection against hacked or compromised wallets to prevent funds and other assets from being stolen.

Blackrock ($BLK): World's largest asset manager, with over $10T in assets under management as of January 2022. The firm has consistently been supportive of the cryptocurrency industry, offering clients direct and indirect exposure to the industry.

Black Hat: An individual or organization that hacks into online protocols and computer systems with malicious or criminal intent.

Block: A series of transactions verified by independent nodes in a system that are translated and communicated to all parties in the network. A block is finalized by a verification process, which is defined by a specific protocol's *consensus mechanism*. Examples include Proof-of-Work, which requires mathematical computation to verify, while Proof-of-Stake requires elected delegates to approve specific blocks.

Block Explorer: Online database providing records of blockchain data, including transaction fees, addresses, and additional metadata.

Block Halving: The programmatic reduction of block rewards established in a Proof-of-Work mining economy. In most PoW economics, block rewards are reduced over time to create a deflationary supply, which is usually expected to be outperformed by appreciation of the underlying asset.

Block Reward: The predetermined reward paid out to a miner for solving the hash of a block on a blockchain. This is the main economic incentive for nodes to contribute computing resources to validate blockchain transactions. Block rewards are provided to miners in Proof-of-Work systems to compensate for electricity and hardware costs in running mining infrastructure.

Blockchain: Distributed ledger technology using peer-to-peer hashing computational mechanisms to track a series transactions in a given system. *Blocks* represent a series of transactions verified by independent nodes in a system that are translated and communicated to all parties in the network. These blocks are *chained* together using quantitative algorithms, preventing changes in the historical record. The technology is used to record data in a decentralized manner, allowing for more complex programs to utilize global data without needing to trust any given counterparty.

Blockchain Bridge: Smart contract application build to create interoperability between blockchain protocols. Users lock assets in the smart contract vault, which in turn mints a new asset of the same value on the new blockchain. This allows users to transfer assets to applications on separate blockchains.

Blockchain Capital ($BCAP): One of the earliest blockchain venture fund managers, founded by Brock Pierce, Brad Stephens, and Bart Stephens in 2013. The company has invested in more than 70 companies with over $275M in assets under management. The company was also one of the first venture capital security token issuers, selling 20 percent of their third fund, called the Blockchain Capital III Digital Liquid Venture Fund as a security token offering. This token now trades on multiple secondary markets in the US.

Blockchain Protocol: Rules and restrictions built on top of a distributed ledger or blockchain to govern how computational systems reach consensus. Maintains and allows for the adjustment of the security and scalability of a network.

Blockstream: Blockchain technology company headquartered in Canada. Led by co-founder Adam Beck, the company creates Bitcoin and digital asset products including a large-scale BTC mining operation, development on Liquid Network, and even satellites used to transmit the Bitcoin blockchain into space.

Blockstream Mining Note ($BMN1): Leading Bitcoin mining company Blockstream issued the first Bitcoin mining security token

($BMN1) in 2021. The token represents a fixed set of hashing power to be mined over a three-year period, netting investors Bitcoin yield at a significantly lower price per coin than buying Bitcoin on the open market. The $BMN1 token raised over $40M USD over eight tranches and has been one of the most successful fundraisers in the industry.

Board of Directors: Elected governing body of a company that sets strategy and oversees the company's management. This group, traditionally averaging between 7–14 individuals in public companies, consists of outside investors and advisors who seek to serve in the best interests of shareholders.

Board Seat: Elected or appointed position on the board of directors, providing a board member with voting rights over the strategic direction of a company. Board members have a fiduciary duty to act in the best interest of the shareholders they represent.

Bond: A class of security representing debt incurred by an issuer with an expectation of repayment in addition to a premium in the form of interest payments. The terms of the instrument can vary from issuer to issuer, but most debt products are structured with fixed interval repayment periods over a series of weeks, months, or years. Bonds are evaluated by rating agencies and are graded on a scale from AAA to D. A higher grade signals to investors the debt is more likely to be repaid, as it is less risky, and therefore an investor should feel comfortable accepting less interest in exchange for their upfront investment. Due to the general stability of the debt markets, these assets are viewed as a much safer option than investing in the stock market or real estate, and the total bond industry is estimated to be over $100T worldwide, which is significantly larger than other asset classes like equities or real estate.

Bored Ape Yacht Club (BAYC): Popular NFT art collection depicted by a series of 10,000 images of apes, all equipped with randomized traits (hats, mouth style, accessories, and so on). Created by Yuga Labs, *BAYC* captured the world by storm, skyrocketing from a mint price of 0.5ETH to highs of more than 100 ETH. Subsequent mints, including *Bored Ape Kennel Club (BAKC)* and *Mutant Ape Yacht Club (MAYC)* saw similar success.

Boston Options Exchange (BOX): Equity options market providing order matching services to brokers and investors. BOX is a subsidiary company of Nasdaq BX, Inc. BOX entered into a joint venture with tZERO to build the *Boston Security Token Exchange*, a US licensed national exchange focused on trading blockchain-based securities. As of 2022, the exchange license has been approved for traditional securities trading.

Boston Security Token Exchange (BSTX): The first national exchange to be approved by the SEC to propose blockchain-based settlements and trades. BSTX is a joint venture between tZERO and the Boston Options Exchange (BOX) to make strides towards the vision of issuing stocks, bonds, ETFs, and security tokens all in one marketplace. ETFs, for instance, can only be issued on national exchanges, not ATSs, which limits that vision under the existing ATS-driven landscape.

"Brick and Mortar" Business: Term referring to businesses that traditionally operate in person in a conventional manner instead of over the internet.

Broker-Dealer: Individual or company that trades securities to a network of investors on behalf of itself or its customers. A *broker-dealer* is paid a commission of the funds raised, and are required to be licensed by FINRA in the US and other regulators worldwide depending on what country in which the business is operating and paying taxes.

Bubble: Term used to describe an unusual or unsustainable economic environment, often headlined by speculation and a collective fear of missing out on the current investment opportunities. Due to their volatile nature, these are often short-lived scenarios.

Bug: Small glitches or errors in a technology's codebase, causing cosmetic or operational problems for a company or application. Usually corrected in regular technology updates published by developers, known as *patches*.

Bug Bounty: A reward offered to a *white hat* hacker for discovering critical errors or vulnerabilities in a computational system.

Bull Market: Term used to describe market peaks and strong economic performance. Bull markets lead to increased buying pressure in the market, which in turn causes asset prices to appreciate and deeper liquidity. *Bull market* exists to describe the opposite trading scenario as a *bear market*.

Call Option: Contract between two parties to exchange a security at a predetermined price. When purchasing a call option on a security, an investor selects a price at which they are willing to buy a security and the term they are seeking before the option expires. Options traditionally come in bundles of 100 shares.

Candlestick: Graphic depiction of an asset's price movements over a period of time. Using a single icon, a candlestick communicates an asset's high, low, open, and close price. Candlestick charts display these metrics over a specified period of time to better communicate the movement of an asset throughout the entire trading window.

Capital Gains: Profits made on investments that have appreciated in value over a period of time. All asset sales resulting in a profit from selling at a higher price than the price at which the asset was purchased, ranging from stocks and bonds to homes and jewelry, are considered capital gains and are taxed as income, with breaks given for long-term investments and holdings.

Capital Loss: Losses incurred on investments that have depreciated in value over a period of time. All asset sales resulting in a loss from selling at a lower price than the price at which the asset was purchased, ranging from stocks and bonds to homes and jewelry, create a capital loss which can be used to offset capital gains for tax purposes.

Capital Market: Financial market that enables the purchase and sale of equities and long-term debt. Can refer to country-specific economies or used to identify the global trading market. Capital markets can also be broken down into private and public markets.

Cash Flow: Stream of money transferred in and out of a company on a consistent basis. Cash payments collected as revenue would be considered inflows, while expenses are considered outflows. Free cash flow (FCF) calculates net inflows from normal business activities after subtracting total outflows over a period.

Central Bank: Financial institution that has control over the monetary policy for a nation or group of nations.

Central Bank Digital Currency (CBDC): A digital form of central-bank-issued currency that is issued and transacted on a blockchain.

Centralized: A relatively small group of individuals or organizations that make decisions on behalf of a larger community. Delegates can be selected through election processes by contributing assets or a variety of other means. These systems benefit from streamlined internal communication, but often suffer without diverse inputs from a larger cohort in a democratic coordination.

Centralized Exchange: A platform to exchange assets that is controlled by one central party. Financial licenses and regulations apply in the country of business in which the exchange operates, and offers liquidity services though market making and investor relations strategies.

Centralized Finance (CeFi): Refers to the legacy financial markets that prioritize efficiency and scale over transparency and iteration. Economic incentives drive decision making that creates identifiable bottlenecks through regulatory licensure, capital contributions, and other material requirements. Third-party intermediaries known as *middlemen* add additional variable expenses that reduce business margins as well as a system's flexibility with respect to new ideas and practices.

Chainlink (*LINK*): Decentralized oracle that stores and transmits data to provide blockchain-verified data feeds to users. The platform aggregates off-chain data sources though a series of nodes acting as the on ramp for new datasets. Uses native currency *LINK* as the primary means of transaction within the network.

Chicago Board of Options Exchanges (CBOE): Largest United States options exchange based in Chicago, IL. The company was founded in 1973 and offers options for thousands of securities including equities, stock indices, and exchange-traded funds.

Child Chain: Additional branched blockchain networks created by a protocol to enforce privacy between unique blockchain ledgers. All child chains operate consistent with the consensus mechanisms and rules of the blockchain protocol, but differences including transaction speed, privacy, and application support may vary for an individual child chain.

Circulating Supply: The number of coins or tokens of a specific asset that are publicly available to buy and sell. If an allocation of tokens is available to trade on a secondary market, it is often considered in circulation calculations. Company treasuries or allocations owned by insiders are traditionally not considered in the circulating supply.

Coin: Term used to describe a singular unit of account for digital assets and cryptocurrencies that was popularized in the *2017 ICO Era.*

Coinbase ($COIN): US-based cryptocurrency exchange that became the first digital asset exchange to go public on the Nasdaq stock exchange in April 2021.

CoinDesk: Cryptocurrency media company covering Bitcoin and other digital currencies. Acquired by Digital Currency Group in 2016.

Cold Wallet: Offline hardware wallet used to store digital assets including cryptocurrencies, NFTs, and security tokens. Private keys are stored inside the physical storage, which works in tandem with proprietary software to access the stored assets for transfer or exchange. Hard wallets are not connected to the internet until connected to a computer or appropriate device to prevent outside actors from accessing the protected assets. Generally considered the safest way to store and protect cryptocurrencies and other immutably held digital assets.

Collateral: Assets pledged in a loan that can be claimed by a lender in the event of a default by the borrower. Different types of loans have different collateralization requirements. Cryptocurrency lending has standardized *overcollateralized* loans to protect against market volatility, requiring a larger pool of assets than what is being provided in the loan. *Undercollateralized* or *unsecured* loans do exist, but they present significant risk for lenders and often come with lower limits and higher rates.

Collateralization Ratio: The ratio of collateral to debt a borrower is offering. Often this ratio is tied to a myriad of factors including the risk profile of the underlying assets, the term and size of the loan, and the current liquidity of a lending pool.

Collateralized Debt Positions (CDP): Defined as a collateralized loan by *MakerDAO*, a CDP is a smart contract system that locks a user's collateral in a protocol and issues a loan in the form of the DAI stablecoin. Not to be confused with a *Collateralized Debt Obligation*, which is a type of financial product backed by a pool of loans.

Collateralized Stablecoin: A crypto asset backed by real assets and investments, designed to maintain a stable price, often pegged to a traditional fiat currency, like the US Dollar, Japanese Yen, or Chinese Yuan. While not always entirely backed by the true fiat currency represented by the peg, responsible stablecoin issuers maintain a very low-risk portfolio of treasury assets and bonds. Without a proper proof-of-reserve system in coordination with a balance sheet to observe an issuer's assets and outstanding liabilities, it is not possible for a customer to be fully confident in a 100 percent collateralized stablecoin, and many controversies have centered around this topic, ranging from Tether's USDT to Circle's USDC.

Collector DAOs: An organization that pools funds together to purchase and issue NFTs. The treasury of assets are governed by a DAO and voting structure often involves tokens used by participants to make decisions as a group.

Commodity: Asset class consisting of raw materials or ingredients used in the production of goods in the economy. Unlike securities, commodities are not considered an investment product and have less stringent rules and compliance requirements worldwide. Rare earth metals such as uranium and agricultural products such as wheat are examples of commodities commonly purchased in *futures markets.*

Composability: The ability for multiple software systems to communicate and interact with each other. This is a dominant ideology in the blockchain industry encouraging companies, protocols, and other developers to build tech solutions that integrate with the larger blockchain ecosystem, thereby allowing for frictionless adoption by users. See *interoperability*.

Compound (*COMP*): Collateralized lending provider offering users yield on staked assets by providing a smart contract protocol enabling lenders and borrowers to leverage staked funds. Powered by the *COMP* governance token.

Computing Power: The amount of output a computational system or miner can calculate in a given time period. Measured in terahashes per second (Th/s) representing 1 trillion (1,000,000,000,000) hashes per second.

Concentration Risk: The measure of exposure to one specific asset, industry, or event in a given portfolio. Excessive concentration can result in extreme volatility and significant losses. Often used to describe the potential pitfalls of an overallocation into an investment opportunity.

Consensus: The act of reaching agreement on a decision or verification of a transaction.

Consensus Mechanism: Different solutions for reaching on-chain consensus including the two most popular solutions, *Proof-of-Work* and *Proof-of-Stake*. Each protocol has nuances in its governance, but many stem from the same few overarching mechanism archetypes.

Constant Product Function: Primary automated market making function pioneered by the *Uniswap* protocol. Defined by the formula $X * Y = K$, where X and Y represent the liquidity pools for two assets being traded on a decentralized exchange. K acts as a constant, measured by the total liquidity of the protocol. Based on these three factors, an asset's price can be determined programmatically.

ConstitutionDAO: Decentralized organization that resolved to purchase one of the thirteen surviving copies of the US Constitution. 17,000 people collectively contributed over $40M to the open auction, but were outbid in the November 2021 Sotheby's auction by hedge fund manager Ken Griffin, whose winning bid was $43.2M.

Corda: Enterprise blockchain technology created by R3 which is used by many banks and institutions to build tokenization products and other distributed ledger applications.

Correlation: Measure of the connection between two events or investments. Relevant when considering the diversity of an investment thesis, many investors strive to build a non-correlated portfolio to prevent concentration *risk*.

Cosmos: Decentralized network of independent blockchains powered by one underlying consensus standard known as Byzantine Fault-Tolerance algorithms.

Coupon: Segment of interest paid on a bond, traditionally expressed as a percentage of the face value of the initial offering, paid in regular intervals throughout the duration of the security.

Craig Wright: Computer engineer and Bitcoin developer who led the *Bitcoin SV* hard fork from *Bitcoin Cash*.

Credit Score: Analyzed historical record of financial activity used by lenders and banks to determine an individual's default risk and associated interest rates to apply to a loan. Expressed in a numerical score in the range of 300-850.

Crypto Capital of the World: Miami, through its cultural acceptance and regulatory support, established a worldwide reputation for being a tech innovation hub in the United States. Powered by Miami Mayor Francis Suarez's zeal in 2020 to encourage venture capital activity during the COVID-19 pandemic, the city became a hotbed for emerging technologies, including fintech, blockchain, and aerospace technology.

***CryptoPunks*:** Popular NFT art collection depicted by a series of 10,000 8-bit pixel portraits, all equipped with randomized traits (hats, mouth style, accessories). Created by Larva Labs in 2017, this collection saw mainstream success in 2020, leading to a boom in NFT related projects over the following eighteen months. The collection was acquired by *BAYC's* creators Yuga Labs in March 2022.

Cryptocurrency: Digital asset used as a method of transferring value between two wallets. Often used as an umbrella term during the *2017 ICO Era* for any token issuance, it is more commonly used to describe network tokens used to interact with protocols in a method familiar to traditional currencies. It uses *cryptography* to mathematically verify transactions transparently.

Cryptography: Field of mathematics evaluating the effectiveness of *encryption* and *algorithms* to secure access to information. It is an important pillar of blockchain technology and critical for creating an *immutable ledger* all parties can access.

***CryptoKitties*:** An Ethereum-based NFT collection notorious for 'clogging' the protocol during the *2017 ICO Era*, this collection of cartoon cats has remained in crypto-industry lore ever since and was one of the first collections to popularize the user of art and gaming in cryptocurrency.

Currency: A base unit of account used in an economic system to facilitate transaction and trade in an efficient manner.

Curve (*CRV*): Ethereum token that powers the Curve.fi decentralized exchange and automated market making protocol.

Custodia Bank: Nationally chartered bank in Wyoming licensed to hold digital assets and cryptocurrencies in custody.

Custodian: A financial institution that holds and manages a customer's assets, including cash and investments, on their behalf to prevent theft or loss of assets. Customer funds may be held physically in cold storage, or digitally through other licensed platforms. Custodians often take agency over its customers' assets, and may seek to insure these assets from government programs and other insurance providers to provide an additional layer of protection. Custodians are regulated firms.

Cybersecurity: Field of expertise revolving around protecting tech and data infrastructure from hacking and unauthorized use by outside parties and potential bad actors. In the blockchain industry, the scope of cybersecurity experts has expanded into financial and economic auditing for automated market making protocols and DeFi applications.

***Dai*:** Algorithmic 1:1 USD stablecoin on the Ethereum blockchain created and managed by MakerDAO. Overcollateralized lending and repayment structure facilitated by smart contracts to allow for borrowing and lending through a decentralized application.

DDoS Attack: A distributed denial-of-service attack is a nefarious attempt to disrupt the normal operations of an internet server by overwhelming a system by flooding the target with fake or synthetic traffic, causing delays or breakdowns in service for normal users.

De Novo: Generalized term used to describe the very first actions of a company or organization.

Death Spiral: A situation in which a bad sequence of events creates a negative feedback loop in an economic system, often leading to a total collapse of a market in a very short period of time.

Debt: A financial instrument involving one party borrowing money or assets from another party at a previously agreed upon interest rate and other terms. The borrower may be required to pay periodic payments over time and must eventually repay their initial loan in addition to the interest rate.

Decentraland (*MANA*): Virtual world browser-based platform that allows for metaverse experiences and interactions. Built on the ethereum blockchain, users can purchase plots of land as NFTs in the native *MANA* cryptocurrency. The land, which is measured as a series of 16 x 16-meter squares, was divided into 90,601 plots at its public launch in February 2020.

Decentralized: A term to describe an organization or operation that is not controlled by any one group or individual, instead managed by a group of separate actors.

Decentralized Application (dApp): A program or product that operates autonomously through a network of smart contracts and market making functions on a blockchain or distributed ledger system.

Decentralized Autonomous Organization (DAO): Legal structure that has no centralized governing body and whose members share a common goal or direction. Voting may be measured using a foundation's governance token, allowing holders to manage interest rate changes, grant programs, and decision-making within the organization and its owned assets.

Decentralized Finance (DeFi): Financial technology built on blockchain protocols that leverage permissionless decentralized applications to replicate traditional financial sequences, transactional systems, and economic processes.

Decentralized Exchange (DEX): Specific decentralized applications that utilize liquidity pools to create permissionless trading markets for cryptocurrencies, security tokens, and digital assets.

Deed: Legal instrument that confirms or passes ownership of a right or interest in a real estate title or property.

Default: The failure to repay a loan or maintain collateral in a leveraged position. A default is followed by the bankruptcy process, in which a person or corporation must liquidate assets to repay outstanding creditors. If the full debt is not repaid, the litigation process evaluates other entities responsible for outstanding obligations.

Demand Surge: A sudden increase in buy-side pressure, often triggered by a recent event.

Derivative Contracts: Financial contract between two parties representing an underlying asset or investment without directly exchanging the asset. Generally considered an independent investment as the price of derivative contracts can diverge significantly from the price of the value of the physical asset.

Digital Assets: Anything existing in the digital world that has value. Usually denominated in a blockchain-based token.

Digital Asset Management: Digital assets can be managed through custodial or noncustodial wallets. A custodial wallet is most commonly operated by exchanges or other centralized parties, allowing customers to trade cheaply or earn interest on their stored assets. Noncustodial wallets can be accessed physically through a hard wallet (also known as cold storage) or via digital wallets such as Metamask.

Dilution: Adding supply to a circulation of assets. It increases the market cap of a trading asset but does not increase an asset's valuation.

Direct Listing: The process of going public by selling existing shares of a company, like employee or treasury shares, instead of creating a new class of stock. This process is usually cheaper than an IPO and does not involve underwriters.

Distributed Ledger: A database synchronized across a decentralized network of computational systems (also known as nodes). The database is accessible by all participants in the network and all changes are tracked and published, providing a layer of transparency in a transactional economy.

Dividend: Distribution of cash flows paid out by a company to its shareholders. Can be a percentage of revenue, profits, or other cash flows. Commonly paid annually or quarterly.

Dollar-Cost Averaging: An investment strategy consisting of periodic and equal amounts of money over a lengthened time frame aimed at slowly increasing asset allocation while decreasing the price impact and average cost per share.

DS-20: Blockchain protocol created by Securitize on the Ethereum blockchain purpose-built for security tokens, allowing for securities to meet compliance requirements on-chain while benefiting from blockchain features such as transferring the asset.

dYdX: A platform providing decentralized margin trading for digital assets, allowing users to receive up to 20x leverage on trades.

Early Adopter: The first customers or users to begin supporting a project well before the general public. Defined as the second tier of the product adoption curve.

Encryption: Converting information and data into code by using formulas that are kept secret to ensure privacy. Without the key to unlock the encryption, a set of raw data cannot be translated back into its original form, thereby preventing unauthorized users from accessing private information.

Equity: An asset defined as shares issued by a company.

ERC-20: A technical standard for creating *fungible tokens* on the Ethereum blockchain. Acts as a base layer protocol for other rules and governance to be applied in order to 'upgrade' the token.

ERC-721: A technical standard for creating *non-fungible tokens* on the Ethereum blockchain. It acts as a base layer protocol for other rules and governance to be applied in order to 'upgrade' the token.

ERC-3643: A technical standard for creating *security tokens* on the Ethereum blockchain. It acts as a base layer protocol for other rules and governance to be applied in order to 'upgrade' the token.

Escrow: Contractual agreement where a trusted third party custodian manages assets on behalf of two or more parties, enforcing conditions agreed upon by all parties prior to the transaction.

Ethereum (*ETH*): Decentralized, open-source blockchain enabling smart contracts and distributed ledger technology. Uses a native cryptocurrency, *ETH*, to power fees and decentralized applications in the network. Conducted one of the first cryptocurrency ICOs in 2014, leading to the 2017 ICO Era.

Ethereum Classic (*ETC*): A previous iteration of the Ethereum network that was a part of a hard fork in July 2016. Operates separately from Ethereum, and uses a native currency, *ETC*, to power fees and decentralized applications in the network.

Euronext: Global stock exchange group centered in the European Financial Sector and headquartered in Amsterdam, Netherlands.

Exchange Traded Fund (ETF): Type of publicly traded investment fund allowing for passive investment into a group of assets that are generally tracked to a specific market index allowing for diversification of a portfolio.

Exchange Tokens: A digital asset native to a cryptocurrency exchange or corresponding blockchain, allowing users to access cheaper trading fees, enhanced liquidity, and other benefits.

Exodus ($EXOD): A digital asset wallet company built in 2015 that services millions of users. It made history as the first Reg A+ fundraise to reach the $75M fundraising goal. As a security token offering, the fundraise trades on secondary markets representing real ownership in the company.

Expected Return: The profit or loss an investor expects to receive based on historical rates of return.

Face Value: Original value of a bond or loan, not including interest and associated fees.

Family Office: Privately held company that handles investment and financial management on behalf of a wealthy family or individual, generally with over $50M in assets diversified across equity, debt, and real estate positions.

FDIC Insurance: A bank account insured by the Federal Deposit Insurance Corporation, a firm responsible for protecting customer deposits in the event of bank failures. All federally chartered bank accounts, like from Bank of America or JP Morgan, are FDIC-qualified and are eligible for a maximum of $250,000 in protection per depositor. FDIC insurance is generally considered the highest form of asset protection for US customers.

Federally Chartered Bank: Commercial bank with an approval from the Office of the Comptroller of the Currency (OCC), a federal agency, rather than a state banking agency. Federal (or national) banks are required to be members of the Federal Reserve System and belong to the Federal Deposit Insurance Corporation.

Fiat Currency: A unit of legal tender in a nation or group of nations that is not backed by a physical commodity or basket of assets. Instead, the value of the currency is determined by faith in the issuing country's government and financial market.

Figure Technologies: Financial services company using their proprietary blockchain solution, Provenance, to create loans, asset management, and payments architecture. The company's headline tokenized product focused on HELOCs (Home Equity Lines of Credit) and now services funds and other security token issuers.

Filecoin (*FIL*): Decentralized storage and computing protocol that raised $200M through an initial coin offering in 2017.

Financial Service Provider: A company facilitating business activities that may include investment, payment, banking, or custody services. Depending on the service provider, state, federal, or international licenses or approvals may be required.

FINRA: The Financial Industry Regulatory Authority is a self-regulatory body that creates and enforces the rules governing all US-registered brokers and broker-dealer firms.

Fixed-Income: A source of revenue standardized in amount and consistent payment schedule. Most commonly valued by utilizing a discounted cash flow model.

FlamingoDAO: A popular investment DAO that turned a $10 million NFT portfolio into a $1 billion dollar value, largely through the purchase of *CryptoPunks* and other top-tier NFT collections. FlamingoDAO governs the decision-making process in buying, selling, holding, or swapping of NFTs. It is one of the first and most prominent leader-less investment organizations. The DAO is limited to a maximum of 100 members at any given time.

Flash Loan: An unsecured or uncollateralized loan often used in arbitrage trading where a user borrows funds and returns the funds in the same smart contract transaction, which is used when moving assets between liquidity pools without affecting an asset's price or slippage rates.

Float: The total amount of outstanding money on a company's balance sheet that is technically owned by a user or customer, but has not been spent or redeemed yet. These assets are not technically owned by the company, but are often used by the institution to earn a passive return.

Floating Rate: An interest rate that changes periodically based on market conditions such as inflation rate, LIBOR, or other benchmark interest rates.

Floor Price: The lowest currently listed price of an NFT in a collection available for purchase. This price is used to determine the current market value of an NFT in the collection, and is used to calculate the total value of an NFT collection.

FTX: Cryptocurrency exchange that faced a high profile bankruptcy and lawsuit in 2022 after reports detailing misuse of assets led to a public discovery of the misappropriation of billions in customer deposits over multiple years..

Fully Diluted Supply: The total number of shares or tokens in an ecosystem, which includes issued and outstanding shares as well as treasury assets and allocations that may be claimed in the future. Used to calculate an asset's total *valuation*.

Fund-of-Funds: Investment strategy focused on investing in a portfolio of investment funds instead of direct investment into assets themselves.

Funding Round: Refers to the term of a securities offering, where a company raises money to fund company operations, growth, and other enterprise opportunities. A company's first private funding round is traditionally labeled the *Seed Round*, and future funding rounds are labeled with the letters of the alphabet in descending order: *Series A, Series B, Series C*, and so on. Private funding rounds are traditionally followed by an initial public offering (IPO) where all outstanding shares are converted into public stock and traded on an exchange. Funding rounds can be in the form of debt and/or equity.

Fungibility: A quality describing the lack of uniqueness between identical assets in a collection. It denotes any asset that can be interchanged with another from the same set without any true distinction in value, appearance, or metadata.

Futures Markets: Auction market where commodities and futures contracts are purchased and sold.

Futures Trading: Transaction between two parties for an asset at a predetermined price that is to be delivered at an agreed upon time in the future. These transactions are finalized months in the future, and may be a less efficient measure of an asset's market value than *spot trading*.

Galaxy Digital ($GLXY): Publicly traded company on the Toronto Stock Exchange providing institutions and clients with asset management, custody, and other financial services in the cryptocurrency and blockchain verticals.

Gas Fees: Blockchain transaction fees paid to the network validators in exchange for cryptographic transactions on a protocol's distributed ledger. Traditionally paid in the blockchain's base network token. These fees can vary based on demand and other factors.

Gemini: US-based cryptocurrency exchange famously founded by Cameron and Tyler Winkelvoss (known as the Winklevoss twins) who were involved in the founding of Facebook before venturing into Bitcoin early on.

Gemini Galactic Markets: Alternative Trading System owned by Gemini and approved for operations in trading of digital assets and securities in 2022.

General Contractor: The primary manager of all day-to-day operations, activities, and communications during the development of a real estate project.

General Partner (GP): An individual or group of people who are responsible for business operations and are liable for the partnership's obligations. Commonly used to describe the direct managers and allocators of an investment fund.

General Soclitictation: Act of advertising a security or investment by using mass communication.

Governance Token: Digital asset used to allow tokenholders to vote on the direction and decision-making of a protocol or other decentralized entity.

Grant DAOs: Decentralized entity focused on deploying capital to benefit a specific protocol or common goal. Grants act similar to charitable contributions and are provided to a sole beneficiary as *non-dilutive capital*.

Gwei (unit of account): Smallest common unit of measurement of Ether. 1 billion *gwei* make up 1 Ether. The term stems from a combination of the word *giga* and *Wei*, the true smallest denomination of Ether, where 1 billion *Wei* make up one *gwei*.

Hack: A nefarious or unauthorized infiltration of a computational system, resulting in theft, compromised security protocols, or other malicious activity.

Halving: An event that reduces the issuance of new digital assets in a Proof-of-Work system. *The Halving* traditionally refers to Bitcoin's reward halving, which happens every 210,000 blocks, approximately every four years.

Hard Asset: Tangible assets and resources with real underlying value, such as real estate, inventory, and commodities.

Hard Cap: Defines the maximum amount of shares or tokens sold during a public or private offering.

Hard Fork: Major change or upgrade to a blockchain network that permanently changes the characteristics of a protocol. The previously aligned ledger is no longer considered the standard consensus, and a new ledger is created beginning on the snapshot date. The previous blockchain ledger still runs in parallel, but software and network participants merge onto the new blockchain, making backwards-compatibility difficult and often impossible for future iterations.

Hash: A type of encryption that involves transforming strings of natural language, letters, and numbers into another value, traditionally represented by a fixed-length key.

Hash Rate: The measure of the computational power in a proof-of-work (PoW) cryptocurrency network or distributed computing system. Calculated by evaluating the hashing output of a computer per second, denoted in H/s.

Hedging: Risk management strategy involving increased exposure to many outcomes of a single event, asset class, or investment to prevent or reduce losses.

Hedge Fund: A limited partnership of investors that uses high-risk investment strategies to generate large returns.

Hester Peirce ("Crypto Mom"): Nominated SEC commissioner with many outspoken pro-crypto policies leading to a consistent outpouring of support by global industry enthusiasts. Led an initiative to codify new regulation known as the Token Safe Harbor Proposal. Despite multiple iterations and industry-backing, no significant changes have been made to digital asset regulation.

High Frequency Trading: Trading strategy that includes using financial and quantitative algorithms to make rapid investment decisions to make a return. Each individual trade might be smaller in allocation, but with a much higher rate of trade, firms are able to collect market returns where individual investors would not be able to functionally perform.

Home Equity Line of Credit (HELOC): A cash loan borrowed against the value of a house or real estate property. These loans are often *overcollateralized,* so the amount available to borrow is less than the total equity value of the property. The equity in a home is calculated as the difference between a property's appraised value and the current outstanding debt or mortgage balance.

Hot Wallet: A cryptocurrency wallet that is connected to the internet, making it vulnerable to hacks. The most common example is crypto held on a centralized exchange, which provides ease of use and quicker trades, but presents the risk of a lost or stolen password leading to theft. Hot wallets are typically a form of software wallet without dedicated hardware.

Howey Test: Court precedent used to determine if a transaction is considered an *Investment Contract,* which would be considered a security and subject to additional compliance measures and enhanced regulatory scrutiny. Based on a Supreme Court lawsuit (*SEC v. W.J. Howey Co*) that directly led to the creation of four criteria used to determine if an investment contract exists: (1) an investment of money, (2) in a common enterprise, (3) with the expectation of profit, (4) to be derived from the efforts of others. If all four criteria are confirmed, rules and regulations as described by the Securities Act of 1933 and Securities Exchange Act of 1934 must be followed. Much controversy has revolved around the Howey Test, as dissenting opinions feel these criteria are too general and are not enforced equally across all violations.

HQLAx: European financial technology firm building distributed technology for banks and service providers built on R3's Corda blockchain.

Hybrid Digital Assets: Digital assets that share characteristics of multiple types of tokens. Examples include security-NFTs or commodity tokens.

Immutable: Permanent and unchanging. Used to describe a blockchain ledger that tracks the full history of transactions within an ecosystem. Blockchains use *cryptography* to secure the ledger and prevent any edits or changes to previous records.

Immutable X: Layer 2 blockchain solution that creates a more scalable blockchain solution for NFTs issued on the Ethereum blockchain.

Impermanent Loss: Describes the loss in real monetary value of a trading position when an asset's price change causes a nominal loss despite no change in the asset size. Most commonly seen in staking assets in liquidity pools, investors may take losses when a token's value decreases. Despite not changing the amount of tokens owned, the change in price relative to another asset they are staking can lead to a decrease in real purchasing power if the asset pool is sold for cash.

Incentive Mechanism: A result or reward that drives the motivation for a set of actions.

Income: Money received in exchange for work, services, or investments that is commonly paid on a regular basis.

Index: A group or basket of assets representing a general investment in a specific industry, vertical, asset class, or investment strategy.

Index Fund: A mutual fund or exchange-traded fund that tracks a particular *index*, allowing investors to passively invest in a basket of assets.

Inflation: Increase in price of goods and services in an economy commonly due to an increase in money supply or the value of a fiat currency.

Initial Coin Offering (ICO): Event at which an issuer sells a crypto asset or token, often crossing lines with unregulated methods of crowdfunding and private fundraising.

Initial Deposit: Minimum amount of money required to open a bank account, invest in an offering, or begin borrowing in a DeFi protocol.

Initial Offering: The first time a product or investment is sold to the public market.

Initial Public Offering (IPO): A public offering registered with the SEC or equivalent government agency that allows for a stock offering to trade on an exchange. They are typically underwritten by an investment bank or group of banks.

Institutional Investor: Large, formal entities including banks, union funds, endowments, and other professional investment companies and asset managers that make sizable investments into public and private businesses. Most have restrictions around what types of investments they are allowed to make, which is referred to as *investment mandates.*

Intellectual Property (IP): Vehicle that represents a creative work or idea, including written ideas, art, songs, and so on that can become legally protected works.

Intercontinental Exchange (ICE): US company that is best known for owning the New York Stock Exchange, among other brokers, lenders, clearinghouses, and other financial service providers around the world.

Interest Payable: The amount of interest expenses accrued that have not yet been paid.

Interest Rate: The amount of interest to be paid per period, often expressed as a yearly percentage of an outstanding loan.

Intermediary: A person or company that acts as a middleman between two counterparties. A trusted third party can add value to a transaction by providing independent validation, licensed approval, or added efficiencies to complicated financial and technical processes. Traditional intermediaries can sometimes take advantage of their strategic position, charging fees or exerting influence over customers, leading to increased adoption in automation and DeFi tools that provide the same services to customers with less friction.

International Issuer IPO: An initial public offering executed by a company based outside of the US.

Interoperability: The ability for multiple software systems to communicate and interact with each other. It is a dominant ideology in the blockchain industry encouraging companies, protocols, and other developers to build tech solutions that integrate with the larger blockchain ecosystem, to allow for frictionless adoption by users. See *composability*.

Intrinsic Value: A measure of an asset's value derived by evaluating the *book value* and the sum of its future cash flows to determine the objective value of an underlying asset before factoring in supply and demand economics.

InvestaX: Singapore-based investment and trading platform for security tokens and digital assets.

Investment DAO: A specific type of decentralized autonomous organization dedicated to investing capital into different companies or people, with the goal of supporting or developing a common goal or protocol.

INX ($INX): US-registered broker-dealer and alternative trading system, allowing for primary offerings and secondary trading for security tokens and digital assets in addition to cryptocurrency trading. Completed an *international issuer IPO* with an $85M offering for its native $INX token, which acts as an *exchange token* with additional benefits such as a profit sharing component.

iOS: Operating system for Apple's iPhone collection. New iterations of iOS are released annually, often in conjunction with the launch of a new hardware device.

iPhone: Flagship cell phone model made by Apple. The most popular cell phone in the United States.

Issuance Platform: Technology platform that creates and distributes digital assets and cryptocurrencies on behalf of its issuer clients.

Jamaican Digital Exchange (*Jam-Dex*): Legally recognized central bank digital currency of Jamaica. In 2022, it became the first digital currency to be declared legal tender in the Caribbean.

JOBS Act of 2012: The *Jumpstart Our Business Startups Act* is a law passed in the United States dedicated to create more viable funding opportunities for small businesses by creating more accessible options within the securities regulatory framework. The law established the Regulation CF and Regulation 506(c) private securities exemptions, while also improving the Regulation A exemption, among other changes to the number of shareholders allowed for private companies, new approved methods of fundraising through online portals, and so on.

Joint Venture: A collective corporation formed by two or more separate individuals, companies, or entities that is separate from any one party's identity.

JPM Coin: Permissioned currency used as the main method of payment between participating JP Morgan clients within the bank's proprietary *Onyx* blockchain network.

K (constant): Represents the product of reserve balances between two assets in an automated constant product market-making function, as defined by $X * Y = K$.

Kairos AR, Inc: Facial recognition software company headquartered in Miami that issued the first dual token offering in 2017/2018. The token gave investors access to equity in the company via the first private company offering in the US using a Security Token and granting investors a bonus 1-for-1 on the FACE Utility Token which happens to be a form of biometric access via blockchain using their proprietary facial recognition technology.

KKR: American investment company that manages private equity, real estate, credit, and other alternative asset classes with over $450B in assets under management. Credited with inventing the leveraged buyout (LBO).

Know Your Customer (KYC): Standards and requirements used to determine the identity and address of an investor or customer of a financial service.

Layer 0: Base blockchain technology consisting of a distributed ledger that is cryptographically secured.

Layer 1: Protocol technology built on top of blockchain technology allowing for interfaces and maintenance.

Layer 2: Scaling solutions for blockchain protocols to reduce costs and increase speeds within a given network. Built on top of a *Layer 1* protocol leveraging batching, sharding, and other technical methods to improve performance.

Ledger: Official record of transactions or bookkeeping entries. Can be kept in physical or digital copies, and can be recorded on a blockchain.

Leverage: Borrowed money, usually *collateralized* by investments or assets owned, that is used to purchase new investments. Acts as a form of liquidity for illiquid assets and is popular in debt, real estate, and private equity markets.

LIBOR: Rate of interest used between banks on the London interbank market. Used as a reference rate when determining interest rates for other loans.

Lightning Network: Layer 2 network for the Bitcoin blockchain that enables smart contracts and other scaling features for Bitcoin.

Limit Order: Indication to buy or sell an investment on a secondary market with a restriction on the price at which an asset is to be purchased or sold.

Limited Liability Company (LLC): A US business entity structure that protects owners from personal liability for its debts and outstanding liabilities.

Limited Partner (LP): A partner in a company or business that is entitled to limited profits in the business and who has limited liability regarding debts and obligations. Traditionally used to describe outside investors into an investment fund without direct operational control

Line of Credit: Revolving sum of money loaned to a borrower they can use as needed and pay back at their discretion as opposed to receiving a *lump sum* with a set payback schedule and term.

Liquid Network: Layer 2 network for the Bitcoin blockchain to enable the issuance of security tokens and other digital assets.

Liquidation: Process of selling a set of assets for cash, commonly to cover outstanding debts and other liabilities during bankruptcy or insolvency.

Liquidity Depth: Current amount of buy and sell pressure from outside investors, or the size of a liquidity pool. Thin or shallow liquidity pools cannot facilitate large orders, leading to extreme *slippage* and illiquidity premiums or discounts.

Liquidity Discount: A comparatively lower price than market value offered by an investor in order to complete the sale of an asset due to a lack of investor demand.

Liquidity Mining: Method of lending assets across multiple protocols to increase yield through multiple platforms. The yield is traditionally accrued through trading fees combined with staking rewards.

Liquidity Pool: Vault of staked assets by *liquidity providers* that is used to power trading and transactions by users of a decentralized application. Contributors to the pool are rewarded with interest, usually in the form of staking rewards and trading fees, as compensation for locking up their funds.

Liquidity Premium: A comparatively higher price than market value offered by an investor in order to complete the sale of an asset due to a lack of supply.

Liquidity Provider (LP): An investor that stakes assets into a decentralized application in exchange for staking rewards, trading fees, and other returns.

Liquidity Risk: Threat of default on current outstanding obligations by an investor or institution due to a lack of cash on hand or assets that can be easily converted into money used to repay debt.

Litecoin (*LTC*): Decentralized peer-to-peer cryptocurrency inspired by Bitcoin. One of the earliest *altcoins*, with a goal of providing a cheaper and faster way to transact permissionlessly worldwide. Its native currency, *LTC*, is built on a modified Bitcoin codebase and is used for network transactions.

Loan-to-Value Ratio (LTV): Financial ratio comparing an asset's outstanding loan amount with the value of the asset's purchase price.

Commonly used in real estate transactions when evaluating the *liquidity risk* of a property.

Loan Origination: Process of creating a new loan that starts with a manual application, progresses with legal and compliance verifications, and concludes with financial distributions.

Lock-up Period: Period of time where a specific asset is restricted from secondary market activity. Can be mandated through smart contracts or through regulatory requirements. See *seasoning period.*

London Stock Exchange: Leading stock exchange based in the United Kingdom.

Long Position: Direct exposure to an asset with an investment goal to capitalize on price appreciation.

Loopring (*LRC*): Ethereum exchange protocol that uses *zero-knowledge proofs* to enable permissionless and private transactions. Uses the native *LRC* token as a base trading pair and a transactional asset within the ecosystem.

Limited Partner (LP) Token: Token representing a liquidity provider's allocation in a liquidity pool that can be redeemed for the underlying staked assets in addition to the rewards earned over the staking period.

Lump Sum: Total amount of money received in a transaction, typically as part of a loan.

Mainnet: The primary, active, fully functional blockchain ledger on a network protocol. Experimental or beta ledgers are known as *testnets.*

MakerDAO (*MKR*): Decentralized autonomous organization built on the Ethereum network that offers collateralized lending and borrowing services using its native stablecoin, *DAI.* Governance token *MKR* offers members the ability to control lending rates and other protocol decisions.

Maker Vault: Staking pool that allows users to deposit cryptocurrency and receive yield paid in Dai. Each separate cryptocurrency has its own vault, like a bank account.

Margin Call: Requirement to deposit additional cash or assets to cover debt exposure due to a decrease in the value of loan collateral.

Margin Trading: The practice of using borrowed capital to invest in speculative assets.

Mark to Market: Measurement of the current market value of a company's assets irrespective of previous valuations.

Market Capitalization (Market Cap): The total value of the circulating supply of an asset or token.

Market Depth: Measure of liquidity for a trading asset. Quantified by evaluating the *slippage* incurred on a new allocation or sale.

Market Maker: An investor, institution, or automated protocol that commits to always buying and selling investments at specified prices.

Market Order: Indication to buy or sell an investment on a secondary market at the current best available price.

Market Price: Current price of an asset on a trading market.

Market Saturation: A situation where additional supply of an asset enters a market, fulfilling outstanding demand and creating potential decreases in asset prices due to subsequent lack of buyer interest.

Market Volatility: A period of extreme price fluctuations in an asset or economy, leading to unpredictable investment scenarios.

Marketspace Capital: Texas-based private equity and real estate firm that is the issuer behind the Myra Park security token ($MYRA).

Masternode: A central point of verification for new blocks of transactions on a network's protocol. Especially relevant in *Proof-of-Stake* and other alternative consensus mechanisms, these service providers act in a similar role as miners in a *Proof-of-Work* system and are rewarded with network fees for their efforts.

Media DAOs: A decentralized organization focused on creating and curating media for users within a context of transparency and accountability by removing centralized corporate financial incentive or bias.

Merkle Tree: Cryptographic structure creating a set of *branches*, each holding individual, secured segments of data in a scalable manner for future access and verification.

Metadata: Ancillary data used as additional context for a primary dataset.

Metaverse: Immersive digital reality that connects all online experiences and applications.

Metcalfe's Law: Technological understanding that the aggregate size of a network can be calculated as the square number of connected users in a system (n^2).

Middleman: See: *Intermediary*

Minimum Investment: Smallest size investment possible for an individual investor in an offering.

Mining: The process of validating blocks of transactions in a *Proof-of-Work* system by solving complex math formulas using computing resources in exchange for rewards.

Mint Numbers: A serial number describing the order in which a specific NFT was minted in a collection.

Minting: The process of purchasing and creating a token that is recorded on a blockchain ledger.

Monero (*XMR*): Cryptocurrency known for using a public ledger with integrated privacy features that allow for anonymous transactions for all users within the network. Uses its native currency *XMR* for transactions between parties.

Money Market: A short-term loan market between banks and other financial institutions. Traditionally, these loans exist in less than one year terms.

Money Transmitter License: Financial license allowing institutions to conduct financial transactions revolving around monetary transmission between states and other jurisdictions.

Mortgage-Backed Securities (MBS): Basket of home or other real estate loans turned into a single investment product sold to investors and institutions.

Multilateral Trading Facility (MTF): Regulatory standard established by the European Union acting to allow institutions to trade securities on a secondary market. Similar to an *ATS license* in the US.

National Securities Exchange: Licensed financial institution that has registered with the SEC under the Securities and Exchange Act of 1934 allowing for trading of publicly traded stocks and other securities.

NBA Top Shot: Marketplace allowing users to buy, sell, and trade collectible "Moments" from NBA games in the form of NFTs. Like sports trading cards, each Moment has a specified rarity and limited supply.

Net Asset Value (NAV): The current value of an investment fund calculated by subtracting outstanding asset liabilities from the market value of all assets in a portfolio. Can be evaluated on a per-share basis by dividing the net value by the amount of issued shares.

Network: Set of connected computers shared between separate, individual nodes.

Network Effect: Economic concept detailing the increase in value of a system or community as the number of users increases.

Network Token: Ingrained payment protocols within a given blockchain network used to transact between nodes and parties.

New York BitLicense: Regulatory distinction in New York, USA allowing a company to conduct Virtual Currency Business Activities in the state of New York or with New York residents.

Node: Electronic computational access point allowing for communication between computers connected to a network. Able to create, receive, and send information over designated communication channels.

Non-Fungible Token (NFT): Digital asset on a blockchain with a unique encoded identifier acting as a serial number to distinguish one asset from another in the same collection.

Non-Custodial: A cryptocurrency wallet owned by a user, giving them full control over their private keys and full responsibility for protecting held assets and funds.

Non-Dilutive Capital: Money received for a business without giving away equity or ownership in the company as part of the investment. Commonly seen through blockchain grant programs.

Office of the Comptroller of the Currency (OCC): Independent bureau of the US Department of the Treasury responsible for the regulation of national banks in the United States of America among other financial institution supervision.

On-Ramp: Financial platform providing users with the ability to use fiat dollars to purchase cryptocurrency and onboard into the blockchain economy.

Onyx: Independent business vertical of J.P. Morgan Chase established to develop technology solutions using blockchain, specializing in payments, settlement and clearing, and loan origination technologies.

Open Source: Software developed and released with publicly-available source code allowing for modifications and improvements by the community. Allows publicly available protocols to be peer-reviewed and transparent for all parties.

Operating Systems: Software technology framework used to create an interoperable program or application.

Optimistic Rollups: Layer 2 blockchain protocol, primarily associated with Ethereum, used to create a more scalable process for on chain transactions.

Options Contract: Agreement between two parties to create a transaction for an asset at a pre-agreed price and date. *Call options* represent an opportunity to purchase a given investment in the future, while *put options* represent an opportunity for an investor to sell an investment at a fixed price in the future. The price at which both options are set is known as the *strike price.*

Oracle: A central point of truth that collects information from many sources to present in an aggregated format. Leading blockchain oracle *Chainlink* collects smart contract data across blockchains, protocols, and other third party nodes to create an accessible on-chain database of varied information.

Order Book: Bulletin board of buy and sell orders for a specific asset sorted by price and the amount of available shares in a given offer.

Overcollateralized: A scenario where the value of assets used as loan collateral exceeds the value of a loan. This is required in most decentralized lending platforms to account for the variability in the prices of digital assets.

PancakeSwap: Decentralized exchange built on the BNB blockchain allowing users to trade BEP-20 standard tokens in a permissionless manner.

Parent Organization: Business entity that owns a majority or controlling interest in a different, independent company often referred to as a subsidiary company.

Patch: A new iteration of software published to a live application that makes changes to a codebase intended to fix identified problems or bugs.

Peer-to-Peer (P2P): Direct interaction between two users using decentralized applications without the interference of a centralized third party.

Peg: Policy requiring a fixed exchange rate for an asset, traditionally quoted in a fiat currency such as the US Dollar or Japanese Yen.

Permissionless: Trait describing applications and systems where users do not need approval in order to use or interact amongst themselves

Perpetual Swap: Agreement allowing investors to gain exposure to an investment without having to own it directly.

Plasma: Ethereum Layer 2 sidechain that forms new "child chains" through an unlimited supply of Merkle trees.

Platform Coins: Cryptocurrency created by a specific project acting as a hybrid between a network token and a transactional token. A project's token may act as both an access token to the project and a payments or rewards facilitator for the project.

Polkadot (DOT): Blockchain platform acting as a decentralized bridge between other blockchains. Uses native cryptocurrency *DOT* within the network.

Polygon (*MATIC*): One of the largest Layer 2 sidechain scaling solutions for the Ethereum blockchain. Uses native cryptocurrency *MATIC* as a network token for staking and fees.

Ponzi Scheme: Fraudulent investment scam using newly invested cash flows to pay back previous investors, leading to a large discrepancy in the expected assets under management of the fund vehicle and the actual portfolio.

Portfolio: Collection of investments across asset classes, including equities, real estate, bonds, cash, and all other assets.

Prediction Markets: Platform allowing users to place bets on the outcome of future events ranging from sports and public events to asset prices and other occurrences.

Price Impact: Estimated change in price of an asset when an individual makes a trade in a liquidity pool.

Pricing Mechanism: Algorithm determining the price of an asset on an open market by using formulas factoring in the size of a liquidity pool and current market demand.

Primary Issuance: The first creation and distribution of an asset to users, typically through a fundraise or airdrop.

Primary Market: Segment of the capital markets where the initial sale of assets and initial offerings are purchased and sold.

Principal-Agent Dilemma: A conflict in priorities between a person or group (the principal) and those making decisions and acting on their behalf (the agent).

Principal: Total amount of money loaned to a borrower. Also known as the *face value* of a bond.

Private Company: A business held under private ownership that is not publicly registered with a federal government and does not trade on public exchanges.

Private Credit: Debt between investors and companies that is non-dilutive and is not traded on a secondary market.

Private Equity: The industry of investing in equity or acquiring private companies.

Private Key: Secret string of numbers used in cryptography to secure a blockchain wallet. NOTE: Do not share your private key with anyone.

Private Security: Investments represented by privately held companies.

Pro Rata: Traditionally used to describe the act of giving each party in a transaction their proportional share of the whole. Directly translates from Latin to "per the rate" or "proportionally."

Product Adoption Curve: Description of the distribution of a general population that segments the adoption of new technologies into five groups: (1) Innovators, (2) Early Adopters, (3) Early Majority, (4) Late Majority, (5) Laggards).

Profit Sharing: Economic system that distributes the profits generated by a company *pro rata* to investors, employees, and other shareholders.

Project Guardian: Joint pilot program with JP Morgan Chase, the Monetary Authority of Singapore (MAS), DBS, and Marketnode

285

dedicated to exploring tokenization and DeFi in regards to wholesale funding.

Proof-of-History (PoH): Consensus mechanism pioneered by the Solana blockchain that uses cryptography to verify periods of time between individual events or transactions.

Proof-of-Stake (PoS): Consensus mechanism pioneered by the Ethereum blockchain that uses staking of assets by nodes to process transactions and verify blocks, removing the need for computational power to solve computational problems, allowing for a reduced carbon footprint, more efficient transaction speeds, and reduced costs.

Proof-of-Work (PoW): Consensus mechanism pioneered by the Bitcoin blockchain that uses computing power to solve complex prime functions to cryptographically secure blocks of transactions.

Protocol: Base set of rules used to determine the core values of a blockchain and sets guidelines for how transactions should be processed and recorded.

Public Security: Assets registered with a federal government and openly traded on stock exchanges.

Public Key: A publicly-visible address for a cryptocurrency wallet used to send transactions and messages through decentralized protocols.

Put Option: Contract between two parties to exchange a security at a predetermined price. When purchasing a put option on a security, an investor selects a price at which they are willing to sell a security and the term they are seeking before the option expires. Options traditionally come in bundles of 100 shares.

Qualified Purchaser or Investor: An individual or entity that is allowed to purchase private and high risk assets, often due to the investor's net worth or sophistication. Qualified purchasers typically hold assets of at least $5 Million.

Quantum Computing: Next generation of computational power focused on the applications of quantum theory on the atomic and subatomic levels.

Quoted Currency: The second of two assets in a trading pair, used to determine the market price of a trading asset in relation to a stable and liquid asset known as the *base currency*.

Ravencoin (*RVN*): Peer-to-peer blockchain forked from Bitcoin enabling smart contracts and distributed ledger technology. Uses a native cryptocurrency *RVN* to power fees and decentralized applications in the network. Purpose-built to enable third-party digital asset issuance.

Real World Assets (RWA): Assets secured by legal structures and physical goods, services, intellectual property, real estate, cash flows, and other valuable items.

Rebalance: Adjusting a portfolio's allocations to better match an investor's investment thesis, which may consist of return targets, risk profiles, and/or specific sector concentration.

Regulation A+ (Reg A+): Private securities exemption in the US that allows for equity, debt, and other securities issuers to fundraise from public markets. Reg A+ allows for US and international investors of any income level to invest in an offering, with a maximum fundraise limit of $75M per year. There is no seasoning period for these securities to trade on a secondary market post-issuance.

Regulation Crowdfunding (Reg CF): Private securities exemption in the US that allows for equity, debt, and other securities issuers to fundraise from public markets. Reg CF allows for US and international investors of any income level to invest in an offering, with a maximum fundraise limit of $5M per year. There is a 12-month seasoning period for these securities sold to the retail public before they may trade on secondary markets.

Regulation D 506(b) (Reg D): Private securities exemption in the US that allows for equity, debt, and other securities issuers to fundraise from private capital markets. Reg D 506(b) allows for US accredited investors to invest in an offering with no total fundraise limits. Investors may self-attest to accreditation themselves without verification by the issuer. These securities may not be *generally solicited*. There is a 12-month seasoning period for these securities sold to investors before they may trade on secondary markets.

Regulation D 506(c) (Reg D): Private securities exemption in the US that allows for equity, debt, and other securities issuers to fundraise from private capital markets. Reg D 506(c) allows for US accredited investors to invest in an offering, with no total fundraise limits.

Unlike *Regulation D 506(b)*, these securities may be *generally solicited* but require investors to prove their accredited status with the issuer. There is a 12-month seasoning period for these securities sold to investors before they may trade on secondary markets.

Regulation S (Reg S): Private securities exemption in the US that allows for equity, debt, and other securities issuers to fundraise from private capital markets. Reg S allows for qualified international investors to invest in an offering, with no total fundraise limits. There is a 6-month seasoning period for these securities sold to investors before they may trade on secondary markets.

Regulatory Sandbox: Government-sanctioned testing environments for financial institutions to develop innovative technological solutions under the guidance and oversight of regulatory authorities.

Rehypothecation: Business model involving financial institutions reinvesting client funds to make a profit, often sharing a portion of the returns with the customers directly, such as a high-yield bank account.

Repo Market: Market for short-term repurchase agreements to be purchased and sold between institutions.

Repurchase Agreement: Short-term debt contract where a party agrees to sell an asset for a specified price with an agreement to purchase the asset at a higher price in the future from the counterparty.

Retail Investor: A member of the general public who is not a professional investor and decides to buy and sell securities through a broker or savings account.

Return on Investment (ROI): Metric used to calculate the percentage return or loss by dividing the net profit by the initial investment.

Revenue Multiple: A method of valuing a business or financial asset by applying an industry-standardized multiple to a set of cash flows.

Revenue Sharing: Economic system that distributes the revenues generated by a company *pro rata* to investors, employees, and other shareholders.

Ripple (*XRP*): Digital intra-bank payment network and settlement system created by US-based Ripple Labs Inc. Uses native cryptocurrency *XRP* as a transactional currency within the network.

Risk Curve: Visual representation of the risk and return of an investment, describing the significant changes in one variable even with small changes to the other.

Risk Factor: A variable of unknown quantity that may lead to increased risk of failure within an economic model or financial system.

Robo Advisors: Algorithms or artificial intelligence programs that make investment decisions on behalf of clients.

Roger Ver: Notorious early investor and evangelist in Bitcoin who built on his public profile as an active promoter of Bitcoin forks such as Bitcoin SV (*BSV*) and Bitcoin Cash (*BCH*).

Rollup: Scaling solution that combines a set of transactions into one datapoint to be processed by blockchain validators.

Royalties: Revenues earned from intellectual property distributed *pro rata* to investors. This is commonly seen in NFT projects, patent licenses, and music deals.

SAFE Note: A *simple agreement for future equity* is a convertible security acting as a note that may solely be converted into equity in the future based on a set of rules defined in the agreement structure.

Sandbox (*SAND*): Virtual world browser-based platform allowing for metaverse experiences and interactions. Built on the ethereum blockchain, users can purchase plots of land as NFTs in the native *SAND* cryptocurrency. The land, which is measured as a series of 96 x 96-meter squares, was divided into 166,464 plots at its public launch in February 2021.

Satoshi (unit of account): Smallest unit of measurement of a Bitcoin. 100 million satoshis make up 1 Bitcoin. Named after *Satoshi Nakamoto*.

Satoshi Nakamoto: Anonymous founder and creator of the Bitcoin blockchain and widely credited for the adoption of cryptocurrency and blockchain technology. Published the Bitcoin Whitepaper to the public on October 31, 2008.

Scalability: The measure of how quickly and cheaply a system can adopt new users to a transactional system.

Scarcity: Declining supply of an asset often coinciding with increased prices on secondary markets.

Seasoning Period: Period of time where a specific asset is restricted from secondary market activity. Can be mandated through smart contracts or through regulatory requirements. See *lock-up period*.

Secondary Market: Section of the capital markets where assets are purchased and sold between investors and other counterparties following their listing on a secondary exchange or marketplace.

Securities and Exchange Commission (SEC): US government agency responsible for regulating the securities markets and spot commodities markets. Generally considered the primary oversight body for investor protection.

Securitization: Process of turning a basket of assets or an individual asset into an investment product for individuals and institutions to purchase in primary and secondary markets by creating a financial wrapper around the asset using an entity.

Securitize: US broker dealer and ATS that offers tokenization services for security tokens sold to US and international investors.

Security: Investment assets including stocks, bonds, partnership interest, futures, options, and other investment contracts.

Security NFT (S-NFT): A security created as a non-fungible asset. One example of a *hybrid token*.

Security Token: A security represented by a digital asset on a distributed ledger or blockchain.

Security Token Group: Financial conglomerate providing consulting, education, media, research, and financial services for the security token industry.

Security Token Market (STM.co): Financial data and media provider for the tokenization industry. Provides all the trading prices of security tokens in one place.

Security Token Offering (STO): A public securities offering allowing investors to participate in an initial offering for a security that may trade on an exchange or marketplace in the future. Typically issued through a broker or issuance platform.

Seed Phrase: Series of words allowing access into a cryptocurrency hard wallet without the need for the private key. NOTE: Do not share your seed phrase with anyone!

Seed Funding: The initial funding round for an early-stage company, often occurring without a functional product and supplied by friends and family of the company founders.

Segwit: Technical term referring to Segregated Witness, a transaction format change to the Bitcoin blockchain that removed specific witness information from being recorded in a verified block.

Series Funding: Successive opportunities for companies to sell a portion of equity in exchange for investment to grow and scale operations. Traditionally beginning at the 'seed' stage, additional rounds of funding follow the alphabet, with a 'Series A' fundraising round followed by a 'Series B' and so on. This trend continues until a business is acquired or goes public via IPO, where fundraising rounds transition into periodic stock sales or purchases by owners.

Service DAOs: Recruiting and talent acquisition agencies for Web 3.0 managed by a decentralized autonomous organization

Set Protocol: Asset management tool allowing users to create, manage, and share portfolios of ERC-20 tokens. Known as *Sets*, each portfolio or basket becomes represented as an ERC-20 token itself, which can then be traded, staked, or utilized across the Ethereum ecosystem.

Settlement: The process of delivering purchased assets and exchanged capital to each respective party and recording it on a ledger. This is the final step of an exchange and renders the agreement completed.

Sharding: Method of segmenting a database into smaller fragments or *shards* to improve efficiency and scalability by reducing transaction sizes.

Short Position: Indirect exposure to an asset with an investment goal to capitalize on price depreciation.

Slippage: Difference between the market price before a trade occurs and the estimated price change following a market order.

Smart Contract: Series of automated commands that allow the creation of programs and applications built on blockchains and distributed ledgers. Acts as complex nested if/then statements allowing for permissionless transactions that only execute when all conditions are met between parties.

Snapshot: An instant recording of the current state of a blockchain ledger at a specified time that captures user addresses and transaction metadata, typically used for airdrops and measuring user engagement such as for voting in DAOs.

Social DAOs: Social media and networking platforms organized, managed, and operated by a decentralized organization made up of its users.

Soft Asset: Intangible assets without real underlying value such as intellectual property and goodwill.

Soft Cap: Defines the minimum amount of shares or tokens sold during a public or private offering.

Soft Fork: Published change to a blockchain protocol that only affects future transactions and consensus, allowing for backward compatibility and no requirement for the implementation of a new ledger.

Solana (*SOL*): Blockchain platform and smart contract protocol using the native *SOL* cryptocurrency for network transactions.

Solvency: The ability to cover and pay all debts with outstanding assets and cash on hand.

Source Code: Text-based file containing programming language that can be executed to run an application or server.

Special Purpose Vehicle (SPV): Financial entity created to fulfill a singular purpose, such as to isolate an asset or financial liability. Traditionally filed in the US as a *Limited Liability Corporation (LLC)*.

Special-Purpose Depository Institution (SPDI): Chartered banks that receive deposits and conduct banking activities. Legally defined in the state of Wyoming to accommodate digital asset custodians.

SPiCE VC ($SPiCE): Venture capital fund launched in 2017 with a focus on digital assets, blockchain technology, and security tokens. It issued a security token backed by LP interest in its first fund under the ticker symbol $SPiCE.

Spot Trading: Transaction between two parties for an asset at a price to be settled on a specific date. These transactions are to be finalized in real time, and may incur more price fluctuations than *futures trading*.

Stablecoin: A digital asset or cryptocurrency designed to have a stable price, traditionally pegged to a fiat currency like the US Dollar, Japanese Yen, or Chinese Yuan. Can be issued by a private company, pegged using algorithmic rebalancing, or issued by a central bank (see: *Central Bank Digital Currency*).

Staking: The process of locking up assets in a smart contract protocol or centralized custodian in exchange for rewards, earned interest, governance rights, and other benefits.

Stock: Equity shares in a publicly traded or private company.

Stock Market: A platform, exchange, or marketplace where stocks can be bought and sold.

STOKR: European broker and issuance platform for security tokens.

Strike Price: The price at which a put or call option can be exercised.

Subnets: Separate, fragmented blockchain network used for alternate or testing purposes.

Supply Chain: Sequence of processes between the creation, distribution, and delivery of a product or service.

Surplus: Extra cash or assets leftover following the repayment of outstanding debt and liabilities.

Sushiswap (*SUSHI*): Decentralized exchange to provide liquidity and trading for Ethereum-based tokens using native *SUSHI* tokens to track liquidity rewards and for governance decisions inside the protocol.

SWIFT Network: The *Society for Worldwide Interbank Financial Telecommunications* system is a communication protocol for banks, institutions, and financial service providers to send and receive information, primarily for efficient global money transfers.

Swiss International Exchange (SIX): Leading stock exchange in Switzerland and pioneer in blockchain technology through its subsidiary Swiss Digital Exchange.

Syndicate: A collection of investors or institutions that join as one registered entity for the purpose of managing a large or complex investment.

Synthetic Financial Products: Financial instruments that simulate other investments on the market without requiring physical ownership of the underlying asset.

Tangible Asset: Physical assets including inventory, real estate, commodities, machinery, and other items of value existing in the real world.

Target Rate: Interest rate used to guide monetary policy.

Target Rate Feedback Mechanism: Algorithm built by MakerDAO that adjusts the *Target Rate* in order to maintain the price stability of the Dai stablecoin.

Terra (*LUNA*): Blockchain protocol and payment platform known for creating the largest algorithmic stablecoin, *UST*, which notoriously collapsed in 2022, leading to the bear market cycle in 2023. The protocol used a dual token structure, headlined by network token *LUNA*, to attempt to balance the stablecoin's price. The protocol and assets were victim to a *Death Spiral* that brought asset prices down nearly 99 percent in less than a week.

Testing the Waters Period: A process to evaluate investor interest in a public offering before the initial offering has begun.

Testnet: Testing environments hosted on a distributed ledger that do not have permanent ramifications on the *mainnet*.

The DAO: The first decentralized autonomous organization founded in 2016 that acted as a venture capital fund. After one of the largest crowdfunding campaigns at the time, the open-source code securing the asset treasury was hacked with hundreds of millions of dollars of Ethereum stolen, leading to a hard fork of the Ethereum blockchain that same year.

Timestamp: Accurate recordkeeping of the date and time a transaction takes place.

Token: Base layer digital asset used as a method of account for transactions on a distributed ledger or blockchain.

Tokenized Assets: Blockchain-based digital representations of tradable assets such as commodities, securities, and stablecoins.

Tokenized Collateral Network: Proprietary tokenization platform spearheaded by JP Morgan building real-time frictionless transfer of collateral assets.

Tokenized Stock Derivatives: Digital assets acting as synthetic derivatives or depository receipts of public stocks traded on the stock market such as Google, Apple, or Tesla.

Tokeny: European issuance platform and infrastructure platform for digital assets and security tokens.

Total Supply: Total amount of an asset that exists and can exist, including all circulating units, locked/vesting units, and treasury shares.

Total Value Locked (TVL): Metric used to measure the amount of assets staked across a blockchain's ecosystem of DeFi tools, liquidity pools, and staking vaults. Measured in either the base network currency or compared across blockchains using fiat currency.

Trade Rejection: Event occurring when a smart contract's requirements are not fulfilled, causing a transaction to fail without third party interference.

Trading Pair: Assets that can be traded for each other on an exchange, typically denoted between a base currency representing a common and very liquid asset, and another asset to be used and quoted in the base currency price.

Transactions per Second (TPS): Measure of the number of transactions that a blockchain network can process each second.

Transfer Agent: SEC-regulated entity that takes agency over the capitalization table of a security, recording and updating a manual ledger of identified shareholders in a secure and auditable manner accessible by all parties in real time.

Transparent: Feature of decentralized systems where any user or observer can access and audit any actions occurring within an ecosystem.

Treasury: Central pool of assets held by an organization to be used for operations, growth, and investment.

Two-Sided Marketplace: An economic platform where both buyers and sellers interact with one another to exchange assets.

tZERO ($TZROP): US-registered broker-dealer and alternative trading system, allowing for primary offerings and secondary trading for security tokens and digital assets in addition to cryptocurrency trading. Completed one of the first security token offerings for its native $TZROP token, which acts as an *exchange token* with additional benefits such as a profit sharing component.

Uncorrelated: Measures how two different assets move in price relative to each other.

Undercollateralized: A loan not fully backed by assets, resulting in a portion of unsecured debt that may not be repaid upon default.

Underwriting: Financial service provider offering initial capital or resources to assume the risk of an offering in exchange for a discount.

Uniswap (*UNI*): Decentralized cryptocurrency exchange that uses liquidity pools and automated market makers to facilitate permissionless trading. Uses native *UNI* token as a governance mechanism to set interest rates and other decisions on behalf of the Uniswap Foundation.

Unregistered Security: Any stock, debt, or other security that has not filed proper regulatory paperwork and has been sold illegally.

Unsecured Loan: Debt that is *undercollateralized* when created.

US Federal Bank Charter: License allowing for financial institutions to provide banking and custodial services in the US.

USD Coin (*USDC*): Open-source, fiat-collateralized stablecoin issued by *Circle* that is pegged to the US Dollar. The stablecoin is *composable* and can be used and accessed from many blockchains including Ethereum, Avalanche, and many more.

Utility Token: Cryptocurrency or digital asset used primarily as a token to facilitate direct services within a blockchain ecosystem such as paying fees.

Validation: Verification that a transaction is true and correct.

Vampire Attack: An economic threat where a DeFi protocol offers higher rates to attract *liquidity providers* to move their staked assets to the newer platform, leading to an immediate drain in liquidity pools of the attacked system.

Vault: Form of *liquidity pool* that stores cryptocurrency for users at a higher level of security than traditional *hot wallets*.

Venture Capital: Investment fund focused on early stage companies and startups with a high potential for growth and exponential returns.

Vertalo: Registered transfer agent and issuance platform for security tokens that offers blockchain-based capitalization table management and issuance services.

Vesting Period: An issuer-mandated *lock-up period* used to incentivize long term commitment of team members and investors, preventing all shares from being accessed until a period of time has passed.

Virtual Machine: An online or cloud-based operating system accessible globally from one physical computer host.

Volatility Shield: Payment feature that locks the fiat value of a purchase at the time of transaction and ensures the amount is delivered to the seller, despite changing cryptocurrency prices.

Wall Street: Street in New York City where many financial institutions are headquartered. Used as a term to describe the traditional financial markets and ideology in the United States.

Wallet: Physical hardware or digital device used to store cryptocurrency and digital assets.

Wash Trading: Market manipulation strategy where an investor repeatedly purchases and sells shares or tokens to realize capital transactions and misrepresent trading activity. Often used to avoid capital gains taxes among other noncompliant activities.

Whale: Term used to describe large investors or institutions that hold a large amount of an asset or investment.

White Hat: An individual or organization that hacks into online protocols and computer systems with the intention of helping organizations improve their internal security. Often compensated via *bug bounties* to reward ethical behavior to improve customer protections.

Whitelist: A list of individuals, companies, or wallet addresses that are explicitly allowed to access or transact within a smart contract system. Often used to prioritize interested users during surprise or scarce public offerings or mints.

Wire Transfer: Electronic money transfer between banks.

Wrapped Token: The process of staking a digital asset on one blockchain and issuing an equivalent synthetic asset on another blockchain for the purpose of more efficient trade.

Y Combinator: US technology accelerator that provides infrastructure, support, and education for multiple yearly cohorts of startups.

Yearn Finance (*YFI*): DeFi platform allowing users to stake funds across an aggregate of lending protocols to maximize yield across the ecosystem. Uses native token *YFI* as a governance token to manage yields and staking allocations for its vaults.

Yield: The amount of interest or return an investment may generate over a period of time. Traditionally expressed as a percentage of the investment principal.

Yield Farming: Process of staking digital assets through DeFi protocols in order to maximize returns across the lending ecosystem.

Yuga Labs: Blockchain technology company that owns and operates the two of the largest NFT collections, *Bored Ape Yacht Club* and *CryptoPunks*, among other digital assets and experiences.

Zero-Knowledge Proof: Form of cryptography allowing users to engage in a transaction and prove validity without knowing the full details of the transaction for maximum security and protection of all involved parties.

ABOUT THE AUTHORS

Peter Gaffney is an industry-recognized expert through his research initiatives and publications within Security Token Group. He acts as a connector between traditional capital markets and blockchain applications on both the institutional and retail levels through the *State of Security Tokens* publication series and *Tokenize This* column. Previously spending time with Global X ETFs and boutique private equity firms, Peter strives to develop the tokenization ecosystem as the next evolution in investment product wrappers applicable to private and public assets alike. His entrepreneurial journey began developing and selling computer games in fifth grade, expanded into the global gaming market through the iOS App Store in high school, shifted towards FinTech through digital assets at the University of Michigan, and found its groove at the intersection of finance and digital asset technology with Security Token Group.

Kyle Sonlin is an accomplished entrepreneur, investor, and advisor with a passion for technology. He has been a leader in the blockchain industry since 2015 and is recognized as a thought leader in the security token industry since its inception. As a founding partner at Security Token Group and Security Token Market, he has built the largest ecosystem of security token offerings worldwide and developed a thriving community of tens of thousands of active users while building a series of proprietary algorithms to enhance liquidity and further adoption of tokenization among institutional parties. Kyle is a sought-after speaker and advisor, leveraging his unique perspective and deep expertise to help issuers navigate the complex landscape of private securities exemptions and drive adoption of the industry to retail audiences worldwide.

Herwig Konings is known as one of the inventors of the security token and for advising the first tokenized private stock offering in the US for Kairos AR, Inc. He founded Security Token Group (STG) and its subsidiaries in early 2018. Prior to founding STG, Herwig founded investor compliance software firm InvestReady in 2013. He has been named Miami Technology Leader of the Year by the Greater Miami Chamber of Commerce and was the winner of the Miami Herald Startup Competition in 2019. He also founded and served as the Managing Director of the Miami Venture Capital Association where he advised countless entrepreneurs and investors on tech transactions, investment structures, and VC mechanics. He has continued to advise and pioneer in the security token space, including helping list the first private (tokenized) US company on a public foreign exchange, helping create a proprietary model for tokenizing carbon credits using a financial wrapper, and being recognized by the SEC for regulation changes they made based on his input.

Made in the USA
Columbia, SC
12 September 2023

22692183R00188